FRANCIS SUAREZ, S.J.

ON THE
FORMAL CAUSE
OF
SUBSTANCE

MEDIÆVAL PHILOSOPHICAL TEXTS IN TRANSLATION

No. 36

Roland J. Teske, S.J., Editor

Editorial Board

Lee C. Rice
Mary F. Rousseau
John L. Treloar, S.J.
Wanda Zemler-Cizewski

FRANCIS SUAREZ, s.j.

ON THE FORMAL CAUSE

OF SUBSTANCE

METAPHYSICAL DISPUTATION XV

TRANSLATED BY

JOHN KRONEN & JEREMIAH REEDY

INTRODUCTION & EXPLANATORY NOTES

BY

JOHN KRONEN

MARQUETTE
UNIVERSITY

PRESS

Library of Congress Catalogue Cataloguing in Publication Data

Suarez, Francisco, 1584-1617.
  [De causa formali substantiali.English]
  On the formal cause of substance : metaphysical disputation XV /
Francis Suarez ; translated by John Kronen & Jeremiah Reedy ;
introduction and explanatory notes by John Kronen.
    p. c. — (Mediæval philosophical texts in translation ; no 36)
Includes bibliographical references and indexes.
  ISBN 0-87462-239-5 (alk. paper)
  1. Substance (Philosophy) 2. Form (Philosophy) I. Kronen, John,
1961 – II. Title. III. Series.
  B785.S823 D 3613 2000
  111'.1—dc21

                                                        99-050569

Printed by Thomson-Shore, Inc., in the United States of America

Marquette University Press is a member of the
ASSOCIATION OF AMERICAN UNIVERSITY PRESSES

MARQUETTE UNIVERSITY PRESS
MILWAUKEE

The Association of Jesuit University Presses

Contents

Introduction

I: The General Nature and Importance of Disputation XV

The importance of Suarez, both with respect to his historical influence and with respect to the intrinsic merit of his philosophical work, is becoming increasingly recognized.[1] Suarez was one of the first scholastic philosophers to write a systematic presentation of metaphysics that was not a commentary on Aristotle.[2] He was so successful in this undertaking that his work was used as a university textbook and as a model for aspiring metaphysicians for over a hundred years, not only by his fellow Jesuits but, perhaps to an even greater extent, by Protestant philosophers and theologians. Nor was Suarez's influence restricted to the scholastic tradition which we are now coming to see was far from dead in the 17th century, but it extended, both through that tradition and independently of it, into the main currents of modern thought. It can be detected in Descartes, Leibniz, Wolff and, ultimately, even in Kant. So pervasive was Suarez's influence on modern thought that Alasdair MacIntyre has been bold enough to assert that Suarez, not Descartes, was the first truly modern philosopher.[3]

Apart from to its historical influence, Suarez's work remains important for its intrinsic merit. Indeed, it could be very reasonably argued that Suarez produced the most perfect incarnation of the type of realistic metaphysics[4] initiated by Aristotle. Though this sort of metaphysics has been under attack for three centuries, it shows no signs of disappearing and has recently been vigorously defended.[5] As long, therefore, as this Aristotelianism remains a live option for philosophers, Suarez's work will remain valuable to those engaged in the philosophical enterprise.

Central to Aristotelian metaphysics is the notion that the world is fundamentally constituted by independent entities called substances, which act according to natures intrinsic to them. These natures make them "powerful particulars," in the parlance of Hare and Madden, and it is such natures which explain why there is regularity, order, and predictability in the universe. Since a belief in substances having specific natures is such an important feature of Aristotelian realism, Disputation XV, which deals with the principle of the nature of material substances, or their substantial form, is central to Suarez's presentation of the Aristotelian metaphysics. In the Disputation, Suarez defended the view, contrary to both dualism and materialism, that material objects are constituted by two co-principles. These are primary matter, which is a determinable stuff common to all of them, and substantial form, which is the specifying principle of material objects giving them their own particular active and passive powers. This metaphysics is opposed both to the atomistic materialism that had already been resurrected in Suarez's day, and that was soon to find such champions as Hobbes and Gassendi, and to the dualism that would be defended, shortly after Suarez's death, by Descartes. Against the first view, Suarez argued that the unity and the active powers of composite substances demands that there be in them a principle of unity and action for which atomism, with its view of composites as complex aggregates of inert material parts, leaves no room. This principle is the substantial form of the composite. Against the second view, Suarez argued that no being that is truly one could arise from a union of two independent substances; hence, both the soul and the body of a human being must be taken to be incomplete substances which together make up one complete being.

Though Suarez defended the hylomorphic view of substance against atomism and dualism, he modified it in ways that adumbrate Cartesian dualism. This is most clear in Suarez's doctrine that matter has a being of its own distinct from form such that it could exist without form,[6] though not by the regular order of nature. Furthermore, according to Suarez matter is able to sustain, independently of form, the accident of quantity.[7] Hence, Suarez's view of matter comes close to Descartes' notion of material substance as an "extended thing." Nevertheless, Suarez would not admit that matter along with quantity could alone constitute a substance. His reasons for holding this are similar to the arguments he used against atomism and foreshadowed the arguments Leibniz would later bring against Cartesianism. The first of these reasons is that a complete substance is necessarily active and, hence, necessarily contains some active powers. But a mere quantified mass has no such powers; hence, it cannot, in itself, be a complete substance.[8] In addition to this mass, or quantified matter, there must be a principle rooting the active powers of things, namely, a form. The second of these reasons is that, for a substance to be essentially one, there must be some principle of unity in it besides mere extended mass.[9] For, insofar as a thing is extended, it is not truly essentially one. Therefore, in addition to extended mass, there must be a substantial form in every complete corporeal substance.

Suarez's view of material substance as being constituted by more than mere extended mass retains some plausibility for those working in the tradition of a realistic metaphysics today. For example, Hare and Madden have forcefully argued that, in order to ground both our common sense view of the world and our science, we must suppose the existence of "powerful particulars" which are similar to Suarez's formed substances.[10] Suarez's view is more subtle than that of Hare and Madden, however, because Suarez insisted, along with Leibniz, that, in order to account for the unity of material substances, we must suppose some substantial principle of unity which is not a material structure or relation, but which is a sort of substantial quality. Furthermore, Suarez's insistence that such a form is necessary in addition to the different active powers of a thing can still be used against the notion that a substance could consist of a cluster or bundle of properties attached to an indifferent substantial core, or, in more recent parlance, a "bare particular."

II: The Specific Problems Addressed in Disputation XV

The basic content and continued relevance of Disputation XV should now be clear; hence, we turn to a more specific consideration of its content. One of the things that made Suarez a great thinker was his impatience with vagueness of any sort and his systematic thoroughness. In this regard Disputation XV is no exception. Never before or since has there been so thorough a treatment of the Aristotelian notion of form. In the course of the Disputation Suarez considered the existence and nature of substantial forms, their eduction, their causality and effect, and their unity. Finally, to be complete, Suarez treated what he called the "metaphysical form," though this is only analogous to the substantial form in the proper sense. We shall briefly summarize Suarez's views with respect to each of these issues, and discuss the main reasons he gave for them. But we must warn the reader that no summary of Suarez, much less one this brief, can give any idea of the exhaustiveness and sophistication of his discussion of substantial form; to get the proper sense of these, one must turn to Suarez himself.

Section I: The existence of substantial forms

The first question Suarez treated in Disputation XV concerns the existence of substantial forms. This might seem a rather odd procedure. One might think it suitable first to give a definition of what substantial forms are, before attempting to prove their existence. Disputation XV does have a short section which presents a very thorough definition of substantial form, but it is the fifth section in Disputation XV. Why did Suarez wait so long to give this definition? The reason is simple: substantial forms are inferred entities, not observables. Their very nature, therefore, can only be established on the arguments which present reasons for believing they exist. Accordingly, Suarez first gave arguments for the existence of substantial forms, and answered objections to positing them, before defining them. Furthermore, he regarded some of these objections as important enough to merit sections of their own; hence, he did not give a definition of substantial forms until he had both argued for their existence and responded, to his own satisfaction, to objections against positing them.

The arguments Suarez gave for supposing substantial forms exist are of two sorts, *a posteriori* and *a priori*. The *a posteriori* arguments briefly are: 1) Human beings are constituted by matter and a substantial form; therefore, other material substances are as well; 2) Substantial forms are necessary to root the various essential properties of things; 3) Substantial forms are necessary to provide an explanation for the return of a thing to its connatural state after it has been altered from without; 4) Substantial forms are necessary to explain why the intense application of one power impedes the application of another power; and 5) Substantial forms are necessary to provide proper *termini* of substantial changes. The single *a priori* argument is that substantial forms are not intrinsically impossible, and are demanded by the order of the universe, the perfection of the universe, and the perfection and unity of material substances.

Sections 2-4: The eduction of substantial forms

Suarez gave several objections to positing the existence of substantial forms. The one he regarded as the most grave focuses on their origin. It takes the form of a dilemma: 1) If substantial forms exist, then they come to be either a) by creation or b) not by creation. Not (a), since this would require continual miracles. Not (b), since when substantial change occurs the form itself must come to be from nothing; but to come to be from nothing is to be created. Hence, there are no substantial forms.

Suarez accused this argument of laboring under a false dilemma since it fails to consider that forms could come to be without being either 1) created or 2) made out of something. In the course of making his case, Suarez argued that creation is opposed not only to making something *out of something*, but also to making something *in something*. Thus, though he admitted that substantial forms are not made out of anything, as that would lead to an infinite regress, he argued that they are made in something, that is, in a matter properly organized to receive a them. In so arguing Suarez gave a very clear notion of what it means for a substantial form to be educed from the potency of matter. It is for it to be made with a dependency, both in coming to be and being, in a properly disposed bit of matter.

After having given a clear account of the nature of eduction in general, Suarez took up some very particular problems concerning the eduction of substantial forms. The first problem is whether or not matter always temporally precedes form in every eduction, and the second is whether or not forms are made as such. Without going into his reasons here, Suarez's answer to the first question is that matter need not *temporally* precede form, but need only *ontologically* or *logically* precede it, insofar as matter is the subject of form. His answer to the second question is that form, as a proper part of a complete substance, is not made as such, though it is itself made from nothing, but rather the composite, which the form partially constitutes.

Section 5: The nature of substantial forms

Having given a barrage of arguments to prove forms exist, and having answered crucial objections against supposing that they exist, Suarez gave a very precise definition of substantial forms. According to Suarez, a substantial form is "a simple and incomplete substance which, as the act of matter, constitutes with it the essence of a composite substance." This differs from the traditional definition of form, which is "an intrinsic cause giving being to a thing." Though Suarez used this definition in defining formal causality in *MD* XII, he did not favor it here because of his disagreement with Thomistic metaphysics. For Suarez form completes the being of a composite, giving it powers particular to a specific sort of substance, but it does not give complete substantial being to a thing; in particular, it does not give the being of matter to a thing. Since, according to Suarez, the Thomists held that form channels the act of existing to matter and thus, in some sense, gives matter its own proper being,[11] Suarez decided not to give the traditional definition of form here, preferring instead one that is more in harmony with his own doctrine of a merely conceptual distinction between essence and existence in finite beings.

Sections 6-9: The causality and effects of substantial forms

In accordance with the general method Suarez adopted in treating the causes of being, after he proved the existence of substantial form and gave a clear definition of it, Suarez went on to treat, in a typically exhaustive manner, of its causality and its effects. The first topic Suarez discussed with respect to a form's causality is its principle of causing. The principle of causing of a thing is the faculty or power *in virtue of which* it causes when it causes. Thus the principle of causing of June Anderson's singing is her vocal chords and her trained musical ability. According to Suarez, the principle of causing of a form is nothing other than the form itself. This is related to the actual causality of the form. For Suarez form, as an intrinsic cause of being, does not cause by creating something distinct from itself in a composite substance; rather, it causes by simply uniting its own essence to the other constituent of the composite. Thus the causality of form is simply its union with matter.

The conditions required for a form to cause are: 1) its existence;[12] 2) its spatial proximity to its subject; and 3) appropriate dispositions on the part of its subject. The first two of these are absolutely necessary (i.e., not even God could bring it about that form causes in their absence); the last is only naturally necessary (i.e., in the natural order dispositions on the part of matter are necessary for the form to inform it, but God could bring it about that form informs in the absence of these. For example, He could bring it about that a human soul informs the body of a cat).

The effects of form are: 1) the actualization of matter and 2) the composite. These are in reality [*ex natura rei*] the same effect taken from the point of view of different relations, in the way that getting a majority of the vote in the general election and being elected president are the same. That is to say, the actualization of matter's potency to be something, say a pig, is *nothing other than* the very constitution of the composite substance of a pig. For Suarez, form gives being to matter only in a certain respect. For example, it may give being to matter by actualizing its potential to be a pig. However, form does not give being to matter by giving matter its own being *qua* matter. In this, Suarez disagreed with the Thomists and their doctrine of the real distinction between essence and existence. Nevertheless, though form does not give being intrinsically to matter by actually constituting that being, matter has such a minimal existence that it cannot naturally exist without a dependency on form; only by the absolute and infinite causal power of God can matter exist denuded of all form.[13]

Section 10: The unicity of substantial form.

A much debated question in the middles ages was whether or not there is more than one substantial form to each substance. The Franciscans held that there is more than one substantial form in higher substances such as human beings and animals.[14] Their reasons for holding this were diverse, and each of them was treated by Suarez in section 10. However, there seems to have been two main reasons for their doctrine. The first is that, as higher substances share certain powers and properties with lower beings but also possess powers peculiar to their own levels of being, several forms must be posited in them to account for their similarity with and difference from lower beings. The second main reason is that there is evidence that lower forms remain in compounds (e.g., it seems that water is present in plants, animals and humans); therefore, it would seem that compounds are characterized by the forms of the elements that make them up as well as by their own peculiar forms. Scotus added a new argument for the view that there is more than one form in humans based upon the metaphysical distance between the human soul and the body. The human soul, he reasoned, is too perfect to immediately inform naked prime matter; hence, in order for the soul to inform a certain piece of matter, it is necessary that matter be first informed with the form of corporeity, which gives it extension and the required organic structure. Scotus thought his theory confirmed by the fact that human bodies do not immediately corrupt after death.

The Franciscan tradition came under strong attack on these points from Thomas Aquinas and his followers. Aquinas argued, in the first place, that it is impossible for there to be more than one substantial form in a single composite since, as substantial form gives substantial being, a plurality of substantial forms yields a plurality substantial beings. But each substance can only have one substantial being since it is impossible for a *single* thing in a category to be *many things* in that category. Further, Aquinas argued that, as a higher form can do anything a lower can, there is no need to posit many substantial forms to account for the higher powers of humans and animals; one form will give the human being, for example, not only the higher powers of reason, but also the lower powers of sensation, growth, reproduction, etc.[15]

Suarez agreed with the Thomistic tradition in holding that there can only be one complete substantial form in each composite, and he further agreed with the reasons the Thomistic tradition gave in support of this view. However, Suarez disagreed with Aquinas and the Thomists in one major respect. Aquinas had argued that all substantial forms are simple and without entitative parts, apparently on account of their function as unifiers of the composite substance.[16] His view seemed to be that a substantial form cannot give substantial unity to a thing unless it is itself fully one. Suarez, however, held that all substantial forms other than the human are composed of parts, and he thought these parts are incomplete substantial forms. This disagreement with the Thomists probably is related to Suarez's view that essence and existence are not really distinct. Such a view forced Suarez to grant more independence to the parts making up a substance, for example, form and matter, and this made him more open to the possibility that a composite substance that is truly essentially one could be constituted out of really distinct, albeit incomplete, substantial parts.

Section 11: Metaphysical form

For the sake of completeness, Suarez rounded off his discussion of substantial form with an account of the nature and reality of metaphysical form. Suarez noted, however, that metaphysical form, in whatever sense it is taken, is not a true form because it is not an entity which, by informing some being really distinct from it, constitutes a complete substantial essence. Metaphysical form is, then, form only by analogy.

Suarez distinguished two sorts of metaphysical form. The first is the complete essential nature of a thing, taken as an individual. Thus, as a human nature is constituted out of form and matter, an individual person's metaphysical form is her body informed by her soul. Such a "form," though it could be said to give a person being, is not really distinct from the person whose form it is, and it does not constitute the being of anything by informing some subject really distinct from it. Nevertheless, Suarez did not hold that any individual's essence is precisely identical with her since she is constituted, not simply by her essence, but by a substantial mode terminating her essence and making it incommunicable to another in the way in which Christ's human essence was communicated to His Divine Essence. For Suarez complete individual essence along with substantial mode constitutes the supposite or hypostasis.

The second sort of metaphysical form Suarez discussed is logical form. This form is equivalent to the difference in a "genus-difference" definition of a thing. Thus, in the traditional definition of human being as "rational animal," "animal" is the genus which is informed or determined by the difference "rational." So "rational" is said to be the formal element in the definition and "animal" the material element. But, as Suarez did not believe that universals really exist and held rather that they are mind-dependent relations, he did not think of differences as really combining with genera to form the real essences of things. Hence, he did not regard logical form as being a form in the true sense of the word. It is rather a form only by a kind of analogy with real, physical forms, i.e., with forms which actually exist and inform a subject really distinct from themselves.

III: Notes on the Translation

Our main source for this translation was the *Opera omnia* edition of the *Metaphysical Disputations* (Vivès: 1866) which is the standard edition. We have also looked at the edition prepared by Sergio Rabade Romeo for the Spanish translation of the Disputations (Madrid: 1960-66). This differs in a few places from the Vivès, and we have indicated in end-notes wherever we have preferred it to Vivès.

Since Suarez's references to other authors are quite detailed, we have, in general, left them as they stand. The exceptions to this are Suarez's references to Aristotle and Plato. Wherever we could find the passages in Aristotle which Suarez refers to, we have given the Bekker numbers for them, and for Plato likewise we have given the Stephanus numbers. We have also supplied the reader with notes giving publication dates and locations for the rarer works Suarez cites, as well as information on recent editions or reprints.

Most of Suarez's references to his own work are to other portions of the *Metaphysical Disputations*. Where Suarez has not supplied the reader unfamiliar with his work with enough information to locate precisely the passage being referred to, we have supplied the Disputation number Suarez has in mind, followed by section and paragraph numbers. So, for example, *MD* XVIII, 2, 3-4, should be read as referring to the 18th Metaphysical Disputation, section 2, paragraphs 3-4. References to Suarez's other works give the volume and page numbers of the Vivès edition.

Among the people we need to thank for their help in preparing this translation are Roland Teske S.J., Jorge J.E. Gracia, and an anonymous reviewer for Marquette. All of these offered invaluable comments and suggestions concerning the style of the translation as well as concerning our interpretation of Suarez. Gracia, in particular, has been an aid to us because of all the work he has done over many years making Suarez's thought more accessible and understandable to the philosophical community. Our greatest debt is, of course, to Suarez himself whose lucid and profound mind made this translation a very rewarding task in spite of all the difficulties and challenges we faced in preparing it.

Notes

[1]Evidence of this can be found in the number of references to Suarez's thought in recent works on the great modern philosophers. For example, in his book, *Leibniz: Determinist, Theist, Idealist* (New York: Oxford University Press, 1994), Robert Adams refers to Suarez's philosophy well over a dozen times, often discussing aspects of it at length. This is in marked contrast to Russell's classic work on Leibniz, which does not contain a single reference to Suarez.

[2]It is often said that Suarez was the first to accomplish this. But before him the Dominican Diego Mas and the Augustinian Diego Zungia wrote complete works on metaphysics which were not commentaries on Aristotle. On this, see Lohr's chapter "Metaphysics" in *The Cambridge History of Renaissance Philosophy*, ed. by Charles Schmitt *et al.* (Cambridge and New York: Cambridge University Press, 1988) pp. 610-611. Mas's treatise antedates Suarez's by ten years.

[3]*Three Rival Versions of Moral Inquiry* (Notre Dame: University of Notre Dame Press, 1990) p. 73. For a criticism of MacIntyre's mentalistic interpretation of Suarez, see Jorge J. E. Gracia, "Metaphysics and Mentalism," in the *American Catholic Philosophical Quarterly*, Volume LXV (Summer 1991) no. 3, pp. 287-309.

[4]"Realism" like both "liberalism" and "conservatism" is both vague and ambiguous. Nevertheless, it can be given a fairly clear and sensible meaning. According to this meaning, a philosophy is realistic just in case it agrees with the common sense view that the world is constituted by a plurality of individual things which differ in kind. These things are thought by common sense to perdure over shorter or longer periods of time and to be characterized by properties which they in some sense have or possess but which do not, strictly speaking, constitute them. Such properties can be divided into two basic sorts, that is, physical and mental.

Though realists such as Suarez support the common sense view of the world, they refine it in two ways. In one way they refine it by positing entities unknown to common sense. Suarez's form and matter are examples of such entities. They are entities Suarez inferred exist in order to explain how the world must be if certain common sense beliefs are true (such as the belief that an animal is one thing in the way a car or a watch is not).

In another way philosophers such as Suarez refine common sense by correcting certain crude and inadequate pictures it can all to easily fall prey to when following too closely the play of the imagination. Thus common sense tends to regard transitive causality as a kind of transfer of the properties of one thing, such as a fire, into another thing, such as a rock heated by a fire. Suarez is adamant that such pictures won't work and that when a fire heats a rock it actualizes in the rock the rock's own capacity to be hot; it does not transfer its heat to the rock.

Opposed to realism are various kinds of idealism, such as that of Kant, who denied that the world is or could be populated by the sorts of entities common sense holds that it is. Kant thought that all common sense objects are mental constructs; they are only phenomenally real and the realm of the thing-in-itself is hidden to the human mind. Thus he thought that even the category of substance, which is for Aristotle and all realists the most real of all the categories and the support for all the rest, is but a concept which the mind imposes on appearances in space and time.

For some very insightful comments about the proper relation between philosophy and common sense see J. Maritain, *Distinguish to Unite or the Degrees of Knowledge*, trans. by Gerald Phelan (Notre Dame: University of Notre Dame Press, 1995), pp. 86-89. For an extremely learned account of the history of the philosophical notion of common sense see William Hamilton, "Of Common Sense," in his edition of *The Works of Thomas Reid*, Vol. II (London: Longmans, Green and Company) pp. 770-803.

[5]We are thinking here of Saul Kripke in *Naming and Necessity* (Cambridge: Harvard University Press, 1980), of Alvin Plantinga in *The Nature of Necessity* (Oxford: The Clarendon Press, 1974), of Roderich Chisholm in *A Realistic Theory of Categories* (New York: Cambridge University Press, 1996), of Baruch Brody in *Identity and Essence* (Princeton: Princeton University Press, 1980), and of Jorge J. E. Gracia in *Individuality* (Albany: State University of New York Press, 1988). Of course, none of these is as Aristotelian in outlook as Suarez. For example, none of them, as far as we can tell, embraces a strictly Aristotelian notion of form and matter, and two of them, namely, Chisholm and Plantinga, defend a Platonic notion of universals. However, all of them defend such Aristotelian doctrines as that persons are individual substances which perdure over time and which are characterized by both essential as well as non-essential properties. And Brody even defends what he himself calls an Aristotelian theory of substantial change.

[6]*MD* XIII, sect. 5.

[7]*MD* XIV, sect. 3.

[8]See the present disputation, sect. 1, para. 17-18.

[9]*MD* XIII, sect. 2.

[10]See their book *Causal Powers: A Theory of Natural Necessity* (Totowa: Rowman and Littlefield, 1975).

[11]Whether or not Aquinas held this view, Suarez was less certain. But he was certain it was the view of the Thomists. See the present disputation, sect. 8, para. 2.

[12]It should be noted that the existence of the form, though necessary for it to cause, is not a causal condition in the most proper sense of the word, according to Suarez. The reason is that a causal condition must be really distinct from that of which it is a causal condition, and nothing, according to Suarez, is really distinct from its existence.

[13] For Suarez form gives matter the property "being actualized by such and such a form," and the property "being a human body"; it does not give it the property "being such and such a form" or the property "being the substance constituted by such and such a form and such and such matter." Thus my soul gives my body the property "being actualized by a human form," but it does not give it the property "being a human soul" or the property "being a human being."

[14]On this see Frederick Copleston, *A History of Philosophy: Vol. 2, Medieval Philosophy*, Part I (Garden City: The Newman Press, 1950), pp. 304-305.

[15]*Summa theologiae*, Part I, Q. 76, a. 4.

[16]*Summa theologiae*, Part 1, A. 76, a. 8. On this matter, see Thomas Harper, *The Metaphysics of the School*, Vol. II (New York: Peter Smith, 1881), pp. 655-672.

METAPHYSICAL DISPUTATION XV
ON THE FORMAL CAUSE OF SUBSTANCE

Introduction

Since the material and the formal causes are mutually related, we shall treat first substantial form and later accidental form, using the same method we used in discussing matter.[1] For whatever is pertinent to the definition of form in general either was touched on in the disputation concerning the causes in common[2] or will be explained more clearly in the following sections of the disputation, which fit together only analogously under the common definition of form.[3] Because of the intrinsic connection between prime matter and substantial form,[4] we shall in this disputation, while treating substantial form, complete our treatment of those aspects of prime matter which we postponed until now. It ought to be said, however, that there will be no discussion of the extrinsic form, which scholars call "exemplary," about which we will speak below, because extrinsic form fits the definition of efficient cause better than that of formal cause.[5] Nor does this discussion concern separate forms, as the angelic or immaterial natures are commonly called on account of their actuality or beauty and not on account of their causality,[6] but we are treating form only as informing or as received in matter since it is that form which has the proper and specific nature of the formal cause.

It is indeed customary to divide form into physical and metaphysical;[8] the prior is that which exerts true and real formal causality, and it is, therefore, that which we must treat most extensively. It is said to be a "physical form," either because it chiefly constitutes the nature of a thing,[9] or because it is investigated principally through the analysis of physical change and is considered primarily in physics.[10] Nevertheless, it is not outside the consideration of metaphysics.[11] This is so, first, because the notion of "form" is common and abstract; then, because form constitutes the essence of a thing; and, finally, because it is one of the principal causes. At the end of this disputation we will consider what is meant by the term "metaphysical form" and the way in which it is said to be a cause.

Section 1
Whether There Are Substantial Forms in Material Things

1. Reasons for doubting that substantial forms exist in material things.[12] The first reason for doubting that substantial forms exist is that substantial forms cannot be known by any experience, nor are they necessary to account for any of the actions and differences we perceive in things. Therefore, they should not be posited without sufficient reason.[13] The antecedent is clear because fire, for example, can be satisfactorily understood as constituted in its being if we conceive of it as a certain kind of substance having perfect and consummate heat conjoined with dryness, even if the substance which is the subject of these accidents is simple. And this joining of the properties of heat and dryness is sufficient for all the actions of fire which we experience, as well as for the distinction between fire and water and for the change of one into the other. Such a change seems to consist in this, namely, that one substance passes from the greatest coldness to the greatest heat, and *vice versa*. This supposition, therefore, is enough for the constitution, distinction, and action of the elements; the same supposition, likewise, is proportionally sufficient to account for the constitution of compounds since they are made out of the mixture of the elements.[14]

2. The second reason for doubting that forms exist is that there is an apparent contradiction involved when one speaks of a form that is both informing and substantial;[15] for either a form is a subsistent thing and needs no sustaining subject, or it does need one. The first sort of form cannot be an informing form because it is a contradiction to suppose that something is subsistent and received in another. Again, the second sort of form is inhering and, therefore, accidental; either way there is no substantial form.

3. The third reason for doubting that forms exist is that, if we posit substantial forms, it is impossible to understand how changes and generations occur unless we suppose that something comes to be out of nothing, which is not possible according to natural principles.[16] The inference is clear because either the whole substantial form exists before its generation, or part of it does, or none of it does. The first alternative cannot be held, for otherwise 1) an infinite number of forms would pre-exist in matter and 2) nothing new would in fact come into being; it would only seem to do so. Nor can the second alternative--that part of the form pre-exists its complete generation--be maintained: First, because in the same part of matter it is impossible for there to exist one part of the form without the whole since substantial form is indivisible; and, second, because, even if part of the form pre-exists and part has to be educed, the latter part would come into being out of nothing, since it cannot come into being from the pre-existing part. There remains, there-

fore, the third possibility, namely, that form comes to be out of nothing, which is, nevertheless, absurd and exceeds the power of natural agents.

4. **The ancient philosophers did not know of substantial forms**. On this question nearly all the ancient philosophers[17] were ignorant of substantial forms, as is obvious from what we reported above concerning their opinions about prime matter[18] or the first subject of natural changes. For, since they thought that the first subject was a complete being in act, they could not recognize the substantial form because substantial form and prime matter, which is pure potency, are, as it were, correlatives. A few later philosophers[19] also denied the existence of substantial forms, at least in the elements. Alexander of Aphrodisias indicates this in his *Commentary on the Metaphysics*, book 12, commentary 12, although there he seems to be merely giving an example and to be speaking analogously.[20] John Philoponus also taught this, in his *Commentary on Generation and Corruption*, book 2, commentary 7,[21] and earlier Galen held the same opinion in *On the Elements*, book 1,[22] and before him Empedocles, who did not deny forms for compounds but for the elements, as Aristotle indicates in *Physics* I, text 50 [189a16], and *Physics*, II, text 22 [194a20-27].

Resolution of the Question

5. It should, therefore, be said that, besides matter, all natural or corporeal things consist of substantial form as their intrinsic principle and formal cause. This is the view of Aristotle in innumerable places. He often reprimanded the ancient philosophers because, having almost passed over substantial form, they directed all their inquiry toward matter.

This opinion of Aristotle is obvious from the whole of Book One of the *Physics*, and from Book Two, chapter 1 [193b7], where he says that form has a more perfect nature than matter. He holds the same thing in *On the Parts of Animals* I, chapter 1 [694b29], and in *Metaphysics* VII, chapter 4 [102b10] and XII, chapter 2, [106b10] where he calls form a "this something" because it completes the substance which is a "this something." And, again, especially in Book Seven of the *Metaphysics*, he calls form "what something is" [1029b12] and gives as the reason why that form is that which constitutes and distinguishes the essences of things.[23]

Again in *On the Soul* II, chapter 1 [412a7-11], he distinguishes substance into matter, form, and the composite, and he calls form "entelechy."[24] Peter Fonseca wrote a great deal and with much erudition concerning this name at the end of Book One of his *Commentary on the Metaphysics*.[25] Scholars, nevertheless, commonly teach that the word "entelechy" is more general and has a wider comprehension than "substantial form," because it properly signifies perfection or the act perfecting a thing. It is customarily attributed to substantial form by *antinomasia*,[26] since such a form is the first act and highest perfection of the substance.

Aristotle also often used other names to refer to substantial form, which we will note below when explaining its causality.[27] Nevertheless, Aristotle was not the discoverer of the truth concerning the existence of substantial forms. Plato recognized their existence before him, as is evident from the *Timaeus*, where Plato calls forms "images of real being,"[51a6] that is, copies of the Ideas, since he posited Ideas only of substances. And before Plato some of the philosophers are believed to have touched on the existence of substantial forms, as is clear from Aristotle in *The Parts of Animals* I, chapter 1 [694b29], and in other places that were cited above.

This teaching concerning the existence of substantial forms is now so commonly accepted in philosophy that it can only be denied through great ignorance. Furthermore, it is so in harmony with the truth of the Christian faith[28] that its certitude is greatly increased because of that fact. Therefore, it is appropriate that proof of this truth begin from a principle certain by faith and evident by the natural light of reason.

The Existence of Other Substantial Forms Can Be Inferred From the Nature of the Rational Soul

6. The first argument for the existence of substantial forms is that a human being consists of a substantial form as an intrinsic cause; therefore, all other natural things also do.[29] The first premise of this argument is proven because the rational soul is a substance and not an accident, as is plain from the fact that it can exist by itself separate from the body since it is immortal.[30] It is, therefore, subsistent of itself and independent of a subject. Hence, it is not an accident but a substance.

Again, that soul is the true form of the body, as faith teaches, and as is also evident by the natural light of reason. For it cannot be an attendant substance or something moving the body from without; otherwise, it would not cause the body to live, nor would the functions of life depend essentially on its union with and presence to the body.[31] Finally, it would not be a human being, as such, who understood, but some other attendant substance. Therefore, a human being consists of a body as matter and a rational soul as form.[32] Hence, this soul is a substantial form because, as we will show below,[33] the term "substantial form" signifies nothing other than a certain partial substance which can be united to matter in such a way that it composes with it a substance that is whole and essentially [*per se*] one, such as a human being.

7. The inference drawn from the substantiality of the human soul is indeed proven by assuming the discussion is about natural things which are subject to generation and corruption. For, in this respect, these things belong to the

same order as human beings, and transformations and changes can occur between them. From this, nonetheless, it can easily be concluded *a fortiori* that the same thing must be said about incorruptible bodies, given our teaching above concerning their matter.[34] Therefore, a human being's composition from matter and substantial form shows that there is in natural things a certain substantial subject fit by its own nature to be informed by some substantial act. Such a subject is imperfect and incomplete in the category of substance and, therefore, always needs to be under some substantial act. This subject, however, is not peculiar to humans but is also found in other natural things, as is self-evident.[35] Hence, it is necessary for the generation and sustenance of the human being, and it remains after the corruption of the human being. All natural things, therefore, which are composed of matter as their subject are also composed of a substantial form, actualizing and perfecting that subject.[36]

Furthermore, from the composition of human beings it is possible to infer that an aggregation of many accidental faculties or forms in a simple substantial subject is not enough to constitute a natural thing. For in human beings there are perhaps more accidental faculties and forms, and more perfect ones, than in other natural things, and yet these do not suffice for the constitution of any complete natural being. In addition to these accidental forms there is required a form to rule, as it were, over all those faculties and accidents and to be the source of all actions and natural changes of the human being and the subject in which the whole variety of powers and accidents is rooted and unified in a certain way. For the same reason, therefore, in the other natural beings there is needed a substantial form distinct from the accidents and more intimate and perfect than they are.[37]

Thirdly, from the same example it is clear that the substantial generation and corruption of a human being does not consist in the acquisition or loss of any accidents, but in the union or separation of the rational soul which substantially informs the human body. Certain accidents prepare the body for this union. Once these accidents are removed, the soul departs and the human being is corrupted.[38] It must be understood, therefore, that the corruption and generation of other natural entities occurs in the same way. For, as can be gathered from experience, there is the same mode of generation and corruption in humans as is found in other things, except for the difference in the perfection and subsistence of the human form, though we would not have inferred this difference between the human and other substantial forms solely from their manner of generation and corruption, unless it were known to us from other facts. Furthermore, *Ecclesiastes* 3 says [verse 19], "The death of man and the beasts are one, and the condition of both is equal, so that just as a man dies, the beasts also die," etc. Finally, all the indications and signs by which substantial composition can be known in humans are found in other natural beings, especially in the living ones, as the following argument will show.

Various Indications of Substantial Form

8. The return of what has been changed to its original state. The second principal argument for the existence of substantial form is gathered from various indications arising from accidents and operations of natural beings which indicate that a substantial form lies beneath them. The first indication can be discerned even in the elements. For if water, for example, is heated, and later the external cause of the heat is removed, the water returns to its original coldness because of an intrinsic force, as experience attests.[39] This is a sign, therefore, that there is in water a certain inner principle from which an increase of cold flows anew after all external obstacles have been removed. That principle which returns water to its original temperature, however, cannot be anything other than the substantial form; therefore, substantial forms exist.

That the return of water to its original state is from an intrinsic force is proven since there cannot be any extrinsic principle of this return. First, because, if this return were from something extrinsic, it would not be essentially [*per se*] and necessary but by accident, since an extrinsic agent would act on it by chance.[40] Then, also, because, if one examines all extrinsic principles which are generally present to water, there is none from which that action could emanate since the only one that is nearby is the surrounding air. This air, however, either is not naturally as cold as the water, or it often happens by accident that it is left as warm as the water itself. Hence, the air also returns itself to its own original state, so far as it is able. The heavenly and universal causes intervene only remotely, and they are by themselves not ordered to an action of this sort, as is commonly known.

9. A refutation of various theories concerning the cause of such a return. The second antecedent, namely, that no internal cause of the return of water to its coldness except the form of water itself can be conceived, is proven; for what else could it be?[41] Some say that in certain parts of the water intense coldness always remains and from these cold parts the other parts, which had been heated, are cooled. Cajetan [Thomas de Vio] thought this was probable in his *Commentary on the Summa Theologiae* I, q. 54, a. 3,[42] and it is attributed to Averroes in his *Commentary on On the Soul* II, commentary 1.[43] But this view is silly and contrary to experience, for by our senses we perceive that all of the water poured in a vase is very hot, whatever part we touch. If there were some parts that were so cold, they would either have been perceived by sense or would at least have tempered the sensation of heat in a part of the water; neither, however, is the case.

And this view is also contrary to natural science since all the water throughout all its parts is uniformly applied in two ways to fire acting naturally. Therefore, the water in all its parts is uniformly acted on in the same way. For what is there that could either impede that action or interrupt it so that it would affect some parts of the water but not others? Likewise, either those parts which are said to retain the cold can be heated, or they cannot. If they cannot, neither can they be corrupted.[44] But if they can be heated, then, if all the water is sufficiently applied to the fire, those parts will also be heated. Or at least there could be a state in which that potency to be heated is actualized and, if that state obtains, that water will return to its original coldness, once the contrary agent is removed, as long as it had not come to the point of the corruption of the water.

10. Others reply that that action does not proceed from any principle distinct from coldness because coldness always remains to some degree, and, as soon as it is not impeded, it immediately recalls itself to its original state. For two things can be distinguished in coldness, namely, its essence and its mode of intensity. Its essence always remains whole, even if its intensity is diminished, and thus from the same essence the mode of intensity can emanate.

But this reply is also false. It is false, in the first place, because a more intense degree cannot proceed from a quality that was diminished; otherwise, even air would be able to make itself hot in the highest degree, and the same would be true of all other things. It is false, in the second place, because it often happens that there are in the water more degrees of heat than of cold; hence, even if the remote extrinsic agent had been removed, the coldness could not have conquered the intense heat. For it could in no way be helped by the subject since matter in itself is indifferent to either accident. Thirdly, this reply is false because otherwise cold and heat could never have remained at peace in diminished degrees, but the one quality would always have expelled the other by perfecting itself all the way up to the ultimate intensity. For on the part of the subject, if it were only prime matter, there would be no impediment, and we are supposing that all extrinsic causes have been removed.

11. **In the elements no qualities virtually contain the primary ones.** Others, finally, reply that it is necessary that there be some internal principle prior to coldness which remains whole, even if coldness is diminished, from which the return to a state of coldness would come. They, nevertheless, deny that that principle is the substantial form because such a change could not immediately arise from the substantial form, but they say it is a certain quality of a higher nature which virtually contains the primary sensible qualities.[45]

This view, nonetheless, can be understood in two ways. In the first way it does not deny substantial form, but places that virtual quality between the substantial form and the primary sensible qualities. Understood in this way, it is not opposed to the truth which we intend to prove. It, nevertheless, weakens the argument which we are pursuing; besides, it ought to be rejected as unfounded and gratuitously invented since it multiplies qualities without foundation or any experiential evidence.[46] For the emanation of an accident from an intrinsic form does not require any intermediate accident; otherwise there would be an infinite regress.[47] Likewise, this view must be false because it is contradictory that there be in the elements some qualities prior to the first. The primary qualities of the elements, according to Aristotle [*On Generation and Corruption* II, chapter 2, 329b17-330a29], are formal heat, cold, moisture, and dryness. Hence, although in compounds there may occasionally be a quality virtually containing heat or cold, that quality is, nevertheless, posterior to the balance of the primary qualities natural to the compound and is not for the intrinsic emanation of the primary qualities in the same subject, but for the production of them by its proper action in external subjects.[48]

This response can be understood in another way so that it intends to do away with substantial form and put a quality in its place. Understood in this way, however, it is easily refuted because that intermediate quality is not directly and in itself sensed but is known from the effect of natural emanation. On what basis, therefore, is that internal principle said to be an accidental quality and not the substantial form? Likewise, that principle is the primary act of matter, composing with matter this natural being which we call water. It is, therefore, a substantial and not an accidental act.[49]

Likewise, that form is the root not only of coldness but also of moistness, density, and the other properties which the element of water requires, for the same argument can be made concerning these. That is, if these qualities are changed through a contrary action from that natural state which water demands, as soon as the contrary action ceases, the qualities will immediately return to their natural state. Therefore, these qualities have some prior form from which they are derived and which remains unchanged. Hence, either to the individual qualities there correspond individual root—so to speak—or virtual forms, something which nature abhors and which is completely unnecessary, or there is one form in which all those properties are rooted and, as it were, gathered, and this seems most true. That form, then, is not accidental, but of a superior order. There is, therefore, a substantial form from which such a return proceeds, as is the common view: Avicenna, *Sufficientia*, book I, chapter 5;[50] Paul Soncinas, *Commentary on the Metaphysics* 9, q. 8;[51] Dominic de Soto, *Commentary on the Physics* 2, q. 1,[52] and others.

12. From this another piece of evidence can be drawn which is a confirmation of the preceding. For it is established by an experience which is almost obvious that, even in inanimate things or the elements, substantial corruption is distinct from alteration. I am speaking specifically about inanimate things so that *a fortiori* the induction will be made universal; for in animate things this is even more evident, as will become clear. We experience that an

alteration—for example, the heating of water or of iron—is sometimes so forceful that the most intense heat is felt in those things; and, nevertheless, if the action of the contrary agent ceases, those things remain whole, or mostly whole,[53] in their own substance and also easily return to the accidental state.

Sometimes, however, the alteration continues to such a degree that a complete transformation of the thing occurs so that, even if the agent is removed, the substance which was acted on can never return to its original state or recover its prior actions or similar accidents. Sometimes a thing is even changed into a less noble sensible substance, such as cinders, slag, etc. Finally, sometimes a thing is entirely consumed in a way that cannot be perceived, because it is transformed into a more subtle and imperceptible body. This, therefore, is an obvious sign that alteration is sometimes simple and remains within the sphere of accidental change, but sometimes it has connected with it a greater change of a thing. This change cannot, however, be explained as anything other than the dissolution of the substantial composite itself as the substantial form recedes. Substantial forms, therefore, exist.

The last assertion is proven because, if the whole substance of the thing always remained equally whole, however far an alteration proceeded, it would in itself always have the same relationship to its accidents. It would after any alteration, therefore, always remain unchanged under any accidents whatsoever, insofar as this depends upon it and when the contrary agent is removed, or it would always return to the same accidents, once those agents are removed.

13. This argument is confirmed because we see that some accidents are so inseparable from certain subjects that, if they are destroyed or greatly diminished, a complete change occurs in their subjects so that they cannot return to their original state by any intrinsic force. That inseparability, therefore, proceeds from a connection of such accidents with some principle intrinsic to these things.[54]

This principle cannot be prime matter or that first subject which remains under every change, because with respect to it there is no accident among those which can be acquired or lost through alteration which is inseparable.[55] Nor can this principle be an accident if we are speaking of the first and radical principle.[56] For, even though one accident is inseparable in relation to another, as rarity is inseparable in relation to heat, or whiteness in relation to a certain balance of the primary qualities, that balance, nevertheless, is inseparable from another prior form of the nature which was abandoned. We must necessarily, therefore, insist upon some form which is first in relation to inseparable accidents. This form is, therefore, substantial and not accidental since it constitutes the proper essence in which the accidental properties naturally and inseparably exist.

14. **The subordination of properties among themselves is an indication of substantial form**. Finally, from this sort of evidence another argument can be drawn. For in one natural being many properties are united which at times are so subordinated to one another that one arises from the other, as the will arises from the intellect. At times, however, they do not have a mutual subordination, as heat and humidity in the air, whiteness and sweetness in milk, or the many senses in an animal. Therefore, this multitude and variety of properties, especially when they are related in the latter way, require a single form in which all are united. Otherwise, they would be merely accidentally gathered in the same subject and, when one was completely destroyed, another would not recede because of that. But experience teaches us that the opposite is the case. This is, therefore, a sign that such accidents which are required in such a subject and exist in a certain number, weight, and measure[57] do not have that connection in relation to the first subject alone, namely, prime matter, but in relation to a composite which, by reason of its form, requires that order of the accidents among themselves.[58]

It is usual to confirm this argument specifically by referring to composite bodies in which we see that certain contrary accidents, when reduced to certain levels, are preserved in the same compound. This, however, cannot come from the qualities themselves, as is clear enough in itself, since they are rather in conflict by their nature. Furthermore, it cannot come from an extrinsic cause or from matter, as is easily seen. Therefore, it necessarily comes from the form. This confirmation, nonetheless, either has no force at all or is not an argument distinct from the preceding ones. For, when the four primary qualities have been reduced to that harmony in which they are simultaneously able to exist in the same subject, they do not need another internal cause or principle in order that they may be perpetually preserved in it in the same state, but only need the removal of the external corrupting agent. For those qualities established at that level are not properly contrary, nor can they have any action among themselves. Indeed, if they could have an action among themselves, the substantial form would not be able to impede or reconcile them. Because of this it happens in the living, even in humans, where the form has the greatest unity, that the form cannot impede action among the various heterogeneous parts. For, though the qualities are so balanced in the individual parts that they agree among themselves in relation to their proper subject, they are not so balanced in relation to the qualities of another dissimilar part.[59]

Therefore, the existence of the substantial form cannot be inferred from the conservation of a balance constituted from contrary qualities, taken by itself. It can, nevertheless, very well be inferred from the fact that in such a balance the qualities are not only permitted, so to speak, to remain in this degree, but are also so connected in it and so required by it that, if one or the other of them is augmented or diminished by an extrinsic agent, when that agent is removed, the balance will return immediately to its prior proportion.[60] This is especially clear in animals; this is, therefore, an obvious sign that such a balance is due to some form in which these qualities are connected. This sign, however, coincides with that concerning the return of a thing to its natural state.

15. **The fact that, when a thing is intensely acting in one way, its power to act in another is reduced is evidence for the substantial form.** This argument is finally confirmed by another indication drawn from the action of certain natural agents. We experience that, if a thing which has many faculties of operation acts intensely through one faculty, it is impeded so that it cannot act through another faculty or so that it cannot act through another with such great force. This is, therefore, a sign that these faculties are subordinate to the same form which operates through them as a principle. For, if they had no subordination among themselves or operated without any common principle, each one of them would operate independently of the others, and there would be no reason why the force of one would impede the force of the others more than if they were in diverse subjects. But the best explanation for this phenomenon is given by supposing that all these faculties are subordinate to the same form. For, since a form is finite in power, while it is intensely applied to one operation, it is withdrawn from another, and it can focus itself with such great force on one operation that its power is exhausted in it.[61]

The antecedent is explained by some in natural things or agents which, while they act intensely to overcome a contrary, are not able to protect themselves entirely from also being partially overcome or influenced by the contrary. This experience, nevertheless, from the reaction undergone by natural agents does not come from the subordination of many faculties to one form, but from the fact that a thing is not always as capable of resisting as of acting.[62] Hence, even the hottest iron, when it heats water, is acted upon in return by the water, although the form of iron contributes absolutely nothing to that action. In fact, the actions of diverse faculties do not intervene in this case, but there is rather the action of one quality, namely, heat, and a passion opposed to it to a certain extent, which comes from the fact that the heat is not as powerful to resist as it is to act. On this point I believe that one can hardly find any experience in inanimate things which would prove the antecedent. For in accidental actions which do not come from life it does not seem that some concurrence of the substantial form intervenes proximately so that by reason of it the action of one faculty is diminished by the force of another.[63]

In living beings, however, and especially in us, we clearly experience such an effect, for when thought is focused interiorly, it often impedes us from seeing things present to us. Again, long meditation often impedes the action of the nutritive part.[64] Nor does it matter if someone should say that this comes from the concurrence of the vital spirits[65] necessary for the operations of these faculties which, while they flow to one faculty, leave another. This is not relevant, first of all, because the very concurrence of the vital spirits with one faculty rather than with another is a sign of one form using these spirits and faculties for two actions; otherwise, there would be no reason why the spirits would flow to one faculty more than to another. The second reason this is not relevant is that intellectual operation is not produced by means of the vital spirits,[66] and yet intellectual effort and attention impede lower actions. Nor can this be attributed to the cooperation of the imagination, which does require the concurrence of the spirits; for intellectual attention, especially if it is very intense and concerned with things of a higher order, greatly reduces even the action of the imagination.[67] Therefore, this sort of occurrence does not come from the vital spirits, but from the occupation of the same soul with some operation.

Causes Demonstrating the Existence of the Substantial Form

16. **Substantial form is not impossible.** The third principal argument for the existence of substantial form can be drawn *a priori*[68] from the proper causes of the substantial form, which are the final, the efficient, and the material.[69] After all, substantial form does not have a formal cause since it is itself a form; hence, no positive argument for form can be gathered from it. We can, nonetheless, suppose that for its part there is no repugnance in there being in natural things such a kind of being or incomplete substance as substantial form. For what repugnance could be imagined or thought of in this?

Again, it is not contradictory that there exist in the nature of things substantial acts of the highest order which are subsistent and do not inform anything, such as the angels. And it is not contradictory that there is a substantial act of a middle order which both subsists and is actuating or informing, as has been said concerning the rational soul. It will, therefore, not be contradictory that there exist substantial acts of the lowest order, that is, which are actuating and not completely subsistent. And these we call substantial forms.[70] Likewise, such an act [i.e., a substantial form] would be contradictory either because it is an act or because it is substantial or because it is contradictory for these two to be joined together in the same thing. But none of these can be stated with probability. It is not contradictory, therefore, for its part that there exists a substantial form.

But, if it is not contradictory on its part, it will readily be proven that it is not contradictory because of the other causes[71] or that it is even necessary. The first two parts of the first antecedent seem evident (*per se notae*).

The first part is evident because it is evident that there really exist in things entities which are acts and perfections of other things;[72] for in that way brightness is an act of something white and understanding an act of one who understands. The second part is evident because it is also evident that there are in things substantial entities since these are the foundation of all the others.[73]

The third part of the above argument remains to be proven, namely, that it is not contradictory that these two properties or natures be joined in the same entity. This, however, is clear, first, because nothing can be found in either of these natures which would be intrinsically incompatible with the other. It is clear, second, because the nature of act bespeaks, of itself, perfection. Therefore, if it is not contradictory for it to be joined with accidental being, why is it contradictory that it be joined with substantial being?[74] Finally, because the nature of a substantial entity looks to perfection without qualification, it seems to conflict more with the nature of potentiality than with the nature of actuality. But the first is not contradictory, as is clear from prime matter;[75] therefore, neither is the second.

A new argument arises from this since potency and act in every genus correspond proportionally to each other, but it is not contradictory that there exists in natural things a substantial potency which is an incomplete and imperfect being in the genus of substance, as was shown above [in *MD* XIII], and is manifest from the composition of the human being. Therefore, it will not be contradictory that there exists an act proportionate to that potency by which the potency can be actualized in any natural thing and that this act exists and is conserved in a way connatural to it.[76]

17. **The existence of substantial form is demonstrated from the material and efficient cause.** And so from this an argument can be easily taken from the nature of the material cause. For, since matter is a substantial potency, it contains in its own genus and in receptive potency every act proportionate to itself; therefore, it is capable of causing every act in its own genus if it is not contradictory for some other reason. Hence, in this respect the substantial material form has a sufficient reason for its being able to exist.[77]

Again, an argument is derived from the efficient cause because, if we are talking about the First Cause, He cannot be lacking power by which He could produce in the universe substantial forms which actuate matter, whether in dependence on or independently of matter, according to various grades and perfections of such forms, on the supposition that they are not contradictory.[78] Therefore, since such forms are necessary in the nature of things, they have been produced by such a cause. If, however, we are talking about proximate causes, we must later see which one is able to intervene in relation to which form.[79] Now it is sufficient to say that such a cause cannot be lacking, if such an effect is necessary to the constitution of natural things; hence, if created causes occasionally lack this power, it pertains to the causality of the

First Cause that He should also supply the function of the proximate cause, which, strictly speaking, only happens in the rational soul in terms of its production.[80] For all other forms are made in such a way that it is not impossible that they be produced by created agents, since they are made with the concurrence of matter, as we will immediately explain.[81] Whether there is, indeed, sufficient power for such a production in created agents, we will discuss in dealing with the efficient cause.[82]

18. **The chief argument for form is from its end**. The chief argument, then, ought to be taken from the end of the substantial form, which is to constitute and complete the essence of a natural being. This end or effect is absolutely necessary in the nature of things. Otherwise, nothing among physical things would be complete and perfect in its own substantial nature, nor would there be the multitude and variety of substantial species which chiefly constitutes the wonderful order and beauty of the physical world.

For this end, therefore, substantial form is absolutely necessary. For, since matter is a very imperfect being, it is not possible for the complete essence of anything to consist in it alone.[83] Second, because matter, insofar as it is the first subject, is one and the same in all natural things. The essence of these things, therefore, cannot consist solely in it; otherwise, all things would be of one essence and would only differ accidentally. Such a state of affairs is incompatible with the greatness and beauty of the universe, which chiefly arises from the variety of species. This seems to be the meaning of the words of *Genesis* I [verses 12 and 31], "Making seed according to its own kind" or "according to its own species." And it often repeats "according to their own species," and "in its own kind," and finally concludes: "God saw all things that He had made, and they were very good," because the complete goodness of the whole universe undoubtedly arises from that variety. This is also sufficiently shown by the variety of powers and operations and by reciprocal generations and corruptions, as has been said. Besides matter, therefore, something must be added to it by which the essence of each thing may be completed; since, however, matter is potency, that which is added to it to complete the essence will be act, for potency implies an essential relation to act.

19. That act, however, which is joined to matter to complete the essence of a thing cannot be an accidental act. It cannot be such an act, in the first place, because no essence which is truly and essentially [*per se*] one is made out of an act and a potency of diverse orders.[84] But the essence of a natural and substantial thing ought to be truly and essentially one; otherwise, the thing would not be one substance. It cannot be such an act, in the second place, because, since matter is a substantial potency, it is not completed through an accidental act, and so it cannot compose a true essence of a natural thing with such an act.

In the third place, it cannot be an accidental act because, supposing it is, I ask of what is it the accident? For either it is the accident of the composite of that act and potency as such. But this is contradictory because, since the composite is intrinsically constituted from such a form, the form cannot be an accident of it, just as whiteness is also not an accident of something white, insofar as it is white, but it is an accident of the subject which is white. Or the form is an accident of matter or the substantial subject, and so I ask again why it is said to be an accident of it. Is it because matter is able to exist with such an act and also without it?[85] But this reason is not sufficient; otherwise, the rational soul would also be an accident of the body. This, therefore, is common to both a substantial act and an accidental act. Or is it because such a form depends on matter for its own being?[86] This reason is also not enough, because the parts of a substance can also depend on other parts of the same substance, and matter in its own way depends on form. There are, therefore, various kinds of dependence, and it is not contradictory for an incomplete substance to depend on a subject of the same order.

Finally, the form which completes matter may be said to be an accident because in its own being it has an entity so imperfect and diminished that it is of an order lower than the whole genus of substance. And this is, first of all, said gratuitously and without grounds. For on what basis is it established that the act of matter, to which matter itself is essentially [*per se*] and primarily ordered and which with matter completes the essence of natural things, is so diminished and incomplete an entity? Secondly, it is incompatible with the end of such a form because, as I said, one substantial essence cannot be composed from a substantial subject and an accidental form, especially since form is that which gives the final grade and completion to an essence. On account of this Aristotle rightly said, in *Physics* I, chapter 6, [189a34] "substance is not composed out of non-substances."[87] It is established, however, that natural things and their essences are substantial and essentially one; therefore, the philosophical teaching concerning substantial forms is absolutely certain.

Solution to the Arguments

20. Of the reasons for doubting originally given, the first two have been answered from what has been said. In reply to the first it is denied that there are lacking in natural things sufficient indications and effects by which one can justifiably arrive at a knowledge of substantial forms.[88] And it is further denied that all actions and changes can be maintained without substantial forms.[89] In reply to the second, it is denied that a subsisting and informing form is contradictory, either in diverse states or even in the same state, as we will explain at greater length below when dealing with subsistence.[90] It is also denied that it is contradictory for a form to depend on a subject and also to be

substantial, as was stated a little earlier.[91] We will show, however, the way in which this dependence differs from the inherence of an accident in the following disputation.[92] The third argument against substantial forms indeed presents a special difficulty which it will be best to treat in the following section.

Notes

[1]Suarez is referring to his treatment of prime matter in disputations XIII and XIV. He first, in XIII, treated matter as the subject of substantial form and then, in XIV, treated it as the subject of accidental form. He will use the same order in treating form, starting in the present disputation with the substantial form and in the next disputation moving on to the accidental form.

Matter is, for Suarez, the primary subject of all forms and the underlying substrate of all change (*MD* XIII, 1). It is the primary subject because all material forms, in some way, exist in it, while it does not exist in anything else. Things other than matter, however, can exercise material causality, insofar as they are subjects for some form. Thus the soul, as the proper subject of the intellect and will, could be said to be their material cause, even though the soul is a subsistent form, not matter (cf. *MD* XIV, 2, 4).

Form is, for Suarez, any intrinsic feature of a thing, which gives it a definite essence or perfection, whether in the substantial or accidental order. Thus Suarez says that substantial form is like a substantial quality of a thing making it to be, substantially, such and such, e.g., a tree, a cat, a man (cf. *MD* XLII, intro., 3). Accidental form, on the other hand, is an actuality, making a thing to be such and such accidentally, e.g., white, round, intelligent, etc.

Substantial being is that being which exists "in itself," not "in another" (*MD* XXXIII 1, 1). Since a human exists in herself, she is a substantial being, and the form, i.e., her soul, that makes her to be a human, is thus substantial. Accidental being, on the other hand, is that being which exists "in another" (*MD* XXXII, 1, 5). Whiteness and intelligence, for example, exist in substances really distinct from themselves, and thus they are accidents.

[2]*MD* XII.

[3]The scholastics distinguished three most general modes of predication: the univocal mode, the equivocal mode, and the analogous mode (cf. Cajetan, *The Analogy of Names*). A term was said to be predicated of several subjects univocally if it is predicated of them in exactly the same sense. Thus "animal" is univocally predicated of "cat" and "dog." A term was said to be predicated equivocally of several subjects if it is predicated of them in entirely distinct senses. Thus "bank" is predicated equivocally of "river" and "financial institution." Finally, a term was said to be predicated analogously of several subjects, if it is predicated of them in partially the same, partially different ways. Thus "wisdom" is predicated analogously of God and creatures because God is infinitely wise by His very essence, whereas creatures are finitely wise by means of an accidental quality, specifically, a habitus (see *MD* XLIV, 13, 10-11).

There are two reasons why the general nature of form is analogous: (1) Its concept can be predicated of both substances and accidents, but substances and accidents, though they both exist, exist in distinct ways, since a substance exists in itself, and an accident exists in a substance, (*MD* XXXI 2, 11); (2) Its concept can be predicated of both material and immaterial creatures, which also exist in distinct ways (see note 6). Suarez, therefore, nowhere treats form as such in a distinct Disputation, but treats different kinds of forms in different Disputations. All forms, however, have in common that they are "intrinsic causes which give being to things" (*MD* XII, 3, 3).

[4]Usually form and matter are treated together in scholastic works which deal with hylomorphism, and most scholastics probably thought that, once they had proven the existence of prime matter, they had *ipso facto* proven the existence of substantial form. For matter, being a pure potency, cannot exist except as informed (cf. Aquinas, *De principiis naturae*, chap.2, para. 17).

Suarez, in contrast to Aristotle and some of the schoolmen, held that matter, though in some sense pure potency, has an existence of its own separate from form (*MD* XIII 9, 5). Therefore, it can support accidents, such as quantity, which are natural to it. It follows that, for Suarez, proving that matter exists does not automatically prove that form does. Thus Suarez treats each in a separate Disputation.

[5]The "exemplary forms" are a sort of Christian reworking of Plato's forms. They are the ideas in the mind of God according to which He knows all possible beings and according to which He creates; hence, the link Suarez made between them and efficient causation (*MD* XXV).

[6]Angels were held by Suarez, and by the whole school of St. Thomas, to lack all matter. Since matter is potency with respect to form which is act, something lacking all matter would be more actual than any material being. But if more actual, then more formal since form is the most actual part of a thing, giving it being of a definite sort, as well as active powers natural to the sort of being it is; for example, a dog's power of vision follows from its very nature as determined by its form (*MD* XVIII, 2, 3). However, angelic "forms," although in some way more formal, because more actual, than material forms, do not exercise formal causality, precisely speaking, because they do not inform anything. Suarez briefly treats the nature of formal causality in Disputation XII 1, 7, and at length below in section 6.

[7]That is, it is a real entity, distinct from matter, which actualizes matter by joining its whole entity to matter (see below, section 6, 3).

[8]Suarez treats metaphysical form in section 11. It either corresponds to Thomas' *form of the whole* (*De ente et essentia* 2, 12) or to the specific difference marking off the specific from the generic nature of a thing. Taken as the form of the whole, the metaphysical form of material things includes matter. Though it includes matter, it was held to be a form in some sense because it is that *by which* (*quo*) a given substance exists. Thus, one might say that a human being is a human being by *humanity*. However, such a form does not properly inform any entity really distinct from itself, and according to Suarez it differs from the substance of which it is the form only modally (for Suarez's doctrine of modes, see *MD* VII 1, 16-22).

[9]Since matter is passive and potential, the active powers of things were said by Suarez to follow from their forms. Thus form is the first principle of action of a thing (*MD* XVIII 2, 3). But if that is the case, then it is the chief constituent of the essence of a thing since every essence is the root of all the active powers of a thing (*MD* II, 4, 6).

[10]By "physics" Suarez meant the science which investigates natures embodied in matter. All science, to some degree, abstracts from matter since matter is the source of relative unintelligibility in a thing and since all sciences are concerned, not with individuals, but with universals (*MD* I, 2, 13-14).

However, according to St. Thomas, whom Suarez followed in this matter, sciences can by distinguished by the degree to which their objects are considered in abstraction from matter. Physics was held, on this view, to abstract from individual or sensible matter, but not from common matter. Thus an anatomist is not concerned with the individual matter of, e.g., Mrs. Jones' heart, but since she is concerned with the human heart, she is concerned with the general *sort of matter* with which human hearts are made. Suarez holds that all sciences which study material natures, insofar as such natures are material, belong to physics. Therefore, the scholastic notions of form and matter, as used to explain the nature of material beings, properly belong to physics for Suarez, though we would call them "metaphysical" or "ontological" notions.

[11]The metaphysician, unlike the physicist, was held by Suarez to abstract from all matter and to consider either 1) those entities which actually exist without any matter, and in this sense metaphysics is reducible to natural theology, or 2) those aspects of all entities, like "substance" or "unity" which are not, formally speaking, material (*MD* I, 2, 13-14). It is in sense (2) that the metaphysician can study form since, as Suarez says, form is 1) in some sense common, that is, it is common to material and immaterial beings, 2) the chief constituent of the very essence of a thing, and "essence" as such, is not a material aspect of a thing, and, lastly, 3) one of the four primary causes, which apply, at least analogously, to all finite beings. Two of the primary causes, namely the efficient and final, apply to all beings, since God is the ultimate final and efficient cause. But He is not a formal or material cause since He does not inform anything and nothing informs Him. All other beings are final and efficient causes as well, and the parts of them are either formal or material causes.

It should be noted that it is probably due to the fact that Suarez is studying form from the aspect of the metaphysician, that he places little emphasis on the "physical" argument for form based on substantial change and instead emphasizes that form is necessary to constitute the complete essence and unity of a thing.

[12]Suarez adopts the style of the medieval disputed question and begins his argument for the existence of forms by presenting objections to the view that they exist. He calls these objections "reasons for doubting." The first of these he answers in section 1, the second he partly answers in section 1 and much more fully in *MD* XXXIV, sect. 5, 14-21, and the third he answers in section 2.

[13]This objection has a contemporary ring to it. Substantial forms, as is true of substance itself (cf. *MD* XXXIX 1, 11-12), cannot be directly experienced by us; we know of them only through inference. But the first objection holds that we have no good reason to infer them since all substances could be composed of a certain simple substantial subject, presumably prime matter, and a number of accidents. Suarez spends most of section 1 of this disputation showing that we *do* have good reasons for inferring the existence of substantial forms and that, indeed, they *are* necessary to complete the essence of any material thing.

[14]The elements, for Suarez, are the four accepted by the ancients: earth, air, fire, and water. In scholastic terminology an element is a substance which is not formed by the mixture of any other substances. Therefore, its sole constituents are matter and an elemental form. Compounds, on the other hand, in *some sense* arise from and are composed out of the elements. Thus, if the elements are merely an aggregate of properties in a simple substance, compounds will be mixtures of those properties in a simple substance.

It was a much debated question in the Middle Ages whether, and to what extent, the elements are actually present in the compounds they compose. Suarez gives his view on this matter in sect. 10, para. 50-51.

[15]This objection to substantial forms seems to adumbrate the objection to them given by modern philosophers such as Leibniz. According to it, a being is either substantial or accidental. If it is substantial, it can exist on its own, and thus cannot inform anything else, nor be a constituent of a composite substance. On the other hand, if it can inform something else, it is an accident and so not substantial.

Suarez's answer, not explicitly spelled out in this disputation, is that an accident is intrinsically ordered to inhere in a *complete* essence, whether or not that essence is a substance or an accident. A substantial form, however, does not inhere in a complete essence, but unites with matter to form a complete essence in the category of substance (cf. MD XVI, 1, 3). Hence, though it is not itself a substance, it goes to make up a substance, and so is "reductively" in the category of substance (*MD* XXXIII 1, 5).

[16]Suarez gave an elaborate treatment of this argument in section 2, para. 1. But the general problem posed by it is clear enough. The argument presupposes that the natural order acts, in general, according to laws inherent in it, and that we should not invoke special divine interventions to explain phenomena characteristic of that order. Substantial changes are phenomena characteristic of the natural order because things are constantly changing from being one sort of substance to being another; hence, such changes should not be explained by invoking divine intervention. But, so the objection runs, if we posit substantial forms, then we must posit that either they existed before coming to be in the composite made from them and from matter, or that they did not. Thus the form of a tree, for example, might be held to come to be when a new tree is generated. If it did not at all exist before it was generated, then it was created. But only God can create, and so such an explanation would resort to miraculous divine intervention. On the other hand, if it pre-existed in matter, there would not be any real coming to be of the tree's form nor, therefore, of the tree, which is contrary to experience. Hence, if forms are posited, one either must deny substantial generation, or one must invoke divine intervention, and neither of these is acceptable.

This problem was generally solved by holding that the substantial form is not made out of nothing but out of the potency of matter. The expression "to be made out of the potency of matter" is ambiguous, but Suarez gave it a clear and intelligible interpretation in sec. 2, para. 13.

[17]Suarez is here referring to the pre-Socratics. His view of them was largely shaped by Aristotle who taught that the pre-Socratics focused on the efficient and material causes to the neglect of formal and final causes. The correctness of Aristotle's view is, of course, another matter.

[18]*MD* XIII, 2, 2. According to Suarez the ancient philosophers did not understand the true nature of matter. In place of an incomplete substance that is pure potency, they posited a multitude of very small, but in themselves complete, substances.

[19]By the "later philosophers," Suarez seems to mean the thinkers of late antiquity. Christian thinkers were not usually referred to as "philosophers," but Suarez does mention here Philoponus, who was a sixth-century Christian thinker.

[20]*In Aristotelis Metaphysica Commentaria*, ed. M. Hayduck, in *Commentaria in Aristotelem Graeca I* (Berlin, 1891).

[21]*Gramaticus in libros De generatione et interitu* (Venice, 1527).

[22]*De elementis libri duo* (Lyon: G. Rovillium, 1550).

[23]Form is here being given predicates which chiefly apply to substance, but which apply to the form in a derivative sense since the form constitutes the substance. See *MD* XXXIII sect. 1 for a detailed account of the various ways in which the parts of a substance can be considered to be themselves substances.

[24]What Aristotle meant by "entelechy" is the subject of some debate, but it seems to refer, in some way, to the dynamic aspect of form, that is, to the form when taken as the root of the active powers of a thing. It was in this sense that Leibniz understood the term when he equated the active power of his monads with entelechy, and their passive power with prime matter (cf. his *New System of Nature and of the Communication of Substances*, in *Leibniz Selections*, ed. by Philip D. Wiener [New York: Charles Scribner's Sons, 1951], par. 3, p. 108).

[25]*Commentarii in libros metaphysicorum* (Cologne, 1615-29; rep. Hildesheim, 1964).

[26]*Antinomasia* is a figure of speech whereby a thing of a certain sort is named after an individual held to exemplify a certain quality. Thus, "He was a veritable *Caruso* in his singing of *Celeste Aida*." Suarez, however, seems to take it to mean something like *par excellence*.

[27]Sect. 5-6.

[28]Suarez is probably here thinking of the Council of Vienne (1311-1312) under Clement V, which taught that the "rational or intellectual soul is truly and essentially [*per se*] the form of the human body" (cf. Denzinger, *Enchiridion symbolorum*, ed. Adolfus Schönmetzer [Fribourg: Herder, 1964], p. 284, para. 902, *De anima ut forma corporis*).

[29]Suarez here adopts an argument for substantial form which is based on metaphysical principles rather than on physical ones (see notes 10-11) and which is very different from the traditional argument for form from substantial change. In it he assumes what he shows elsewhere (*De anima*, Disp. 2, Q. 3), namely: 1) the soul is able to exist apart from the body and 2) the soul is the substantial form of the body.

[30]For Suarez's arguments for this proposition see his *De anima*, Disp. 2, Q. 3.

[31]The soul, by definition, is the first principle of life (cf. Aquinas, *ST* I,75,1). But if it is the principle of life, it does not cause life in an extrinsic substance but is itself the intrinsic, so to speak, principle of life. If the soul merely moved the body as the angelic forms move the heavens, the body, strictly speaking, would be dead, not alive (cf. *ST* I,76,1).

[32]This inference seems rather quick, but makes sense in the light of what Suarez has already said in a previous disputation concerning the four causes (*MD* XII). Granted the body is distinct from the soul and indeed is material, since it is sensible and extended, and granted that the soul, though substantial, actually informs the body and makes it to be the living body of a human being, the soul is by definition for Suarez the substantial form of the human body.

[33]Sect. 5.

[34]Suarez had argued in *MD* XIII, 10, 8, that the heavenly bodies are made of matter just as the sublunar or terrestrial bodies are. There was some debate about this in the Middle Ages because the heavenly bodies were held to be incorruptible and the main traditional argument for the existence of matter was from substantial change (*MD* XIII, 10, 2-3). Suarez argued, however, as did Aquinas, that the fact that the heavenly bodies are sensible and extended shows they are composed of matter since quantity and the other sensible properties are rooted in matter.

[35]There are three reasons why it is evident that material substances other than human beings have in them prime matter according to Suarez: 1) because of the fact that humans assimilate such things into themselves and are transformed into such things after death, which would not be possible without a common underlying subject; 2) because all corporeal things are sensible and extended, and such properties must arise from a passive principle common to them all (see preceding note); and, finally, 3) because the passive principle in humans called prime matter must always be in need of some form. Hence, when it is not under the human form, it must be under another material form; therefore, other corporeal substances are constituted out of it and their own respective forms.

[36]That corporeal substances other than the human have in them, not only matter, but also form, follows from two facts. The first is that matter alone cannot complete the essence of anything; this is spelled out clearly in para. 19. The second is that such things are not only similar to humans in being sensible, extended and mutable, but are different from humans and from each other due to certain essential features which could not have arisen from matter since matter is common to all corporeal substances; hence, there is in them a principle which determines matter, namely, form.

[37]This argument is not very clear as stated here but what Suarez intends by it becomes clearer below (para. 20). It is, in effect, a response to the first reason Suarez gave for doubting that substantial forms exist. This reason asserts that we can conceive of the essence of natural things as consisting of a cluster of accidents in a simple subject. Such a simple subject would presumably be prime matter. A contemporary form of this view might hold that subject to be a "bare particular." Hence, on this view a corporeal substance would be constituted by prime matter and a certain collection of accidents. Suarez holds, however, that these accidents must be related and organized in some way if we are to have a unified substance. They must be so organized by being rooted, so to speak, by or in the substance itself. Matter, however, cannot root them, as is made clear below (para. 13), because it is indifferent to all of them; hence, they must be rooted and thus unified by a substantial formal principle.

[38]Suarez holds substantial change to be a fact, though he argues for it at length in *MD XIII*, sect. 1, and, more briefly, later in this disputation, para. 12. Substantial change could not consist in a mere alteration of features in a substance, according to the scholastics, since such an alteration leaves the substance intact, e.g., when a man gains weight. Hence, they held that substantial change is a change of a more radical kind in a substantial principle, i.e., prime matter, which bears and changes substantial determinations or features, i.e., substantial forms.

[39]The physics of this example, which depends on the notion that coldness is natural to water, is outdated but the general point can still be made. It is based on the idea that some features of a thing are essential to it in such a way that, even if these features are for a time removed by the action of an external cause, the features will return once that cause ceases acting, owing to a force or principle intrinsic to the thing. Thus one might cut the leaf of a plant, robbing it of its natural shape and size, but the plant will itself return the leaf to its natural size and shape, and this must chiefly be ascribed to a power intrinsic to the plant.

[40]The argument here is that something that always happens cannot happen by chance. Hence, if an extrinsic agent caused water to return to its natural coldness, then, since water always does return to its coldness, unless the heat is so intense that the

water evaporates, this must be due to something that naturally and perpetually acts on the water. The only causes which naturally and perpetually act on the water are the surrounding air and the heavenly bodies, since they perpetually influence the earth. But, Suarez argues, neither of these can account for such a return of water to its original coldness; thus, no extrinsic cause can.

[41]Now that Suarez has proven that the cause of the return of water to its coldness is not an extrinsic cause but some intrinsic cause, he must prove that it is neither another accident in the water, nor matter, but a substantial form. By so doing he will prove that such a form must be posited in order to account for such a phenomenon.

[42]*Sancti Thomae Aquinatis Opera omnia cum commentariis Thomae de Vio Caietani*, Leonine ed. (Rome, 1891).

[43]*Aristotelis Opera cum Averrois commentariis, supp. 2* (Venice: apud Junctas, 1562).

[44]The notion here is that if any part of water could not be heated, which is an accidental change, it could not be substantially changed either; for anything which could not even be accidentally changed, *a fortiori*, could not be substantially changed. But, according to Aristotelian physics, all sublunar bodies can be substantially changed. In that case they can be accidentally changed as well. Hence, all the parts of the water can be heated.

[45]Suarez here considers the view that the principle that causes the water to return to its original coldness is neither some degree of coldness always present to the water, nor the water's substantial form, but some quality distinct from either, virtually containing coldness. Javelli held this in his *Metaphysics*, VII, q. 9. This answer to the present question is probably based on the Thomistic notion that no finite substance immediately acts by reason of its substantial form but only by reason of some intermediate power really distinct from the substantial form (*ST* I, 54, 1).

Suarez's position on this matter is curious. On the one hand, he held that it is not impossible for finite substances to act immediately, and indeed he held that with respect to their properties or necessary accidents they do act immediately (cf. *MD* XVIII, 3, 4,). On the other hand, he also held that all the specific powers we can enumerate in finite substances are really distinct from those substances (ibid. 19-22). Hence, he thought that any contingent actions of substances are mediated by powers distinct from them, but that those actions productive of the necessary and natural attributes of a substance, as coldness was held to be with respect to water, are caused *directly* by the substance's form, albeit as an instrument of the substance which produced the form.

[46]Of course, on the Thomistic view that a finite substance cannot directly act by means of its form, this hypothesis does not multiply forms *needlessly*. But on Suarez's view, according to which finite substances can directly act, it does.

[47]Suarez is arguing that if *every* accidental form flowed from the substance by means of another accidental form, there would be an infinite regress. But the Thomist is not forced to hold this. He can hold, for example, that the first necessary properties of a thing are directly caused in it by the agent that caused the thing to exist. This is what John of St. Thomas explicitly held in *Naturalis philosophiae; Pars IV*, ed. by P. Beato Reiser (Turin: Marietti, 1820), Question II, Art. II p. 65. Suarez himself inclines to the view that the *remote* cause of the necessary properties of a thing is the generator of the thing (*MD* XVIII, 3, 14).

[48]The argument here is that the primary qualities are necessarily the first qualities of any thing, not emanating from any other quality, but only from the form. Hence,

Suarez wants to hold that any quality virtually containing the first would not give the first to its subject but would be the means by which the subject might cause one of the primary qualities in another subject.

[49]The notion here seems to be that whatever roots the necessary or essential properties of a substance must itself be constitutive of the substance's very essence. Hence, it must be a substantial and not an accidental form.

[50]*Avicennae peripatetici philosophi ac medicorum facile primi Opera omnia* (Venice, 1508; rep. Frankfurt-Main: Minerva, 1961), pp. 13 ff.

[51]*Quaestiones metaphysicales acutissimae,* ed. Jacobus Rossettus Vincentius (Venice, 1588; rep. Frankfurt-Main: Minerva, 1967).

[52]*Super octo libros Physicorum quaestiones* (Salamanca, 1555).

[53]Since substantial forms are incapable of alteration for Suarez, it seems strange that he would say that such substances remain "mostly" whole. He cannot mean that they remain mostly iron, or mostly water, but only that they remain mostly whole in terms of their quantities, or that they remain mostly whole in terms of the degree to which their natural properties are still present in them.

[54]Since for Suarez all essences have certain accidental properties natural to them, if an essence or form is still present, so will its natural accidents be. But after certain changes the natural accidents of the substantial essence that existed prior to the change are no longer present; hence, the substantial essence is no longer present.

[55]Matter as such, which is a purely passive principle, cannot give the sufficient reason why certain accidents are inseparably connected to a given substance. But all substances, since they are essences, must have certain essential accidents which are inseparable from them. Hence, there is in them something more than matter.

[56]Since it is the nature of an accident to exist in another, one cannot have an infinite series of accidents, each of which exists in another accident; one must stop, eventually, at a thing which is not an accident, that is, at a substance which exists in itself.

[57]This is an allusion to the book of *Wisdom* 11:20.

[58]Suarez here appeals to the unity of substance to establish the existence of substantial form. A substance cannot consist simply of matter since matter is pure potency (see below para. 18, also MD XIII); hence, it cannot consist of matter along with a heap of accidents either. The reason is that accidents have between themselves only an accidental unity and cannot grant essential completion to a substance. Besides, if there were no form grounding the accidents and providing a sufficient reason why some were inseparably bound to the substance and others were not, the properties which one enumerated as essential to a thing would be arbitrary and relative to one's language or particular interests. That is probably why some contemporary philosophers have trouble with the notion of a substantial essence; cf. Irving Copi, "Essence and Accident," in *Naming, Necessity and Natural Kinds,* ed. by Stephen P. Schwartz (Ithaca and London: Cornell University Press, 1977), pp. 80-81. For once you get rid of the form as the *single* principle which gives determinate substantial being to a thing and which causes the necessary properties of it, defining essence becomes a matter of picking out certain features of a thing as opposed to others. But then one can always say that the features of a thing which are considered essential are relative to one's point of view. Thus *qua* white thing, for example, it is not accidental that a white rose is white. And in order to substantiate the claim that, nevertheless, the white rose's very nature as a white thing is not essential to *it*, one must be able to say *why* some features are essential to it and why

whiteness is not among them. And *that* seems to require positing a single substantial principle which, in virtue of its very nature, demands certain features, even if, as Suarez points out, such features are not directly demanded by each other.

[59]The meaning here seems to be that there is not *one* mixture of the primary qualities in a compound but many different ones, at least in those beings which have heterogeneous parts. Thus, the distinct mixtures of the diverse parts might not agree, e.g., when the stomach secrets acids into the throat, they burn the throat, even though the same acids do not burn the stomach. Suarez says this has to do with the mixture of the qualities themselves, not the form, as is proven by the fact that the form cannot prevent the mixture of the various parts from being incompatible with each other.

[60]According to Suarez, the fact that in compounds various opposing qualities harmonize does not prove the existence of substantial form, but rather the fact that, after the balance of these mixtures has been upset by an extrinsic cause, that balance automatically returns, once the extrinsic cause recedes. Thus a certain acid might upset the balance of qualities in the stomach and burn it but, once that acid is removed, the body naturally causes the stomach to return to a natural state of balance among the chemicals in it. As Suarez notes, this is the same argument as the one above concerning the return of the proper qualities of a substance after they have been done away with by an extrinsic cause.

[61]A finite agent has a finite power of acting, so it makes sense that it cannot do several actions at once, just as the mind cannot focus on several different topics at once. But if there were no substantial active principle in a thing, which is what form is, Suarez thinks it would be difficult to explain why, when one faculty of a thing is active, the others are not. For if they were not all different capacities of a single substantial active principle, each could act without affecting the others.

[62]Suarez holds that iron does not actively heat, as it were, by a power natural to it, but by an accident produced in it by some extrinsic agent. Thus, the fact that when iron heats water it is also cooled by the water, does not follow from the fact that the form of iron is directing itself to its faculty of heating and so is unable to use its faculty of resisting. Rather, it follows from the fact that the quality itself of heat is less able to resist being acted on than to act.

[63]Inanimate things, although they act, do not seem to have the power of spontaneously focusing their actions and, hence, this argument for form does not hold with respect to them. For more on why animate beings require the concurrence of their substantial forms in exercising vital acts, whereas inanimate beings do not require the concurrence of their substantial forms in exercising acts connatural to them, see *MD* XVIII, 5

[64]That is, intense thought can make one insensible to hunger.

[65]The vital spirits were certain very fine bodies which ancient, medieval and renaissance physicists posited as necessary for the operations of the senses. They were a sort of adumbration of the nervous system.

[66]Suarez, like most scholastics, held that the intellect so transcends matter that it makes use of no corporeal organ in carrying out its function (*ST* I, 75, 2). Hence, it could not make use of the spirits to do so either.

[67]The imagination was the faculty most scholastics associated with the brain (*ST* I, 84, 7). This faculty was held to produce internal images, whether visual, aural, or tactile. For the scholastics, concepts are distinct from mental images, and represent aspects of reality which cannot be imaged, e.g., one cannot make an image of

God or an angel, for they have no sensible qualities; hence, Suarez's assertion that the intellect, especially if it is contemplating spiritual things, reduces even the action of the imagination.

[68]By an "*a priori* argument" Suarez means an argument for the existence of a thing from its proper causes. Until now he has argued for the existence of substantial form as necessary to explain certain natural phenomena, i.e. he has argued from effects to their cause. Now he is going to give a more certain, as well as a more abstract, demonstration of the existence of substantial form, based on metaphysical principles central to his philosophy.

[69]Suarez will show that the substantial form *can* be produced by the efficient cause and that the material cause and the final cause of substance *demand* that it be produced.

[70]This argument is rather odd and, moreover, requires a knowledge of scholastic metaphysics in order to be properly understood. The reason why it is not a contradiction to suppose that forms of a superior order exist, which subsist on their own but do not inform, is that being is act and so, the more actual a being is, the more possible its existence is. For a greater degree of act and, hence, of existence surely is more possible than a lesser one. But a form without any matter is more actual than either matter or a composite made of matter and form.

Again, for Suarez, the human soul must be subsistent, because immaterial, and yet must be the form of the body (for reasons spelled out above, in para. 7). But Suarez holds that if forms of such a degree of perfection and act can exist *and* can inform matter, then forms of a lesser degree will be able to exist and inform matter since there will be less of a "metaphysical distance" between them and matter.

[71]Suarez is referring to the efficient, and especially the material and final causes. He discusses the efficient cause in *MD* XVII-XXI. He says this cause is extrinsic, unlike the material and formal causes, and causes, not by communicating its own being, but rather by instilling being in another. He discusses the final cause in *MD* XXIII. It is, generally speaking, "that on account which something is or is made" (sect. 1, para.7).

[72]Suarez is here speaking of accidental forms, which he thinks we know exist from experience, though he is clear that we do not directly sense *that* such forms are accidents, even though we do directly sense *them* (*MD* XXXVIII, 1, 12).

[73]A "reductive" proof for the existence of substances is found in *MD* XXXII, 1, 5.

[74]Since act is a perfection, if there are accidental acts there can be substantial acts because the former is less perfect than the latter and, hence, less likely to exist. But Suarez thinks we experience the existence of accidental acts, for example the color of a leaf, or the warmth of a stone.

[75]This supposes the demonstration of the existence of prime matter found in *MD* XIII, 1-3. Granted that demonstration, the argument given here is that substantial being is a very perfect mode of being and perfection and act go together. Hence, if there can be a substantial potency, there can be a substantial actuality. But there is a substantial potency because there is prime matter; hence, there can be a substantial actuality.

If one were to object to this argument on the grounds that the principle that perfection, actuality and substantial being are intrinsically linked together make it impossible for there to be a substantial potency, Suarez would respond that all things are to some extent actual and perfect. Thus, to say a thing is potential is to say it is actual in some respect but that it can be informed by a new entity. Therefore, with respect to the entity that can inform it, it is potential. For Suarez matter is not wholly potential or imperfect, but is so only relative to form (cf. *MD* XIII,5).

[76]Suarez is here arguing that if there is a substantial potency, i.e., an incomplete substantial entity, such as matter, which needs completion by another, more perfect, substantial entity, it must be possible for there to be an actuality which could complete it; for a thing is said to be potential only insofar as there could be an actuality which could complete it.

[77]In other words, the existence of substantial form is almost a corollary of the existence of prime matter, if we have proven prime matter exists. We have already seen the reason for this in note 4. For Suarez, however, form is not so easily inferred from the existence of matter, as it would be for Aquinas; indeed, Aquinas never proves matter without, thereby, thinking he has proven form. For according to Aquinas matter cannot exist without form--so if matter exists, so must form (*De principiis naturae*, chap. 2, para. 17). According to Suarez, matter can exist without form, but it naturally needs or demands form since it is incomplete without it (*MD* XIII, 5, 11).

[78]The First Cause, or God, can produce anything that is not contradictory. But form is not contradictory and matter seems to demand it. Hence, the First Cause will produce it to complete matter; therefore, it exists.

[79]Cf. *MD* XVIII, 2.

[80]The production of a human being requires the special intervention of the First Cause because the human soul is subsistent. But Suarez thinks the production of all other forms does not require any special intervention of the First Cause because such forms are not subsistent and they can be educed from the potency of matter (see below, sect. 2, 13, and *MD* XVIII, 2).

[81]In section 2 of this disputation, para. 13.

[82]*MD* XVIII, 1.

[83]This is fairly evident if one remembers that matter is almost completely passive, having in itself no active qualities, and able to be directly informed only by quantity (cf. *MD* XIII, 5, 11). Such an imperfect being obviously could not constitute the complete essence of anything, insofar as every essence is a determinate *what*, having both qualities and active powers (*MD* II, 4, 6).

[84]A common axiom of the scholastics was that every kind of potency has an act corresponding to it and in the same order as it, and *vice versa*, unless the act is *pure act*, which can admit no potency. Thus, if a potency is accidental, it is essentially completed by an accidental act and, if substantial, by a substantial act. Matter, being a substantial potency, cannot be essentially completed by an accidental act. Furthermore, since substances and accidents are in different orders of being, a substantial potency and an accidental act can only give rise to an accidental unity, such as "white man." But substances are necessarily essentially one, so that a substantial potency must be completed by a substantial act. For Suarez's view of the distinction between accidental and essential unities, see *MD* IV, 3.

[85]The principle employed in this objection would seem to be that any form which can exist in a subject or not in a subject without the corruption of the subject, is an accidental form. This objection is based on a definition of accident common to the scholastics (cf. Ockham, *Summa logicae*, I, ch. 25). Suarez rejects this definition of accident because he thinks that all really distinct essences can, by the power of God, exist separately. Thus, for Suarez accidents are essences which are ordered, not just to any subject, but to a subject which already has a complete substantial

essence. Matter, however, has no complete substantial essence without form; hence, form is not an accident of matter, even though matter could, by the divine power, exist without form, and *vice versa*; see below sec. 9.

[86]For Suarez such forms depend on matter in the sense that they are incomplete without matter and so cannot naturally exist without it. Without matter they could not act since all their actions, except only the actions of the higher powers in humans, require physical organs. God, however, could preserve them without matter, as He could preserve a human being without air, even though a human being naturally depends on air to exist (cf. sect. 8).

[87]Form must be reductively in the category of substance since it is a constituent of substance (cf. *MD* XXXII, 1, 16).

[88]Suarez showed this especially in sections 8-15.

[89]Suarez has argued that form is needed 1) to account for substantial change, 2) to account for the inseparability of certain accidents from substances, 3) to account for the return of certain accidents to their substances after having been destroyed by extrinsic agents and, above all, 4) to give complete substantial being to substances. Hence, if his arguments are good, he has given ample grounds for the belief that there are substantial forms, contrary to the first reason for doubting their existence.

[90]*MD* XXXIV, 5, 14-21.

[91]Cf. para. 16 above.

[92]MD *XVI*, 1, 13. The basic point is that an accident inheres in an *already complete* essence, whether that essence is substantial or accidental; whereas the substantial form *completes* an essence, since matter is incomplete on its own. Hence, form in actualizing matter does not inhere in it in the way an accident does in a substance.

Section II
In What Way Substantial Forms
Can Come to Be in Matter and from Matter

1. **The Nature of the Difficulty.** The reason for doubting that substantial forms can come to be in and from matter was touched on in the preceding section.[1] For the substantial form is a thing distinct from matter. Therefore, either it is something before its generation, or it is nothing. If it is something, it is, therefore, a substantial form before it comes to be since that thing is indivisible and is essentially a substantial form.[2] That thing, therefore, cannot be something before generation without being a substantial form. This, however, is impossible, first, because otherwise there would be no substantial generation and, also, because there would be incompatible substantial forms existing simultaneously in matter.[3]

If the other alternative is chosen, namely, that before generation the form is nothing, it follows that a form comes to be out of nothing, which is contrary to the axiom of the philosophers: *Nothing comes to be out of nothing.* Nor is it satisfactory to respond that it is not the form which comes to be but the composite, while the composite comes to be from matter, and thus there is nothing that comes to be out of nothing. This is, I say, not satisfactory because this reply consists more in words and in a manner of speaking than in reality. For the form really did not exist before generation, and afterwards it does exist; therefore, it came to be. Again, this reply is not satisfactory because the composite does not come to be except insofar as it is composed out of matter and form; it is, however, not composed except out of real entities.[4] Finally, this reply does not suffice because when the whole composite is corrupted, the form truly ceases to exist and passes into nothing; for it was something before and afterwards it is nothing. Therefore, when the whole begins to be, the form also comes to be.[5]

2. **The belief of the ancient philosophers is rejected.** Because of this difficulty the ancient philosophers denied the existence of substantial forms, and they judged that all things come to be only through changes in accidents. Their opinion has already been disproved by the demonstration of the existence of substantial form and of generation and corruption. But we now add that the ancient philosophers did not solve the difficulty by denying substantial forms, unless they would also deny accidental forms which truly and really come to be as new and unless they, for this reason, would say that there is no change in things, except perhaps change in place. They would have to say that things only seem to change because those things which were seen are

now hidden and those which were hidden are now seen. It is perfectly obvious how absurd this view is. Our claim is evident because the same difficulty can be raised concerning accidental form, for that form also, when it exists, has its own reality and entity.[6] Either, therefore, it was something before it came to be, or it was nothing. If it was something, then it did not come to be. If it was nothing, then it comes to be out of nothing. Hence Anaxagores, as we saw above, conceded that all forms were actually present in the atoms, and from their various ways of coming together he accounted for the composition of all things, but that opinion was sufficiently refuted above.[7]

The First View Is Given And Interpreted In Various Ways

3. **Albert the Great is acquitted of holding this opinion.** Once the ancient philosophers, therefore, have been set aside, there are various opinions concerning this matter among later philosophers. The first opinion is that all forms actually exist in matter, but not as whole and complete, because those who hold this opnion see that their whole and complete existence destroys true generation and corruption of things and involves a manifest contradiction since these forms are incompatible with one another and since the same argument holds for accidental forms which are at times properly contrary to one another.[8] But these philosophers say that form actually exists in matter according to a certain inchoate state.

In his *Commentary on the Physics* I, q. 7, Domingo de Soto attributes this opinion to Albert at the same passage tract. 3, chap. 3.[9] Benedict Soncinas, on the other hand, in his *Commentary on the Metaphysics,* VII, q. 28, denies that this is Albert's opinion. And, indeed, Albert only says that in matter, which is the subject of forms, there is a certain confused state of the same forms. This state, however, he declares to be nothing other than an habitual potency by which matter includes forms in itself. He indicates, however, that this confused state by reason of which form is said to pre-exist in matter is something distinct from the nature of matter: "Nor do I intend," he says, "to say that part of the form comes from inside and part from outside; rather, the whole comes from the inside and the whole comes from the outside." In saying this, he indicates that the form comes from inside, that is, it pre-exists in matter according to its essential being, and for this reason he says that "the agent does not act to produce the form's essence, but the form's being." And in this sense he had said that the "whole form is from outside," that is, it is produced by an efficient cause insofar as the existential being is concerned.

Although all of these things have been said very obscurely, they can be brought in line with the correct meaning, if by "essential being" we understand merely being in potency, which is not produced by a natural agent but is already presupposed in matter. Hence, in his *Commentary on the Metaphys-*

ics V, treatise 2, chap. 12,[10] Albert also says that the whole form is from inside according to potential being, and from outside according to actual being, and in his *Commentary on the Physics* VIII, chapter 4, he also calls the potency for form an "inchoate form." We rightly understand by that "confused state" the potency of matter itself, which Albert himself calls a "habitual power." He only seems to distinguish the potency of matter from the matter itself which concerns another question dealt with above, and it could probably have been explained by a distinction of reason and not by a real distinction. For in the same place and in the same way he distinguishes in a genus the nature of the genus from the power by which it contains the differences.

4. Another opinion is reported by Durand of Saint Pourçain in his *Commentary on the Sentences*, dist. 18, q. 2,[11] which posits in matter certain possibilities for forms which do not remain when forms are produced, but are converted into them. In this way he avoided asserting that forms are made out of nothing, but from these possibilities. However, Durand does not report any source of this view, and therefore we cannot with certainty state the meaning of it. Nevertheless, it is hardly believable that by that possibility such authors understood something really distinct from matter and form, but only the essence with the possibility for form, which others say is in objective potency.[12] And yet, if this is all that is meant by this opinion, it proposes nothing novel in order to explain that form is not created; after all, even things which are created are made from such a possibility. De Soto,[13] finally, reports another opinion of Peter Auriol in his *Commentary on the Sentences* 2, dist. 18,[14] that form pre-exists in matter according to a part from which it is completed by the action of the agent, and thus it does not come to be out of nothing. But John Capreolus does not report this opinion from Auriol, nor was I able to find it in any other author.

5. In whatever sense, therefore, it is asserted that some thing distinct from matter itself pre-exists in matter in order that form might be produced from it, it is improbable and completely useless in solving the difficulty which we are concerned with. The first point is evident because it is impossible to understand what that thing would be or what sort of entity it would have, since it is either a substance or an accident. The latter is not asserted by those authors who hold this view, nor can it be held. The first reason is that an accident is not an intrinsic and inchoate state of the substantial form, but can at most be a disposition for the reception of the substantial form.[15] The second reason is that, even supposing the accident pre-existed, that would not avoid the problem that the whole reality of the form would come to be out of nothing because an accident is not anything belonging to the substantial form.[16]

But if the second alternative, namely, that the pre-existing entity is a substance, is held, it will be again asked whether that substance is matter, or form, or the composite. It cannot be the composite, as is self-evident.[17] Nor can it be matter because it is supposed to be a thing distinct from matter. Nor can it be form because the form is what begins to be through generation. Perhaps it will be held to be the form in imperfect being. But against this I will further object, since I presuppose that the discussion concerns the actual being by which a thing is a true and actual entity outside its own causes. For it would be very silly to speak only concerning possible being, because according to that being one does not posit in matter a true thing distinct from matter, a thing which is outside of nothing and is a form in imperfect being.

6. Speaking, therefore, concerning such a thing which has true and actual being even though imperfect, I ask how from that thing form can come to be a complete being, that is, whether it is through an intensification or through the transformation of the one into the other. Besides these ways no other can be conceived. For in the first way the original entity which was imperfect remains, when its imperfection is removed by something which is added to it. In the latter way, however, that imperfect entity is destroyed and a perfect one takes its place, whether through the conversion of the one into the other or in some other way. Those two ways form, therefore, an immediate contradiction; hence, it is impossible to conceive any other way which would not be reduced to one or the other of these two.

The first way [i.e., by intensification], however, does not seem at all likely: first, because the substantial form cannot become more intense or less intense, as I will show below,[18] and second, because otherwise all substantial forms which can be educed from it would actually pre-exist in matter at, of course, a less intense level, but still in accord with some real and actual entity. And thus an infinite number of actual entities would be simultaneously in matter since forms can be infinitely multiplied. This, however, is clearly absurd, first, on account of the infinity of entities,[19] second, because of itself matter does not have such innate forms emanating, as it were, from its own proper entity. Nor is there some agent by which they are made, nor are they themselves owed to matter itself so that we should imagine that God infused them or created them along with matter.[20] A third reason is that, even if we posit those imperfect entities, the same difficulty remains, namely, how there comes to be that level or part of the entity which is added to the preceding. For it absolutely begins to exist though it was nothing before. After all, in forms which are intensified, the second level of the form does not properly come to be from the first, except perhaps as from a *terminus a quo*. In this way the latter level comes to be from a decrease in intensity or limitation of the prior, which is a privation of the later level, rather than from the positive entity itself of the prior level.[21] Therefore, the fact that one level is presupposed does not do away with the fact that the second level was nothing until it received being through the action of an agent. Concerning that level, therefore, the same difficulty remains, namely, how it does not come to be out of nothing. Finally, according to this opinion, true substantial generation and corruption is destroyed because there would only be an intensification and a decrease in intensification of forms.[22]

7. Nor are there lacking equally efficacious arguments against the latter way [i.e., by change of one into the other] of understanding this. For, first, from that way it follows that infinite entities are presupposed in matter, since one cannot imagine that one and the same entity is the inchoate state of all forms. For, if when one form comes to be, its inchoate state is destroyed and done away with, while the others remain, and if it can happen this way to all of them in turn and respectively, it is, therefore, necessary that all these entities be distinct from one other.

Second, if a perfect form comes to be from an inchoate state through change or conversion, the one only comes to be from the other as from a *terminus a quo*.[23] Therefore, the whole entity of the form, which was actually nothing before, comes to be. For one cannot say that the entity of the form pre-existed on account of its preexisting inchoate state, since they are distinct things, one of which perishes, when the other begins to be. Therefore, that imperfect entity is useless in explaining how a form does not come to be out of nothing. For that inchoate state is not anything that is a part or level of that form which comes to be. But if a relation to a positive *terminus a quo* is necessary or sufficient in order that something does not come to be out of nothing, then that inchoate state is not also necessary for this. For the contrary or incompatible form which is always driven out when another is introduced is sufficient, since the generation of the one is the corruption of the other.[24]

Third, it can be asked whether that imperfect entity which is cast out and the perfect form which is introduced are of the same essential species or of distinct essential species. For, if they are of distinct essential species, then each one is perfect in its own species, and if one casts out the other, they will be incompatible with each other; therefore, to posit those inchoate states is nothing other than to multiply forms in matter without any benefit. For, in order that one form should come to be from an incompatible *terminus*, a single contrary or incompatible form suffices and is presupposed in every case. But if those entities are of the same species, no reason can be given why one should cast out the other or why one should come to be in the subject in which the other actually pre-existed.

8. **The difference which Aristotle posited between matters of diverse artifacts.** But you will object that in *Metaphysics*, book VII, text. 29 [1034a22], Aristotle says that in matter there is some part of the thing to be made and locates the difference between artificial and natural things in the fact that in artificial things there is only presupposed matter apt to obey the artificer, while in natural things there is something of the form to be introduced.[25]

This is proven because, otherwise, the natural generation of a complete substance would not be greater than the production of an artificial thing in its matter.

I respond to this that Aristotle calls the aptitude of matter for the form a part of the thing to be produced. Both St. Thomas and Alexander of Hales[26] explain this passage in this way, and it could be understood to refer to a part, not of the form as such, but of the whole composite. But the proper interpretation of the passage is that Aristotle does not call matter itself the part, but some active power which is occasionally joined to matter and which cooperates in the generation or production of the thing. For Aristotle is there wondering why some things which are produced by art are also at times produced by chance and without art, such as health, but at times never happen to be made without art, such as a house, and he answers that the reason is that at times in the matter from which or about which the art operates there precedes some part which can be a principle of motion or operation. For example, health is preceded by the warmth of the animal, which happens to be excited or increased from other causes apart from the art and thus produces health without the art and by a certain chance. But sometimes there is no active power in the matter of the art, for example, in stones and wood, and therefore a house cannot be made from these without art.

Aristotle, therefore, is not speaking about an inchoate state of forms, as St. Thomas and Duns Scotus[27] correctly noted, but about a power which is at times in matter for beginning an action. This interpretation was also given by the Commentator[28] and by Alexander of Aphrodisias. Hence, it is false and entirely unsupported by the text of Aristotle to suppose that he is there establishing the difference between natural and artificial things. For he is only establishing a difference between artifacts, and in the same book in text 31 [1034a31], Aristotle indicates that the same thing happens in natural things, as St. Thomas noted. For at times the passive subject from which a natural thing is generated is only in passive potency, and in that case something can be generated from it only by an extrinsic natural agent. But at other times it has some seminal active power joined to it, which is a *quasi* part of it, as is evident in the case of seed or in a grain of wheat, and in that case it happens that the effect comes to be without another extrinsic agent.

To the confirmation of the above argument I respond that generation is natural on the part of the natural passive potency and, consequently, also on the part of the natural active potency which corresponds to the passive potency. But in artificial things there is not so much a natural passive potency as there is an obediential potency,[29] to which there does not correspond a natural active potency, but a rational or ideal potency, as we will explain a little below.[30]

Not All Substantial Forms are Created

9. **Plato and Avicenna are exonerated of error.** The second opinion belongs to others who, overcome by the difficulty touched on, said that all substantial forms come to be through creation. Albert the Great reports this opinion in his *Commentary on the Sentences* 2, dist. 18, art. 12,[31] and some attribute this view to Plato in the *Phaedo* [100d-101], because he said that the forms are introduced into matter from the separate ideas, and to Avicenna in *Sufficientia* book I, c. 10, and book IX of his *Metaphysics*, where he says that the same forms are induced by a separate intelligence, the tenth intelligence, which he said presides over the sublunar world and comes after the nine which preside over the nine celestial bodies. But though these two philosophers perhaps erred concerning the productive principle of substantial forms, about which we will speak later when treating the efficient cause,[32] it is not, nevertheless, clear that they erred concerning the mode of producing these forms. Nor did Aristotle attack Plato for this reason, but because he introduced the separate ideas without a reason, since material substances can be generated by things similar to themselves.

This argument has more weight against Avicenna. For Plato perhaps did not place the ideas outside of the divine mind, and he said the forms were introduced from them, as from a universal principle which does not exclude the proximate agents. Avicenna erred, however, in attributing the creation of lower intelligences to the higher and the introduction of substantial forms to the lowest intelligence. It is not, nevertheless, established that he said that all the lower forms are made by creation. That is why Benedict Soncinas, in his *Commentary on the Metaphysics*, book VII, q. 29, thinks that Avicenna's opinion can be defended as probable. We will speak about this in the place already cited concerning the efficient cause,[33] and again below when treating of the created intelligences [i.e., the angels].[34]

But whoever held that opinion, it is improbable if it is taken as universal. Regarding the rational soul it is true and Catholic doctrine, but regarding the other forms it is false, since, otherwise, all substantial forms would be subsistent and independent of matter in their coming to be and, consequently, also in their being.[35] This is absurd; otherwise, the souls of brute animals would be immortal.[36] The inference is clear because creation is the production of subsisting things and does not depend on a material cause, as we will show below.

Second, the reason implied above weighs against this opinion, namely, that, if the substantial forms are created for the reason given, the accidental forms are necessarily also created, for an accidental form also comes to be out of nothing of itself and does not actually pre-exist in the subject either according to its totality or according to a part. If this is conceded, it follows further that, just as the introduction of the substantial form is not brought about by natural agents for this reason, so the production of the accidental form is also not. And thus it finally follows that the natural agents produce nothing at all, which we will show below is most absurd.[37]

Resolution of the Question

10. **A prior assertion about the rational soul.** It is a true and peripatetic view that among substantial forms some are spiritual, substantial, and independent of matter, though they truly inform matter,[38] while other forms are material and so inherent in matter that they depend on it in their being and their coming to be. Only human souls are of the first group, for we are dealing solely with informing forms,[39] and concerning these one must concede the inferred conclusion in the difficulty touched on, namely, that they come to be out of nothing by true creation. This must be shown more at length in the proper place. Now it is sufficient to say that it is a necessary consequence of the principle posited, on the supposition that these souls do not pre-exist before being united to bodies, a point which is certain by faith and by the principle that they are true forms of the body.[40]

In fact, even if they pre-existed, they could not possibly come to exist except by creation because they are not beings necessary from themselves and possessed of being from their own quiddity,[41] as we shall demonstrate as a universal claim below, partly in the disputation concerning the efficient cause,[42] partly when demonstrating that there is only one uncreated being. If, however, the rational soul does not have being except by the action of another and is supposed to be before the body, it is in a certain way clearer and more evident that it has being by creation because it is made out of nothing and without the concurrence of a subject or of a material cause.

I say that it is in a certain way clearer because, now when the disposition of body is required in order that the soul might come to be, it can seem that it is not so properly creation, because it comes to be with some concurrence of matter. It is, nevertheless, true creation because on the part of the body there is no concurrence that is essential and in the genus of material cause[43] for the very being or coming to be of the rational soul. But there is, as it were, a certain occasion that demands the creation of that soul, and without this occasion it is not owed to the soul that it should come to be, nor could its cause be determined to its production.[44] However, that the body or matter does not of itself influence the coming to be or the being of the rational soul is clear from the fact that the rational soul, when separated from the body, retains its own being. Therefore, it does not depend on a sustaining subject in its being; hence, neither does it depend on one in its coming to be, because the coming to be of a thing is of the same sort as its being. Therefore, conversely, the subject itself or matter also does not have an essential influence on the being or coming to be of such a soul. For these two are correlatives or rather are the same thing, namely, the dependence of the effect and the influence of the cause.[45]

11. **The axiom, *Nothing comes to be out of nothing*, ought to be limited**. Hence, the principle, *Nothing comes to be out of nothing*, taken universally concerning all causes and effects, is false[46] and contrary to natural reason, as the example of the rational soul itself shows, and also the example of prime matter, which was touched on above, and we shall add more examples in the following. But understood concerning the power of a finite and natural agent it is true.[47] Hence, one ought to concede concerning this form that proximate natural agents do not have the power to produce it, but that the proximate agent disposes the matter, while a separate intelligence produces the form,[48] not, of course, a created intelligence, as Avicenna thought, nor an idea that is separate and existing outside of God, but God Himself whom we shall show below is the sole cause of all things which come to be through creation.

12. **Prime matter is a natural potency for the rational soul**. You will say that it results from this view that prime matter is not in a natural potency with respect to the rational soul, which seems problematic. The inference is evident because an active natural potency corresponds to every passive natural potency, but there is no active natural potency which can produce this form in matter. Therefore, there is no natural passive potency in matter either.

Some concede the inference both on account of the argument given and also because, if matter were in potency with respect to the rational soul, when this soul comes to be, it would be said to be educed from the potency of matter. But this opinion is unsatisfactory. For, if matter were not in natural potency with respect to the rational soul, the generation of a human being would not be natural since it would not be natural either because of an active or passive natural principle.[49] It is likewise unsatisfactory because matter is naturally disposed for ultimately receiving the rational form, and such a form is owed to it according to the order of nature when it is disposed in that a way. It is, therefore, in natural potency with respect to the rational soul.

I respond to the objection by denying the inference. To the first argument I answer that a natural potency primarily and essentially ought to be considered in relation to its connatural and proportionate act. The rational soul, however, is a natural and proportionate act of matter, and for this reason matter also is a natural potency with respect to that act.[50] Hence, from both there comes to be a certain natural being which is essentially [*per se*] one, and matter itself is connaturally conserved under such an act. But with respect to what concerns the active potency, there can, first of all, be a natural active potency for uniting such an act to such a potency, and in this way a natural active potency now corresponds to the passive natural potency. Second, although this form can be made only by God, in this action, nevertheless, God acts according to the manner and order owed to natural things, and this suffices so that He may be said to operate in the manner of a natural cause and so that a sufficient active potency may correspond to the passive potency.[51]

To the other argument, I respond that it is one thing for matter to contain the form in potency, and quite another for it to be in potency to the form. The first of these indicates a power for causing the form since a cause contains the effect in its own genus. But the second only indicates a capacity for receiving form. Matter, therefore, is in natural potency for receiving the rational soul, but does not, nevertheless, contain it in its potency since it is not able to cause it. For this reason the rational soul is not educed from the potency of matter because nothing is educed except from that which contains it and because eduction connotes the causality of matter on form, as I shall now explain.[52]

13. **All substantial forms, except the rational form, come to be from a previously existing subject.** Secondly, one should say concerning all other substantial forms that they do not properly come to be out of nothing, but are educed from the potency of the pre-existing matter. And for this reason, in the production of these forms nothing comes to be contrary to the axiom: *Nothing comes to be out of nothing*, if it is rightly understood. This assertion is taken from Aristotle in *Physics* book I, *passim*, and in book VII of the *Metaphysics* [1032a20], and from other authors, whom I will immediately mention. This point can be briefly explained. For to come to be out of nothing is said in two senses: One is to come to be absolutely and simply; another is to come to be produced out of nothing. The first is properly said concerning a subsistent thing because to be belongs to the same thing to which to come to be belongs. That, however, properly is which subsists and has being, for that which inheres in another is rather that by which something else is. For this reason, therefore, substantial material forms do not come to be out of nothing because they do not properly come to be. And this is the reason St. Thomas gives in the *Summa theologiae* I, q. 45, a. 8, and q. 90, a. 2, and it will be explained more by what we shall say.

If one takes "to come to be," therefore, properly and rigorously, to come to be out of nothing means for a thing to come to be according to its whole being, that is, without presupposing a part of the thing from which it might be made. And for this reason, when natural things newly come to be, they do not come to be out of nothing because they come to be out of a presupposed matter of which they are composed, and thus they do not come to be according to their entirety, but according to some part of themselves. But although the forms of these things really newly receive their whole entity which they did not have before, nevertheless, because they themselves do not come to be, as we said, they also do not for this reason come to be out of nothing. But, if one takes the expression "to come to be" in a wider sense, one cannot deny that the form has come to be in the way in which it now is and was not before, as is proved by the reason for doubting given in the beginning of the section.

For this reason one ought to add that, if "to come to be" is taken in this wide sense, to come to be out of nothing not only removes the function of a material cause, which is an intrinsic component of that which comes to be, but even the function of a material cause which essentially causes and sustains the form which comes to be or comes to be together with it.[53] For we said above that matter is a cause of the composite and of the form that depends on it; therefore, in order that the thing might be said to come to be out of nothing, both modes of causality must be denied, and the axiom ought to be understood in the same sense in order that it might be true: *Nothing comes to be out of nothing*, that is, nothing comes to be by the power of a natural and finite agent, except out of a presupposed subject which essentially concurs in the production of both the composite and the form, if both[54] are produced in the same way by the same agent.

From these points, therefore, it is rightly concluded that substantial material forms do not come to be out of nothing because they come to be out of matter which in its own genus essentially concurs in and has influence on the being and coming to be of such forms. For, just as they cannot exist except as attached to the matter by which they are sustained in being, so they also cannot come to be unless their production and penetration is sustained by the same matter. And this is the proper and essential difference between production out of nothing and out of something, and on account of it, as we shall show below, the prior mode of production, but not the latter, surpasses the finite power of a natural agent.

14. **What it means to be educed from the potency of matter is explained in various ways. The first way.** From this it is established that these forms are not properly said to be created, but to be educed from the potency of matter, and many labor at explaining what it means to be educed from the potency of matter, both in their commentaries on *Physics* I and in their commentaries on *Metaphysics* VII. St. Thomas briefly explained both passages in *Summa Theologiae* I, Q. 90, a 2, ad. 2. For, since these forms do not come to be out of nothing, they are not created because to be created means to come to be made out of nothing. But even though these forms are contained in the potency of matter and come to be by an action of an agent outside, as it were, that potency, this does not mean that they exist outside of matter, nor that they do

not actualize the potency of matter and inhere in it. It only means that, since, before they come to be they are only contained in potency and in their cause and after they come to be they are actually and outside their cause, they are, therefore, made from the potential being of matter, in which they were contained,[55] and they are educed into act by the power of the agent with the concurrence of the same matter.

You will say: Therefore, for the same reason things are educed from the potency of the agent because they are also contained in it virtually and potentially, and from this being in potency they are educed into act by the action of the agent. I respond to this by absolutely denying the inference because those words in all propriety signify the function of a material, not of an efficient cause. And so, both the efficient cause and the matter can be said to contain the effect, though in a different way, for the agent contains it eminently or virtually, but matter contains it only in a receptive or passive potency.[56] When, therefore, form is said to be educed from the potency of matter, this specifically denotes the function of the material cause, but by its own power the agent is properly said to educe the effect from potency into act.

15. **The second way**. It is also customary to explain what it means for the form to be educed from the potency of matter in another way, namely, that it means to come to be in matter with a dependence upon it in being and in coming to be, and this fits all substantial forms, except the rational form. This explanation differs only verbally from the preceding, because, as I said above, the fact that matter contains something in its potency implies causality or power of causing on the part of matter in its own genus. Therefore, for form to be drawn out or to come to be outside of the potency of matter in which it is contained is nothing other than for it to actually come to be in matter, with matter itself concurring in its own genus through its potency for the coming to be and the being of such a form. But this is itself for form to come to be with a dependence upon matter in coming to be and being, and this is only a difference in explaining eduction through the relation of effect to cause and, conversely, through the relation of cause to effect.

Likewise, another explanation comes to mind; although it does not contain anything different from the preceding explanations, it does, nevertheless, more fully clarify the point and is more suitable for explaining several difficulties. For form to be educed from the potency of matter means that it comes to be by the same action by which the composite comes to be from pre-existing matter which does not come to be through that action. St. Thomas seems to have intended this explanation when he said that the form is not created but educed because it is not the form which is of itself produced, but the composite, while the form is produced along with the composite from pre-existing matter. And by induction it is established that this happens in all forms which are educed from the potency of matter. But an argument can be given, because eduction consists in the fact that there is an action or change intrinsically and essentially dependent on matter. But through this action the form comes to be and is at the same time united with matter. Therefore, through the same action the composite first essentially comes to be, and such a form is produced along with it and becomes actual outside the potency of matter. Therefore, the eduction of the form from the potency of matter is very well explained by this action.

Corollaries From the Preceding Solution

16. **The rational soul is not educed from the potency of matter.** And from this one now understands better what we said above, namely, that the rational form is not educed from the potency of the matter because it is neither contained in the potency of matter so that it could be educed out of it, nor does it come to be or exist in dependence on matter, nor does it come to be by the same action by which the composite is made or by which it is united to matter. For the rational form comes to be in itself, at least by a priority of nature, and receives its own being as independent of matter, and afterward it is united to matter by another action by which the whole composite is generated.[57]

17. **Whether the forms of heavenly bodies are educed from the potency of matter.** Second, from what has been said we are freed from another difficulty which arose here concerning the heavenly forms, namely, whether such forms can be said to be educed from the potency of matter.[58] For according to the previous interpretations it seemed that we ought to affirm that they are educed. For those forms depend in their coming to be and in their being on their matter. Therefore, they are educed from the potency of it. For, if they depend on it in their coming to be and their being, they are caused by the matter; therefore, they are contained in its potency. Therefore, when they come to be in act, they are educed from its potency. Nor is it satisfactory to respond that these forms do not come to be, but come to be along with their composites, because the forms of generable things also do not come to be, but come to be along with their composites, and yet they are said to be educed because of their dependence upon matter and containment in it.

One should, nevertheless, say along with the common opinion, that these forms are not truly educed because, where the whole composite is not generated, the form also cannot be educed. The *a priori* reason for this is that, as was above touched on,[59] there is a single action by which the heaven is produced in its totality, and by which not only the form but also the matter comes to be, and this action is the entire and complete creation of the whole and the concreation of its matter and form. And for this reason there is in this case no eduction of the form from the potency of matter.[60] When, therefore, a form is said to be educed which depends in its coming to be and in its being upon matter, it is understood that in that case the proper coming to be and proper action which presupposes matter in such a way that the matter does not come to be through it tends toward the form itself or the formal being which is communicated by it. And, similarly, when the form is said to be educed from the potency of matter because it was contained in matter's potency, it is presupposed that matter exists in potency with respect to the form before it actually has it. But though the matter of the heaven is in potency to its own form, it demands by its nature that it is not in potency with respect to it, because this being in potency includes a privation.

Notes

[1] Sect. 1, para. 3

[2] The notion here is that a substantial form cannot be at all except as a complete form since it is that which gives substantial being to the substance. As such, it is itself substantial, and substantial being does not admit of degrees (see below sect. 10,44). Therefore, if it pre-existed in matter, it would already constitute with the matter a complete substance and there could be no substantial generation.

[3] The reason for this is that, since matter can acquire any and all substantial forms, if any substantial form pre-exists in matter, they all must. This, however, is impossible since some substantial forms have incompatible properties, e.g., the substantial forms of fire and water.

[4] The idea is that, since the composite is made out of real entities, if it comes to be, *some* real entity must come to be besides the composite itself, even if it is only one of the parts making up the composite. This seems correct unless it be supposed that the forms of all things have always existed and at some time are placed in a bit of matter. Suarez would hold that this notion is absurd since most material forms need matter to naturally exist (e.g., the form of a rose) and all of them, even the human soul, need matter to be complete.

[5] Suarez is here supposing that the corruption of a thing is the reverse of its generation. But when a thing corrupts, its form ceases to be. Therefore, when it is generated, its form must come to be.

[6] For Suarez, there are real accidents which really modify the being of substances, e.g., the redness of a rose. Since these accidents are real and have their own essences, they have their own proper existence according to Suarezian metaphysics. Hence, when they begin to modify a substance, they are really made and come to be. This is contrary to the views of such thinkers as Descartes and Leibniz who held that an accident is just a substance in a certain state (e.g., the redness of the rose is the red-rose). In this way accidents include the being of their subjects. (On this see Leibniz's *Theodicy*, part one, paras. 27, 89.)

[7] *MD* XIII 2, 3-5.

[8] For example, hot and cold.

[9] Perhaps de Soto had the following passage in mind: "Materia enim est subjectum formarum in entibus, et habet in se habitum confusum formarum, qui habitus imperfectus est et indistinctus, et hic habitus si accipiatur in materia communi, est sicut in genere remota." *B Alberti Magni, Opera Omnia, Vol. 3, Liber primus physicorum,* ed. by Augusti Borgnet (Paris: Vivès, 1890), trac. III, c. III, p. 50.

[10] *Metaphysicorum Lib. XIII, Opera Omnia,* Vol. VI, ed. A. Borgnet (Paris: Vivès, 1890).

[11] *In Petri Lombardi Sententias theologicas commentariorum libros II* (Venice: Guerra, 1571; rep. Gregg, 1964).

[12] By "objective potency" the scholastics signified the potency of a mere possibility, all of the properties of which are internally compatible. As such, an objective potency has existence only insofar as it is or could be the term or "object" of the power of an agent capable of bringing it about.

In contrast to this sort of potency the scholastics distinguished the potency of a real and existing being capable of some further actualization (e.g., a lump of clay). Such a potency they called "subjective potency" because it inheres in an existing subject.

[13] *Commentariorum fratris Dominici Soto Segobiensis...in IV Sententiarum* (Salamanca, 1572).

[14] *Commentariorum in primum [-quatrum] librum sententiarum* (Rome: Vatican, 1596-1605).

[15] That is, accidents can make matter apt for receiving certain substantial forms. So the shape and internal organs of a fetus makes it apt for receiving a human soul.

[16] Suarez is insisting that an accident can in no way help to intrinsically constitute a substance; substances can only be made from other (incomplete) substances. Therefore, pre-existent accidents cannot really help solve the present difficulty.

[17] The reason for this is that the composite is what is made as such when a new substantial form is produced since it is what is primarily intended by generation, and the form is intended only insofar as it contributes to the being of the composite.

[18] Sect. 10, 44.

[19] Suarez is here following Aristotle's view that an actually infinite plurality is impossible. The reason is that an actuality must be definite. But any definite plurality of things is some determinate number, no matter how large, and, hence, is finite.

[20] The argument sketched here is a dilemma:

1) If forms pre-exist in matter, then either (a) they naturally emanate from matter or (b) they are concreated in matter by God.

2) Not (a).

Support: Matter as pure potency doesn't have the inherent perfection to give itself substantial forms.

3) Not (b).

Support: Matter's own essential being does not include substantial forms.

4) Therefore, forms do not pre-exist in matter.

[21] For example, a higher degree of heat is not exactly made from or out of a lesser degree, but a lesser degree could, in some sense, be made from a higher degree of heat. Or, again, a greater amount of something, say a larger snowball, isn't properly speaking made from a smaller amount of that thing, but a smaller amount is made from a larger one.

[22] That is, the production of more or less of a thing is an accidental not a substantial change. So, if forms came to be by augmentation, they would come to be by an accidental, not a substantial change.

[23] In other words, it is not made *from* the prior form as from some part of it; if it were, we would be talking about augmentation. It is only improperly made from it in the way a dead rabbit is made from a rabbit, or in the way wine is made from water, as opposed to wine's being made from water's *matter*.

[24]That is, all natural generation involves corruption. So when a rabbit is killed, prior to the eduction of the corpse form, the form of the rabbit ceases to be and the rabbit corrupts.

[25]So, for example, wood is a chair in potency only in the sense that a carpenter could make it into a chair. A seed, on the other hand, has some sort of intrinsic power in it contributing to its becoming a tree, and in this sense it seems to have in it the nature of what it will become in the way the wood, at least as ordered to the chair, does not.

[26]*In duodecim Aristotelis Metaphysicae libros* (Venice: Simon Galignarius de Karera, 1572).

[27]*B. Ioannis Duns Scoti Quaestiones super Libros Metaphysicorum Aristotelis*, Books VI-IX, ed. R. Andrews, G. Etzkorn *et al.* (St. Bonaventure, NY: St. Bonaventure University, 1994).

[28]*In Libros Metaphysicorum Aristotelis* (Venice: apud Junctas, 1574). "The Commentator" is Averroes.

[29]By "obediential potency" Suarez meant a kind of passive ability creatures have for receiving properties which they are not naturally ordered to. Of such a power is the soul's passive ability to receive supernatural graces (*MD* XLIII sect. 4).

[30]*MD* XLIII 4,17. Since the matter of an artifact does not, by its natural form, *tend* towards the accidental forms imprinted on it, Suarez and other scholatics referred to its ordering to such forms as an obediential power. These forms are impressed on their appropriate matter by a mind which contains them ideally, i.e., in thought.

[31]*Commentarii in II Sententiarum, Opera Omnia*, Vol. XXVII, ed. A. Borgnet (Paris: Vivès, 1894).

[32]*MD* XVIII 1,15.

[33]*Ibid.*.

[34]*MD* XXXV 6,1-14.

[35]This follows for Suarez from his definition of creation. For, in order for a thing to be created, it must not only not be made *out of* any thing else—and this applies to all forms, but not to their composites—but must be made so that it does not naturally require to be sustained *in* something.

[36]That is, since they would not naturally require their bodies to subsist, the souls of brutes would *naturally* survive death, i.e., they would survive death without any miraculous action on God's part.

[37]*MD* XVIII sect. 1.

[38]Suarez felt the need to assert this because in his time certain radical Aristotelians held the soul to be mortal. The most famous of these was Pomponazzi, who seemed to have influenced Cajetan in his denial that natural reason could prove the immortality of the human soul. On this see F. Copleston, *A History of Philosophy: Vol.3, Late Medieval and Renaissance Philosophy, Part II* (Garden City: The Newman Press, 1963), pp. 158-159.

[39]That is, only with those forms which inform or actualize matter. Suarez says that the angels, who are pure spirits lacking bodies, are also called forms, but analogically due to their beauty and actuality (see sect. 1, the introduction).

[40]A true corporeal form naturally requires matter to sustain it in a way analogous to the way accidents require a substance to sustain them. Since this is the case, such a form could not exist prior to being united to matter.

[41]To possess being by its own quiddity, an essence must simply be independent of anything else for its existence. For Suarez, only God has such independence.

[42]*MD* XX 1,15-22. Suarez thinks he has both *a posteriori* and *a priori* proofs for this.

[43]That is, the body does not so sustain the being of the soul that the soul could not naturally exist without it.

[44]The reason for this is that, although the soul has a being of its own independently of the body, its being is incomplete and imperfect without the body.

[45]Cf. *MD* XVIII sect. 10.

[46]It is false because not all effects need to be made from something. This is known naturally because reason can tell us that there can only be one uncaused being. Since this is the case, the principle that *nothing comes from nothing* is false if applied universally concerning material causality. It is true, however, if applied universally concerning efficient causality. Were it not true, a thing could simply pop into being.

[47]That is, no finite agent can create *ex nihilo* (see *MD* XX sect. 2).

[48]That is, the parents of a human child prepare matter for the human soul by molding the organs of a human being in the fetus.
  It should be noted that not all of the Church Fathers taught that the human soul is created by God. Tertullian, for example, did not. And the Lutherans insisted that every human soul other than that of Adam and Eve is produced directly by its human parents. The Lutheran J. A. Quenstedt (1617-1688), one of the representatives of the so-called Protestant Orthodoxy or Protestant Scholasticism of the 17th century, used both a theological and a philosophical argument to prove this. The theological argument is based upon Scripture and on the theological principle that God could not cause sin. Since, according to the Lutherans, original sin inheres in the soul and not the body, it could not be passed on in a physical way from parent to child. Thus, if God created the children of Adam *ex nihilo*, He would have infected their souls with original sin, which is contrary to His perfect goodness. The philosophical argument is that it is natural that like be generated by like and, hence, that humans should be born of human parents. Were this not the case, beasts would be more perfectly the cause of their children than humans are, which is absurd since beasts are less perfect than humans (cf. Walther's edition of Johann Baier's *Compendium theologiae positivae*, [St. Louis: Concordia, 1879], I, cap. II, under sect. 22). For information on the Protestant Scholasticism represented by Quenstedt, see, for the Lutherans, R. D. Preus, *The Theology of Post-Reformation Lutheranism*, (St. Louis and London: Concordia, 1970) and, for the Reformed, R. A. Muller, *Post Reformation Reformed Dogmatics*, (Grand Rapids: Baker, 1993).

[49]This is another way of putting the philosophical argument of the Lutherans. I don't know whether Suarez is here referring to Lutherans or other Catholics. It seems, however, that if he were referring to contemporary Catholics, he would have given their names; hence perhaps he is referring to Lutherans, albeit to Lutherans who wrote before Quenstedt.

[50]The point seems to be that a substantial potency (p) is a natural substantial potency *iff* there is some substantial act (a) which so actualizes (p) that it composes with (p) some complete substance, regardless of whether (a) is produced by another finite being or by God.

[51]The idea here is that even the production of human souls is natural in the sense that God only produces such souls for bodies that have been formed by human beings and that are by their nature ordered to rational souls as to that which completes them.

[52]Matter is the material cause of all substantial forms other than the human form. The reason is that it sustains them in a way analogous to the way substance sustains accidents so that substantial form could not naturally exist without the sustaining causality of matter. But matter is not, strictly speaking, the material cause of the soul because it doesn't sustain the soul as a subject without which the soul could not naturally exist. It is, however, actualized by the soul and further contributes certain perfections to the soul, i.e., organs necessary for its vital operations, and in this secondary sense, as receiving and completing the soul, it is its material cause.

[53]There are two senses of material causality Suarez is distinguishing here. In the first sense, a thing (m) is the material cause of an entity (e) *iff* (m) is a constituent part of (e). In that sense matter is a material cause of the composite but not of the form since the form is not made from matter. In another sense, a thing (m) is the material cause of an entity (e) *iff* it sustains or supports it in being as its proper subject. In this way a substance is the material of its accidents, and matter is the material cause of substantial forms.

[54]The composite is made from matter in the sense that matter is a part of it while the form is not so much made from matter as it is made *in* matter. In these ways, then, the finite agent depends upon matter in producing the composite and the form and thus it does not properly create either.

[55]The language of matter "containing forms in potency" is confusing, but Suarez is fairly clear that the potency of matter for form only amounts to its being able to receive and sustain a form efficiently produced *in it* by something else.

[56]That is, the efficient cause contains its effect by containing in its own essence the perfection of what it can bring about, while matter contains its effect only by being able to receive it and sustain it as its subject.

[57]Here Suarez is clear that matter exercises no true material causality on the soul. It is, however, joined intimately to the soul to create with it a substance more perfect in being than either matter or the soul alone. Furthermore, it in some sense receives the soul and is actualized by it and in this way exercises a *quasi* material causality.

[58]The stars and planets presented a problem for the scholastic theory of eduction because the forms of such heavenly bodies were held to be inseparable from the matter with which they were created, and yet they were not held to have ever been generated.

[59]Perhaps a reference to *MD* XIII, sect. 13.

[60]Suarez's reasoning here seems to be that, since a heavenly body is a perfect and incorruptible whole, it is created instantaneously in two parts which are so ordered to each other that they are naturally inseparable. Hence, the celestial form, as one of the two parts constituting a perfectly united whole, cannot be said to be educed from matter, although it is truly sustained by matter. Compare this to the way in which a soul is created in the first instance of its existence along with its proper accidents, i.e., the intellect and will.

Section III
Whether Matter Temporally Precedes Form in Every Eduction of the Substantial Form

1. This difficulty arises from the preceding solution, and knowledge of it is necessary for grasping more fully the origin or eduction of such a form. The difficulty is best explained in the forms of the elements under which this matter of generable things[1] was created when it was first produced. And regarding these it is asked whether they were educed from the potency of matter or not.

To some it seems that the judgment about these forms and about the heavenly forms is the same, because the elements too were then not generated, but created. Therefore, their forms were not educed, but concreated.[2] Also, because matter was never in potency to those forms, because it was always in act under them,[3] they were, therefore, not educed because, as we said, eduction in the proper sense indicates a relation to a subject which was previously in potency.

Likewise, in the beginning, matter and its form were simultaneously concreated by the same action by which the earth was created; therefore, there was then no eduction.

Thirdly, when an angel or a soul is created, its powers are not educed out of the capacity of the subject because they are concreated;[4] therefore, much less will substantial forms be said to be educed which are concreated with matter of whatever sort.[5]

Fourthly, when the angel is created, its subsistence or personality is not educed from the potency of its nature, though it is concreated;[6] therefore, the forms are similarly not educed. And so, for these reasons the conclusion seems to be drawn that it is necessary that matter temporally precede form in order for eduction to take place.

2. For other reasons, however, the argument concerning the forms of the elements seems very different from that concerning the heavenly bodies. For the latter are such that by their nature they require that they are made by the same action by which their matter is made, but the former rather presuppose matter created through a proper and distinct action, and they are introduced into it by another action, even in their very first condition. Therefore, that action by which the form is introduced cannot be anything but true eduction. The antecedent is proven; for that action by which the elementary matter was created is such that it continues the same up to now by conserving the same matter. But the action which terminated in the form or the composite ceased when that composite was corrupted. This is a sign, therefore, that

those actions are really distinct from each other by their very natures [*ex natura rei*].

Nor can it be said that those actions were merely parts, constituting one action; otherwise, it would even now have to be said that one action is constituted out of the conservation of the matter and the eduction or generation of the form. For, if there were one composite action by which this part of earth were created and later this earth were corrupted and converted into a plant, the action would cease with respect to that part by which the form of earth is conserved in that matter, and in its place another action would come along because[7] the form of a plant would be introduced into the same matter. But the action which terminated in the entity of the matter always remains the same.[8] Therefore, if that action in itself is only a part and constitutes one complete action with the action which introduces or conserves the first form, for the same reason it constitutes one action with that action by which there is introduced the second form which takes the place of the first.

The inference is proven because the nature, proportion, union, and aptitude is absolutely the same in these actions as in those. It is also proven, because otherwise that action conserving matter would be in itself only a part and suited for composing one total action, and yet it would now remain perpetually incomplete and without the composition due to it. This conclusion also seems plainly false because the action by which matter comes to be is true creation and the same action continuing is the action by which it is conserved. But one action is not composed of creation and generation.[9] Therefore, they are two actions and not two parts of the same action. Hence, even in the first condition of things these actions come about as distinct from one another, even though they were united temporally.

In accord with this discussion, then, it is clearly concluded that for true eduction it is not necessary that matter temporally precede the form. For of those two actions, that one which is posterior by nature has the true character of eduction, since it depends essentially upon a matter which does not come to be through it, but is presupposed as created. And this is confirmed. For, if we imagine that God first produced that matter unformed and after some time introduced form into it, no one would deny that this was true eduction. But, though this later action were joined to the earlier in the same instant, it would have the same nature. Therefore, it is a true eduction.

3. You will say: By a similar argument it would be proven that the form of the heaven is educed from the potency of matter because, if God at an earlier time created that matter without form and later introduced form into it, He would then have educed the form from the potency of matter.

I respond by denying the inference, and as proof of this I deny what has been assumed, because even in that case, the heaven could not be said to have been made through generation. And, consequently, its form could not be said to have been made through eduction, because that action by its very nature does not presuppose matter already made. For the fact that in that miraculous case it does presuppose matter is accidental and does not change the nature of the action. And perhaps that action by which matter comes to be or is conserved without form or under another distinct form would not be the same in nature as that by which it comes to be under its proper form. And, therefore, in the previously mentioned case, when the form of the heaven was introduced into the pre-existing matter, the prior action by which it was conserved stripped of form would have ceased, and a new action would have begun by which from then on the whole heaven would have acquired being. This action would actually have been a true and total creation, although it would perhaps not be so called on account of the pre-existing matter.

But if one should argue, as seems probable, that God conserves that matter through the same action by which He conserved it before and that He introduces the form of the heaven through another entirely distinct action, in that case, if it is possible, we will admit that the latter action is the eduction of the form of the heaven and that, consequently, the heaven is generable in a miraculous and extraordinary manner. We deny, nevertheless, that according to its own nature the form of the heaven comes to be by such an action, as the form of an element does. The heaven, however, was at this point made in a mode proportionate to its nature, and thus the inference is not similar.

We derive the difference between the heaven and an element from the incorruptibility of the one and the corruptibility of the other. For, since the matter and form [of the heaven] are inseparable by their nature, they demand that they are produced through one action indivisible in itself, whether absolutely or at least from the nature of the thing. But since the matter [of generable things] is in itself separable from any form whatever by division, the actions which introduce the forms can vary, given the same matter. And, therefore, the action through which such a matter comes to be and is conserved is distinct and by its own nature is presupposed for any action which introduces a form.

4. **An further objection satisfied**. But someone will again say that, even if these statements are true, the first form concreated with this lower matter cannot, nevertheless, be said to be educed from the potency of matter because its matter did not temporally precede it as existing in potency to such a form.[10] For it is not enough that it precedes it by the order of nature. For the matter of the heaven also precedes its form by the order of nature in the genus of material cause.[11] In fact, some add that for the eduction of the form it is necessary that certain dispositions also precede the form in the matter,[12] something which cannot be said in the creation of the elements.

But this point about dispositions seems irrelevant. For remote dispositions[13] usually temporally precede the form by accident, as it were, on account of some inefficiency of the agent. But if God in one instant transforms water into wine, those dispositions do not temporally precede, and yet this is true generation and eduction. An ultimate disposition, however, never temporally precedes the introduction of the form.[14] However, in the way in which it precedes by the order of nature in natural generation, it also preceded in the first creation of the elements. For that union of the form to the matter which was then produced was really produced along with the same dependence upon the ultimate dispositions which it now has in any element. Therefore, it was produced with the same causality on the part of the dispositions; therefore, it was produced with the same order of nature since this is derived from the causality.

But concerning prime matter itself, this is what we contend, namely, that in order for the form to be educed from its potency, it does not seem necessary that the matter precede the form by the order of time as deprived of all form, but that it is enough that it precede it by the order of nature.[15] In this way it is clear that the creation of the matter of the elements was prior to the introduction of their forms, even in their creation. For those two actions, as we explained, were subordinated so that the introduction of the form essentially presupposed the creation of the matter upon which it depends as upon an absolutely necessary cause.

5. **A distinction is made between the matter of the heaven and of an element with regard to their concurrence for the production of their forms.** That, however, this priority suffices can be confirmed in many ways. First, *a priori* from what was said; for it is enough that the introduction of the form is an action of the same nature as that which would be posterior to it in duration, if God first created the matter without form and later informed it. For a temporal interruption alone does not suffice to make those actions essentially different. Therefore, the same priority of nature suffices for the eduction of form.

Second, by an analogy; for, if, in the same instant in which air is created, it is illuminated by the sun, that light is educed from the potency of air.[16] For I presuppose that other illuminations come to be through eduction, as I shall show below. But the air would on that occasion precede the introduction of light only by the order of nature, as is clear; therefore, the same priority of nature suffices for the eduction of form. The major is evident because that illumination is a proper and real [*per se*] action distinct from creation.

Third, from the difference between the matter of the heaven and the matter of an element, with regard to its priority to form. For there is a twofold difference which should be noted which is especially pertinent to the subject. The first is that the matter of the heaven does not without qualification precede the introduction of its proper form even by the order of nature, because it has a necessary connection with it so that it cannot be created without it in a natural way.[17] The matter of fire, however, does without qualification precede the introduction of its form by the order of nature because it does not have an intrinsic connection with the form of fire, but could be created under other forms.[18]

The second difference, which clarifies the preceding, is that the matter of fire is prior in such a way that, by the power of the action through which it is created, it could exist under the privation of the form of fire. And in this way not only matter, but matter as in potency is said to be prior by nature, not because in reality it has a privation annexed to it, but because from the power of the action through which it was created it does not lack a privation, but another action is necessary by which it may be informed, and this action can have the true nature of eduction.[19] The matter, however, of the heaven is informed by the same action by which it was created and, although according to the proper nature of causing, it is said to be prior by nature, it is, nevertheless, in no way said to be prior by nature as existing in potency and under privation in some way.[20] And, therefore, it does not have that priority of nature which is necessary for the eduction of the form. Hence, I think it is most probable that there is a great difference in nature between the first information of the matter of generable things and of heavenly ones.

Resolution of the Question

6. On this topic I, first of all, judge it to be true that in the creation of a corruptible thing, whether of an element or of any other thing, those two actions which were explained above are involved. Henry of Ghent pointed this out in *Quodlibetal Questions* I, q. 10,[21] citing Augustine in *Confessions* book XIII, c. 33,[22] where he says that matter was made from absolutely nothing, but its visible appearance was made from formless matter, although Augustine there speaks indifferently about the heavens and the elements. Nor is there a reason why this should seem strange, since in the conservation of fire or another similar thing two actions are involved, as is satisfactorily shown by the argument that, when one ceases, the other continues. But, according to the teaching of St. Thomas, conservation, strictly speaking, is the same action as production; therefore, there are two actions involved. Furthermore, in the conservation of a human being, three actions are involved, namely, the conservation of matter, the conservation of the soul, and the conservation of the union or of the whole composite. It is correctly inferred from this that these are distinct, because, when the latter action ceases, the other two remain,[23] and thus the argument is also correctly drawn that the same three actions are involved in the production of the human being. Therefore, the case is the same analogously in the other material substances.[24]

7. Secondly, I also judge that it is true that the action through which the matter of generable things is informed in the first instant of its creation is the same in nature as the action by which it would be informed by the same agent, God, even if the creation of matter preceded it temporally. This is proven by that argument that a temporal interruption or simultaneity has nothing to do with making the actions essentially different. It is likewise proven, because those actions agree in their formal or total terminus and in the principles or causes upon which they depend.[25] Therefore, there is no reason to distinguish them essentially.

From this it is further concluded that the action by which this matter is informed, even in the first instant in which it is created, is not creation, if we are speaking strictly and considering that action by itself. This is proven because, if that action took place at a later time, it would, in the opinion of everyone, not be creation; therefore, it was not creation when it took place then, because it has the same nature. And an *a priori* argument for this is that that action depends upon matter which is presupposed by the order of nature. Nor is it a problem that the earth is said absolutely to have been created in the beginning,[26] because plants and animals are also said to have been created, though it is certain that the forms of these things were not introduced through creation in the strict sense,[27] and also because the earth is said to have been created, not because of that union taken by itself, but as joined to the action by which the matter of the earth was created.[28] For, because those two actions were produced at the same time and in the manner of one action, the earth is said to have been created by them. Hence, although by the same word it is said that "God created heaven and earth," it is not necessary that the manner of the creation or action which was involved in the production of the two was the same, except with regard to that which is common to both, namely, to be made from nothing. But with regard to the other facts, each thing is created according the manner and capacity of its nature.

8. And from this I, finally, conclude that there remains a question only about the word, that is, whether the eduction of the form from matter applies, even if matter does not precede the eduction by duration, but only by nature, or—what amounts to the same thing—whether that first production of the form of the earth ought to be called its eduction from the potency of matter. For, if the word "eduction" only signifies the positive nature of that action by which form comes to be in dependence in both its coming to be and its being upon a matter which is not created by that action, but is presupposed as created, it is really eduction, as the arguments already made show. But if the word "eduction," in addition to this positive and real nature, denotes a negation or an extrinsic denomination,[29] namely, that the subject itself is not produced simultaneously with that action, even if it is created by

another action, it will in that way not be able to be called eduction, as is self-evident, but it is said to be concreation in the sense to be immediately explained.

And it, of course, seems that the word "eduction" is more frequently taken in this latter meaning, and, therefore, one ought to speak in that way with the many, although it is necessary to understand and explain the issue with the few. And according to this way of speaking the arguments produced for the prior opinion can be easily reconciled and conceded. And yet, in order that they may not seem to contradict our explanation of the matter, it will be necessary to propose solutions to them.

Answers to Objections

9. The very first objection, which is taken from the heavenly forms, has already been resolved, and the difference between corruptible and incorruptible bodies has been established.[30] The second objection, which is taken from the proper meaning of the verb "to educe," is also admitted by us, if it only regards a way of speaking and an extrinsic connotation. But if it regards the positive reality and action, we deny that it is of the nature of eduction that its subject should temporally precede it. For a priority of nature is sufficient, as has been explained by us.

The third argument rests on the word "concreation," about which one should observe that one thing can be said to be concreated with another in two ways: in one way, because it is created by the same action by which something else is created, in the way in which the matter and form of the heaven are concreated with the heaven. And when the form is concreated in this way, it is not educed, as has been explained in the case of the form of the heaven. In another way something is said to be concreated because it comes to be at the same time as another thing which is created, even though it is not produced by the same action. In this way grace is said to be concreated with the angels, and in this way the form of the earth is also said to be concreated with its matter. And what is concreated in this latter way can be produced by an action which is really the same in nature as eduction, though it is not called by that word on account of the simultaneous creation of its subject.

From this the solution to the fourth objection is also clear. This objection was taken from the concreation of the powers in the substance of a soul or an angel. This ultimate argument brings forth a special difficulty concerning the eduction of an accidental form which could be treated here in the fourth place. Nevertheless, because we will devote the following disputation to accidental form, we shall more appropriately explain it there.[31]

10. **Whether substantial modes are educed from the potency of matter.** But the fifth objection presents another difficulty concerning the substantial

modes, whether, namely, they should be said to be educed from the potency of their subject as, for example, subsistence is educed from the potency or capacity of the nature which it terminates. And the same difficulty arises concerning the mode of the union of the form with respect to the potency of the form or of the subject. In fact, one can also ask about substantial generation itself whether it is educed from the potency of matter.

Concerning all these one should briefly say that there is in these a certain mode or participation in eduction, but that it does not, nonetheless, belong to them properly as it does to the substantial form. For subsistence does not come to be through a proper action. Besides it does not properly inform, and consequently it is not related to its nature as to a subject and a proper material cause.[32] Hence, in this respect it cannot properly be said to be educed. It imitates eduction, however, in this way, namely, that in its being and its coming to be—whatever that might be—it entirely depends upon the nature which it intrinsically [per se] terminates and actualizes in its own way, as we shall explain at greater length in dealing with subsistence.

Substantial generation, likewise, does not come to be so much as it is the road through which a substance comes to be; hence, it is not so much educed, but it is eduction itself. Nevertheless, in the way in which generation itself comes to be when a terminus comes to be through it, it is also educed from the potency of matter by which it is materially caused, as we said above,[33] and it depends essentially upon matter in its coming to be and in its being, which two factors are the same in generation. Finally, the judgment ought to be the same concerning the union of the form to the matter which is not, nevertheless, educed as such [per se], but the form is educed as united to the matter, and thus also the union is, so to speak, co-educed with it. This indeed seems to be said correctly in the case of material forms.

11. **Whether the union of the rational soul with matter is educed from the potency of matter or of the soul itself.** In the rational soul, however, a peculiar difficulty is encountered[34] because in one respect that union seems to be educed because it comes to be as such [per se] through a proper action distinct from that by which the form comes to be. I say, however, that union comes to be as such as a formal terminus since the adequate terminus is the human being. This is enough, however, for proper eduction because, as we will immediately explain, form is never as such (per se) the essential terminus of an action except as a formal terminus and as that by which something is. Therefore, that union of the soul with the body is properly and as such educed. Likewise, it essentially depends, both in its coming to be and its being, upon a body as upon a material cause; therefore, it is properly educed.

But it argues for the contrary that this union is a kind of spiritual mode; therefore, it cannot be educed from the potency of matter any more than the soul itself can be. The inference is clear because it is impossible for something spiritual to be contained in the potency of matter. But the antecedent is evident because that mode immediately affects the soul itself which it unites to matter; it is, therefore, proportionate to it and, consequently, spiritual as the soul is. And this is confirmed because, if the form is not contained in the potency of matter, neither can the union be contained in it, because the union is only a mode of the form. Therefore, if the form is not educed, neither can the union be.

To this one should say that this mode of union is a sort of medium or chain between the form and the matter, and it, therefore, touches and affects both in some way and, hence, depends on both in its coming to be and in its being. As a result this mode of the rational soul, although it is in its own entity something spiritual, nevertheless participates in the conditions of a material thing because it both completely depends upon matter and is in its own way extended along with matter, although it does not have extension on the side of the soul. For this reason, therefore, this mode can be educed from the potency of matter, although it is not adequately nor primarily educed from the matter alone.[35] For it is also educed from the potency of the soul which it intrinsically [*per se*] first affects and which it unites to matter.

Notes

[1] That is, the matter of sublunar bodies which constitutes the substratum of the world of generable and corruptible substances. This was contrasted to the ungenerable matter of the stars and planets which the scholastics held could not naturally corrupt, i.e., could not naturally lose their forms and gain new ones. To say this is simply to say that *only* God could effect the corruption of a heavenly body.

[2] According to the opinion Suarez here sketches, the elements were not generated because God created sublunar matter at the beginning under the simple forms of the elements. The elemental forms have as their immediate substrate primary matter, while they themselves combine to form the proximate substrates of compounds, plants, and animals.

[3] That is, it never existed lacking those forms.

[4] Suarez distinguished between the substance of a human soul or of an angel and its various powers, e.g., the intellect and will. He held these powers to be really distinct accidents of the substance, informing and perfecting it, analogous to the way in which substantial forms inform and perfect matter (see *MD* XVIII, sect. 3). Hence, the human soul functions as the material cause of its various powers, and the latter, therefore, might be held to be educed out of the soul, although the opinion Suarez here describes denies this, holding instead the view that such powers are concreated with the soul.

[5] This is an *a fortiori* argument. Since the accidental forms of the human soul are not educed according to this opinion, but concreated with the soul, it follows that the substantial forms of the elements which, *qua* substantial, are more perfect than the soul's powers cannot be educed but must be created at the same time as the matter they inform is. They must be created because creation is a more perfect way of

becoming than eduction, and substantial forms, being more perfect than any accidents, ought to be created if the soul's accidental powers are.

[6]This, of course, parallels the preceding argument from the powers of the soul. For Suarez the subsistence of an individual substance is a certain mode or way of being causing the substance to exist *in itself* or independently of another as a subject supporting it (see *MD* XXXIV 2,20). Such a mode is really distinct from the individual substance of a finite being and could be removed from such a substance. Indeed, the human nature of Christ had no subsistence of its own but subsisted by sharing in the subsistence of the divine nature according to Suarez (*MD* XXXIV 2,11).

[7]We have followed the Rabade edition here which has "quia" in place of the "qua" in the Vivès.

[8]For Suarez a being created from nothing is conserved by the same action as that by which it was created (*MD* XXI 2,3). Matter, being simple, was created, not generated, and so is now conserved by the same action through which it was made at the beginning of the world.

[9]The eduction of a form is not a true creation, as we have seen, since it occurs *in* a pre-existing matter, but the production of matter *is* creation since matter is not made from or in any pre-existing stuff. Hence, the creation and preservation of matter, which are one action, cannot form a partial action with the eduction of any substantial form, as the two actions are of a different ontological order.

[10]That is, when matter was created, it was created *under* the forms of the elements and did not exist even for a moment bereft of all form. Hence, the objection claims that the forms of the elements were not introduced into a pre-existing matter and so were not educed.

[11]That is, as the subject of the form of the heavenly body, the matter of such a body has an ontological priority to its form according to material causality.

[12]For example, a piece of wood must be disposed by the accident of dryness in order for the form of fire to be introduced into its matter.

[13]A remote disposition would be a disposition rendering some matter apt to be affected by an agent. For example, fire cannot act on wood until the wood is dry.

[14]An ultimate disposition is so connected with a certain substantial form that it exists only with the advent of such a form and do not merely prepare the matter for the introduction of the form. For example, the human brain only begins to exist with the advent of the human soul and *vice versa*.

[15]Something (X) precedes another thing (Y) by the order of nature *iff* (Y) depends for its being on (X) regardless of whether or not (Y) came to be *after* (X). Thus, the proper accidents of a substance, such as the intellect and the will in the human being, depend upon the substance in such a way that the substance is prior to its accidents by the order of nature, even if it never naturally exists bereft of all accidents.

[16]The scholastics conceived of light as an accidental form able to be educed in certain bodies by fire or by the sun.

[17]Again, the reason is that the matter of a heavenly body is naturally ordered to *one and only one* heavenly form.

[18]For example, the form of air or of water or of any other substantial form, whether elemental or not.

[19]That is, the creation of generable matter does not, as such, include within it the eduction of any form since eduction and creation are of two different orders. Hence,

matter, as created, includes within it the privation of a form, which form must be introduced in it by a distinct act of eduction.

[20]The notion is that the matter of a heavenly body does sustain its form and so is prior to it by material causality. However, it is by nature so ordered to its form that both it and its form are properly created by a single action. The reason is that neither the matter nor the form of a heavenly body can naturally exist in separation from the other. In sublunar substances, however, the matter can, and does, naturally exist without any particular form which it might sustain, i.e., matter existing under the form of fire can naturally exist without *that* form, though not without *some* form.

[21]*Quodlibeta magistri Henrici Goethals a Gandavo* (Paris, 1518).

[22]*Confessions* in *Patrologia Latina*, Vol. XXXII, Migne, ed. (1841), pp. 661ff.

[23]That is, after death both the human soul and the matter that constituted its body remain. Hence, the acts conserving these also remain, but the act conserving their union necessarily ceases. Indeed, the death of a person is only conceptually distinct from the cessation of the union of her soul with her body.

[24]The same, analogously, because the forms of substances other than the human soul do not subsist and, hence, are not properly created but rather educed (see sect. 2,13-15).

[25]The notion here is that, as the effect of the two actions is the same, viz., the composite, the two actions themselves must be the same in nature.

[26]Suarez is here considering a theological objection based upon the words of *Genesis* 1, "God created heaven and earth," and he interprets "heaven" to refer to the heavenly bodies.

[27]Suarez is perhaps here following a generally held theory that the forms of plants and animals evolved from the elements (cf. Thomas Harper, *The Metaphysics of the School* [London: Macmillan, 1979-84], Vol. II, p. 730 *passim*). Or perhaps he is simply resting upon the common view that the forms of plants and animals were not created because they don't subsist.

[28]That is, the matter of earth was created by one action, and simultaneously it was informed by another action.

[29]A thing is named extrinsically by its relation to a form or essence it does not possess. Thus urine is named healthy because it is a sign of health and not because it possess the form of health. On the other hand, a thing is named intrinsically from some form really characterizing it, as an animal is named healthy from a form of health that is *in* it.

[30]See para. 5.

[31]*MD* XVI, sect. 2.

[32]The reason is that subsistence is a *mode* and not a *res* in the strict sense. On the nature and existence of modes see *MD* VII.

[33]*Vide MD* XIII 4,5.

[34]The reason is that the rational soul is created, not educed (see above, sect. 2,10).

[35]The reasoning here seems to be that the union of the soul and the body is educed because it is *that by which* the composite is constituted, and thus it shares in the nature of an educed form. See below, sect. 4, para. 5.

Section IV

Whether, When Form Is Educed from Matter, It Comes to Be As Such [*per se*]

1. This difficulty arises from what has been said in the previous sections and [the answer to it] contributes to explaining them more. For, since it was said that eduction is an action by which form comes to be in matter in dependence upon the matter in such a way that by that action matter does not itself come to be, it seems to follow from this that through that action only form primarily and as such comes to be, which is opposed to what Aristotle said in *Metaphysics*, VII, texts 26 and 27 [1032a13ff], and in book VIII, text 4 [1042b9ff].

The inference is clear, because through that action only form according to its totality is educed from non-being to being. A whole, however, does not come to be except insofar as it arises from the parts which were already produced. Therefore, form is that which comes to be both as prior and more properly. As prior, because, in order that a whole might be put together from the parts, it is necessary that the parts should be presupposed as already having being. More properly, because that which is educed in terms of its own entity from non-being to being comes to be more properly than that which is only put together from already existing things.

2. In this matter the first opinion admits what the argument given seems to prove, namely, that the form properly and as such comes to be. This is gathered from Albert the Great in his *Commentary on the De Anima*, book II, tract. I, chapters 1 and 3,[1] where he says that among these three, matter, form, and the composite, form is properly and primarily a being, a position which Zimara also defends at length in *Theorems* 20.[2]

Others distinguish two actions, even in the production of material forms: one by which the form comes to be, and the other by which it is united to the matter. Concerning the first action, they concede that it as such and primarily terminates in the form, although the latter action primarily terminates in the composite. This opinion is found in Durand of Saint Pourcain, in his *Commentary on the Sentences* II, dist. 1, q. 4, at the end.

Resolution of the Question

3. Both of these views, nevertheless, are false. Concerning the second we will speak extensively below when explaining the various modes of causing of an efficient cause.[3] Now an argument which can be easily taken from what we

have already said is sufficient to refute that view; for material forms, which
are the only ones this discussion concerns, do not exist, with regard to their
own entity, without the material concurrence of a subject. But the subject
does not influence the form except insofar the form is united to it, as has been
established from what was said above concerning the material cause.[4] Therefore, such a form cannot come to be through an action which does not unite
the form to a subject. The two actions, therefore, cannot be distinguished in
reality, but only according to reason or according to inadequate concepts or,
at the very most, according to the parts which are essentially joined to one
another, as we will explain in the place referred to.[5]

4. **The terminus of the action is twofold.** But the first opinion is really
opposed to Aristotle in the places cited. The Commentator follows him in
the same places and in his *Commentary on the Metaphysics*, book XII, com. 12
and 18, and St. Thomas follows him in the same places and in I, q. 45, a. 4
and 8, where he adds in the solution to the first objection that forms do not
come to be as such but only accidentally [*per accidens*]. This observation ought
to be understood in a sound way, taking the word "accidentally" in the wide
sense in which it means the same thing as "along with another." More properly, therefore, this form is said to be co-generated, as the same St. Thomas
signifies in that question, a. 4, and in q. 65, a. 4. This same view is held
expressly by Scotus in his *Commentary on the Metaphysics*, book VII, q. 10; by
Antonius Andreas in the same place, q. 9;[6] by Zimara in *Theorems* 100; and
by Soncinas in his *Commentary on the Metaphysics*, book VII, q. 23.

The reason, however, is that what has being as such and primarily comes to
be as such and primarily, since coming to be tends to being. But that properly
exists which subsists. Therefore, that properly comes to be. These forms, however, do not subsist,[7] but the composites which arise from them do subsist.
Therefore, the action properly and principally terminates in the composite.

This is confirmed because the action is one, as we presuppose; therefore,
the adequate terminus of it is also one. But this cannot be form because the
composite truly comes to be and it is not the form. Therefore, the terminus of
the action is the composite. For the sake of greater clarity a twofold terminus
is often distinguished, namely, *that which* and *that by which*, or that which
comes to be absolutely and that by which something else comes to be. The
composite, then, is the *terminus which* or *that which* because it comes to be as
such and primarily. For it is most of all intended in generation, and generation ultimately terminates at it. This is clear from an analogy with artificial
things since a house is what is as such and primarily constructed, and so on.
The *terminus by which*, however, is the form because it comes to be in order
that through it the composite might be constituted.

Hence, because the verb "to be educed" properly indicates only a relation to this terminus *by which*, the form is properly and simply said to be educed from the potency of matter, but not the composite. However, the verb "to be generated," or "to come to be," indicates a principal relation to that which is or to what comes to be, and thus it is simply said of the composite and not of the form.[8]

5. To the argument for the contrary opinion I respond by denying the consequence because, if we are speaking of an order of time, the form does not come to be before the composite, nor is the converse true. If we are, however, speaking of an order of nature, the composite not only comes to be first, but also it alone, absolutely speaking, comes to be through this action, while the form only comes to be along with it.[9] And, although we grant that in some genus of cause the form is by nature educed first, as if in the order of execution, the action, nevertheless, is not undertood, absolutely speaking, to have been terminated, nor is that which is as such and primarily intended understood to have been produced, until the whole composite exists.

Nor does it make any difference that some part of the composite and not of the form is presupposed. For it is necessary to distinguish four kinds of actions. One kind is an action which is only productive and not unitive, and this always terminates in a simple thing and, therefore, can of itself terminate in a partial entity, if it is naturally able to be produced in this way. And such is the creation of the rational soul, and the same thing holds for the creation of prime matter, in my opinion.

Another kind of action is only unitive and not productive of the components, as is the generation of a human being. This kind of action, without any controversy, terminates only in the composite as *that which is* and in the union as *that by which*.[10]

Again, there is another action which is productive of some composite so that it is simultaneously unitive and co-productive of all components, and such an action is the creation of the heaven which clearly as such and primarily terminates in the composite, but concomitantly terminates in the matter and the form.

Finally, there is another action which is simultaneously unitive and co-productive of one component apart from any presupposition of the other part. And such an action is the eductive action about which we are now speaking, and thus it is of its nature that its adequate terminus newly comes to be in such a way that no part of it is presupposed already to exist.

6. And from this we incidentally infer that this view is true not only in the case of substantial forms, but also in the case of accidental ones, even if Scotus in the passage cited above, Antonius Andreas, and others held the opposite view on the grounds that from an accident and a subject there comes to be

something one by accident, something which does not seem to be able to come to be through any true [*per se*] action or causality. But the view we have set forth is true. For Aristotle speaks universally, and he uses examples drawn especially from accidents. And finally, in text 32 [1034b7] he expressly and in particular teaches this about accidental forms. For, as he says in the same place, the argument is the same because for even better reasons accidents do not come to be as such, but as united to subjects and from subjects. Nor does it matter that they are accidental beings [*entia per accidens*], since they have a real, true, and physical composition[11] which that action intrinsically [*per se*] implies. And, therefore, through that action there comes to be as such and primarily an accidental composite since that action itself is also accidental.

Notes

[1] *De Anima, Opera Omnia*, Vol. V, ed. A. Borgnet (Paris: Vivès, 1890).

[2] *Theoremata* (Venice: Valgrisium, 1564).

[3] *MD* XVII, sec. 2.

[4] *MD* XIII, sec. 8,9.

[5] Probably a reference to *MD* XVII, sec. 2.

[6] *Questiones Antonii Andreae super XII libros metaphysicae* (Venice, 1514, 1523).

[7] Suarez is here arguing against the notion that there are two actions in the eduction of a substantial form, one producing the form and the other uniting it to the matter. Suarez's argument against this is that, as material forms naturally depend upon matter in both their coming to be and their being, there could be no natural production of material forms apart from the action joining them to matter. Only God could miraculously produce material forms separated from matter, making up by His infinite efficient causality for the lack of material causality naturally due a material form (see below, sect. 9).

[8] Both the Vivès and the Rabade edition read "of the form and not of the matter," [*de forma et non de materia*] but the sense demands "of the composite and not of the form."

[9] Again, the reason is that only the composite subsists, while the form is sustained in matter and is a part of the composite.

[10] This sheds light on the passage above, sect. 3, para. 11.

[11] That accidents have a physical composition with their subjects does not entail for Suarez that they are corporeal. Rather, it simply entails that they are real entities really distinct from the subjects which they inform. In this sense, to say that they physically inform their subjects is not different from saying that they really, rather than merely conceptually, inform their subjects. This is in contrast, for example, to the way in which the transcendental properties, e.g., unity or perfection, "inform" their subjects since such properties are only conceptually distinct from their subjects.

Section V
Concerning the Proper Nature of the Substantial Form and the Nature of Its Causality

1. **A description of form in general.** From what was said about the existence of substantial form and about the way it comes to be, one can easily understand what form itself is and what sort of causality it has. We can include both of these in this brief description: Form is a certain simple and incomplete substance which, as the act of matter, constitutes with it the essence of a composite substance.[1]

In this description substance is put in the place of the genus in accord with the way in which substance is divided by the Philosopher into matter, form, and the composite. And by that part of the definition this form is distinguished from accidental forms which are not substances. It can also be distinguished from substantial modes. For, although these are reducible to the category of substance, they are not substances in the proper sense.[2] Hence, they are not counted by Aristotle in that division because they are not, properly speaking, substantial entities, as form is, which is for this reason called a substance. The words "simple and incomplete" are added so that by the first word form is distinguished from composite substances and by the second from separate substances.[3] The latter are sometimes called attendant forms, such as those forms which move the celestial bodies, which really do not serve the function of a formal cause, but exercise a certain efficiency. Hence, they are not substantial forms in the sense in which we are now speaking of them.

2. **The way in which substantial form is said to be the act of a physical body.** The remaining part of the definition distinguishes form from matter which is also a simple and incomplete substance, but as potency, while form is the primary act of that potency. And therefore, Aristotle, in *On the Soul* book II [412a22], defined the soul as "the act of a physical body" etc. This definition can be easily adapted to form in general, if by the term "act" we understand "substantial act," as it ought to be understood, and if we only say that form is the act of a physical body, removing the remaining part which distinguishes the soul from the forms of inanimate bodies.

We can, however, understand by "physical body" either matter itself, insofar as it is the other part of a composite nature which, in order that it may be informed by the form, is always presupposed by the order of nature in its own genus of cause, as modified by quantity and other proximate dispositions. And for this reason it can be called a physical body. Or we can understand by "physical body" the natural being itself which consists of matter and form and whose act is said to be form as constituting it. In this way Aristotle also defined soul as "the act of a living being" or "the act by which we live" [412a27-28].

We have, therefore, explained both relations in the part of our description already mentioned. For substantial form is an incomplete substance in such a way that it is the act of matter, the act, I say, either as actually informing or as prepared by its nature to inform matter. For the words in the definition, as they say, express an aptitude, and so the rational soul is included, even if it is separated from the body. And from this there comes, as a result, that it composes with matter the essence of a natural being which is a composite substance. Therefore Aristotle, in *Physics* II, c. 3 [194b27-28], says that "form is the nature of a quiddity or essence," that is, it is what completes the essence of a natural composite and what distinguishes it essentially or quidditatively from others.

3. And from this the causality of form is also explained. For, since form is essentially act, it, therefore, intrinsically includes a transcendental relation[4] to that of which it is the act and to the actualization which it exerts on it. Therefore, the nature of form can scarcely be explained except through a relation to its causality. In it we can consider those four things which we see in all causes, namely, the formal principle of causing, the conditions necessary for causing, the causation itself, and the effect which is caused.[5] All of these must be explained one by one, as we have done in the case of matter,[6] though, with what we have said there presupposed, we can deal with them more briefly here.

Notes

[1]This definition Suarez gives of form contrasts with the more traditional one which is that "form gives being to a thing" (*forma dat esse*) or, more expansively, "Form is an internal cause, through which a thing is what it is, or it is that which gives being to a thing" (N. Hunnius, *Cannones logici*, [Wittenberg, 1621], p. 176). The traditional definition is not necessarily in conflict with Suarez' but is too ambiguous to have been favored by him. For Suarez form is *one* of the *incomplete substances* which constitutes a composite. Form thus does give being to the composite, and it also actualizes the capacity of matter for being a certain sort of thing. However, form does not, as such, bestow the proper being of matter upon it but only gives it being of certain sort. Since the Thomists interpreted the traditional formula, *Forma dat esse,* to mean that form bestows matter's *own* being upon matter, Suarez did not use it in defining form, though he did use it when describing *formal causality* in *MD* XII 3,3.

[2]On the substantial modes and on the notion of being "reductively in" a certain category, see *MD* XXXIII, sect. 1. Certain modes were called substantial by Suarez because they contribute to the substantial being of the composite, e.g., the union of form and matter.

[3]These are, respectively, the angels and God. Such substances are complete on their own and do not need to inform any subject to constitute a complete thing. This is

in contrast to the human soul which, though it can exist without matter, is not complete without it. Suarez says that God and the angels are analogously called forms because of their beauty and actuality (see the introduction to sect. 1).

[4]A transcendental relation is a relation which does not require the actual existence of both terms of the relation. The form of a thing is transcendentally related or, in other words, naturally ordered to matter and is so even if, through a miracle, it is conserved without matter. Opposed to transcendental relations are predicamental relations which *do* require the existence of both terms of the relation, e.g., the spatial relation of a figure skater to the ice he is skating on requires, among other things, that both he and the ice exist.

[5]Cf. *MD* XII, sect. 2.

[6]In *MD* XIII sect. 7-9.

Section VI
Concerning the Nature of Formal Causality

1. Three subjects can be included under this heading, namely, the principle of causing[1] which is, as it were, the first act, the necessary conditions of causing in this way, and that principle of causing in second act.

2. With regard to the first, it should be said that the principle of causing is nothing other than the entity and nature of the form itself which causes through itself and through its own entity by presenting itself, so to speak, to the matter or the composite.[2] For this it does not need another faculty or power distinct from itself, but through itself it is essentially suited for exerting this causality. Hence, just as we said above[3] that we do not distinguish in matter between the principal and proximate principle of causing because the receptive potency, through which it causes, is not a property of it, but is the matter itself essentially, so in the form we can consider a certain *quasi* potency or aptitude for formally causing which remains, for example, in the separated soul, even if it does not actually inform. And this aptitude is the proximate principle of causing formally.[4] It is not, nonetheless, distinct from the chief principle because that aptitude is not a property added to the entity of the form, but is the essential nature and specification of it. For form is essentially actualizing act; the aptitude for actualizing is, however, of the essence of such an act.

This is also the case because from matter and form there is produced something essentially [*per se*] one, since they are not united by the mediation of any property or accident, but immediately through themselves on account of the mutual proportion and aptitude which they have to each other through their own incomplete entities which pertain to the same genus, as is gathered from Aristotle in *Metaphysics* book VIII, c. 6 [1045a5-1045b20], and *On the Soul* book II, c. 1 [412b5-9], where the Commentator notes it, com. 7, along with other scholars.[5] St. Thomas comments on this in his *Commentary on the Metaphysics* book VIII, and in *Against the Gentiles* book II, c. 70, and in I, q. 76, a. 7, as well as theologians in their commentaries on the *Sentences* II, dist. 12, especially Scotus, q. 1,[6] and Durand of St. Pourcain, q. 2. Therefore, just as in the case of matter one should not imagine a distinct potency which mediates between matter and form, so also in the case of form one should not think of a potency which is something distinct from the form itself.

You will say: How can form which is so distant in its nature from matter be immediately united to matter through itself? This seems especially difficult in the case of the rational soul which is spiritual. I respond, in the first place, that there is not so great a distance that form and matter do not agree in a genus.[7] I respond, secondly, that distance is not a hindrance if there is a due proportion. For, as Plato said in the *Timaeus*, mutual proportion is, as it were, a bond between things which are united very closely and intrinsically [*per se*] [31c3-32b1]. But this proportion consists in the nature of act and potency and in the natural and essential aptitude and mutual relation which they have between themselves.

Conditions Necessary for the Form to Cause

3. **Actual existence.** With regard to the second point about the conditions necessary for exercising this causality, it seems that three conditions can be assigned. The first is the actual existence of the form itself; with regard to this one must hold different views according to different opinions about the existence of a creature and about the nature of the distinction it has from essence.[8]

It seems, however, that no one holds that existence is properly said to be a condition necessary for the cauality of form. For, if existence is a thing distinct from essence, it cannot be said to be a condition for form to cause, but a condition of the effect, either in the genus of the formal cause, insofar as form is said to give being, or in the genus of the efficient cause, insofar as some say that existence flows from essence, or, as others think, in the genus of the material cause, insofar as form completes the essence which is the proximate receptacle of existence.

But if existence is not really distinguished from the actual essence, the existence of the form cannot properly be said to be a condition necessary for causing. For a requisite condition, if we are speaking properly, is distinguished from the very nature of the causing. Existence, however, cannot be distinguished in that way according to this opinion since form causes through its own actual entity, because it cannot be understood actually to cause except as something having its actual entity and outside its causes and, therefore, as something having existence.

And this view ought to be given further proof. For, just as the actuality of the form is not a condition distinct from the nature of the causing or of the actualizing, so neither is the existence which is intimately included in the actuality itself. But as to whether it is necessary that the existence of the form be prior to its causality, one should say that it is not necessary that it be prior in the order of duration since such priority is irrelevant. In fact, it is not naturally possible because existence is not owed to form until a subject immediately suited to receive the form demands it, and once this subject is given, the form naturally informs it, as soon as the form exists. Again, it is not necessary that the existence of the form be prior by the order of nature understood as some point or moment in which it exists and does not inform, since this is neither necessary for the priority of nature nor can it be understood in forms which depend on matter, as is clear from what was said in preceding sections. A priority of nature according to some genus of causality can, however, enter in and is necessary. For the causality of the form depends upon its very entity and existence. Hence, it is necessary that there be a natural order between the existence and the causality of the form from which is derived a priority *from which*, as they say, but not *in which*. We will have more to say about these priorities later.[9]

4. **The intimate closeness of form to matter.** Another necessary condition can be assigned: the presence or intimate closeness of the entity of the form to the entity of matter. This condition has been most correctly assigned and is so necessary that without it the form could not produce its formal effect, even by the absolute power of God. For who could understand that a substantial form locally distant from a body constitutes a substance which is essentially (*per se*) one? This composition, then, comes to be through an intimate union which is not, of course, local presence but something distinct from that, and yet it necessarily requires local presence. This can be further explained and made convincing from things said above on a similar issue concerning matter,[10] for in this regard the same argument holds for the form.

5. **Dispositions connatural to the form.** A third condition can be assigned: a suitable disposition on the part of matter which form necessarily requires in order that it can bestow its formal effect.[11] Some think this disposition is so necessary that even by the absolute power of God form could not inform matter, if every disposition were lacking, especially quantity. Henry of Ghent holds this in *Quodlibetal Questions* book VII, q. 17. Yet whatever it is, whether on the part of matter or of quantity, which makes it impossible that the one be separated from the other—something which we cannot treat until the disputation on quantity[12]—if it is once supposed that matter can be conserved by God without quantity, which we think more likely, it will not be impossible that God conserve such matter in that state informed by substantial form. For there is no connection so essential between form, as exercising its own intrinsic formal effect, and these accidents, that God could not conserve form without them.

There is not, therefore, involved so absolute a necessity, but experience itself teaches that this condition is necessary in a natural and physical way.[13] From this, after all, there comes the natural corruption of the thing by which form is separated from matter and which begins with the loss or corruption of the dispositions. This is a sign, therefore, that such dispositions are at least conditions necessary by reason of the nature of the thing, in order for form to inform matter. Whether these conditions precede or follow upon the form by the order of nature must be investigated from what was said in the preceding disputation.[14]

The Causality of the Form is Explained

6. With regard to the third point concerning the actual causality of the form itself, it is not easy to explain what it is; nevertheless, from what was said concerning matter, we can proceed to explain it by analogy. And, first of all, it seems certain that such causality is something really distinct by nature from the entity of the form.[15] This is proven since, just as to act is something in the nature of the thing, so to inform also is, because it is to cause truly, really, and physically. Again, whatever it is, it is in the thing itself separable from form. For it is in fact separated in the case of the rational soul, and in the case of any substantial form it could be separated by the absolute power of God. For the form can be conserved outside of matter, just as quantity is conserved, because the reason is the same or greater.[16] Therefore, by the nature of the thing it is distinguished from the form.

7. **The union of the form with the matter is the causality of the form.– The distinction between the causality of the efficient cause and the formal cause should be noted.** Secondly, it should be said that this causality can be nothing else besides the actual union of the form to the matter. This is proven first from a sufficient enumeration of possibilities, because it is not the matter, or the form, or the composite; therefore, it is the previously mentioned union. Besides these, nothing else can be thought of, and the antecedent is self-evident with respect to all its parts. For concerning the form it has already been proven, and the same argument proves this *a fortiori* concerning matter. The composite, however, is the ultimate effect of this causality, as will be stated immediately; therefore, it is not the causality itself.[17]

Likewise, the composite includes the entity of matter and form, while the causality of form, taken by itself, cannot include all these.[18] Moreover, if the union is posited and anything else whatever is taken away—apart from those things which were mentioned—the form necessarily exercises its causality. If, however, all these other things are posited and the union is taken away, it would be impossible for the form to exercise its causality. This is, therefore, a sign that such causality consists in the union.

The major is evident because, if form is united to matter, it necessarily communicates itself through itself to the matter, that is, not by efficiently causing another similar perfection, but by communicating to the matter its own perfection and entity and in this way actualizing matter. And from this there also arises a substantial composite nature which is essentially [*per se*] one, but in this consists the whole causality of the form and its whole effect which, if the union were taken away, could not remain, as is self-evident; therefore, the causality of the form consists in its union with matter.

Hence, one should note here the difference between the union which we said is the causality of the form and the action which we will later say is the causality of an efficient cause.[19] For its action is the causality of an agent in such a way that the agent, insofar as it is acting, remains entirely outside the effect. For, although it communicates itself through action, it does not do so by giving itself through itself to the effect, but by conferring upon it some similar entity. But union is the causality of form in such a way that, by means of it, the form offers itself either to the matter or the composite. For it is an intrinsic cause causing through itself.

In this sense it could also be said that the causality of the form includes in itself the entity of the form or that this causality is the form itself, not taken by itself, but taken as united to matter. But in this way of speaking the cause is confused with its causation, and the nature of the causing as if in first act is confused with causation, which is like a second act.[20] Therefore, more formally and more precisely, this causality is said to consist in the union itself.

8. **A minor doubt.** But a difficulty arises because this union takes place in two ways in the case of different substantial forms. In certain forms there is a pure union, that is, without the form's inherence or dependence, as it is in case of the rational soul.[21] In the case of other forms, however, there is a union which is also a dependence and *quasi* inherence of the form in matter. The first sort of union, therefore, cannot be the formal causality of the rational soul because it comes from it by efficient causality; efficient causality, however, is very different from formal causality.

The antecedent is clear. For, by the very fact that the soul is created by God in a properly disposed body, it immediately unites itself to matter as if by a natural impulse in producing the union. For, since the soul is naturally inclined toward that union and has present to it a proper subject perfectible by it, there is no reason why it could not join itself to a body as if by its natural weight, as Henry of Ghent thought in *Quodlibetal Question* XI, q. 14, and Peter Auriol as well, according to John Capreolus in his *Commentary on the Sentences* book IV, dist. 43, a. 3, q. 2,[22] and Richard of Mediavilla thinks it probable in his *Commentary on the Sentences* a. 3, q. 2.[23]

Likewise, the second sort of union cannot be the formal causality of other forms because through the union those forms are caused by matter and depend upon it in their own being.[24] Therefore, the same forms cannot be the causes of the same union; therefore, the union cannot be the causality of such forms. For the causality comes from that cause which has the causality, just as action comes from an agent, and therefore it presupposes the existence of such a cause.[25] Nor is it intelligible that the same thing or mode is the principle or road, as it were, whereby the form is caused and which the form causes.

This is confirmed, because above in *MD* XIII, sect. 1, we said that the form cannot be the formal cause of generation because through generation it comes to be and is educed from non-being to being. Therefore, for the same reason, it cannot be the cause of the union and, consequently, the union cannot be its causality. The consequence is evident, both from the parity of the argument and also because generation itself seems to be the same thing as union, since it was said that these forms come to be and are united by one and the same action.

9. **Whether the soul is intimately united to a properly disposed body.** To the first part I respond that the opinion of Henry of Ghent, which is mentioned in it, is rather uncertain, as can be seen in Scotus in his *Commentary on the Sentences* IV, dist. 43, q. 3, a. 3 and in Capreolus, in that place in his *Commentary on the Sentences*, q. 2, a. 3. For perhaps the union of the rational soul and the body is produced either by the power of the seed and the dispositions from the father or, if it comes from the father only as one providing a disposition, it will be made effectively by God alone by Whom the soul is created. But that it is produced by the soul itself is not shown by any sufficient argument. For, although the form by its own nature is suited to enter a union and, therefore, is naturally inclined toward union, it does not follow from this that it is able to enter a union. For those aptitudes or powers are diverse, one of which is not necessarily inferred from the other, just as matter also is suited to be united to form and is, in its own genus, inclined toward such a union, and yet is not able to enter such a union. For, just as a receptive potency and the desire grounded in it are of a different nature from an active potency and its inclination, so the potency, so to speak, or formal aptitude and the inclination grounded in it are of a different nature from an active potency, nor is there any sufficient reason why an active potency should be inferred from a formal aptitude, especially since in all other forms it seems more probable that the union does not come from the form by way of efficient causality.

Secondly, even if that opinion is admitted, the conclusion drawn from it must be denied. For, even if the union of the form to a sufficiently disposed body flows from the rational soul by way of efficient causality, there can, nevertheless, still be a formal bond by which the soul is joined to matter as act to potency. And it is not contradictory that the same union comes from the soul in two kinds of cause, namely, the efficient and the formal, or that it is an effect of the soul as an efficient cause and also that it is the principle of formally causing the whole composite. For no contradiction is involved in these diverse relations.

10. The union which is the causality of the form is caused by the form and by matter–Various ways of understanding the union. To the second part I respond that the same union is caused by the form and by the matter and by the efficient cause, each in its own genus of cause, because it depends on all of them. Hence, it is no contradiction that the same union, insofar as it is from the form, is the path, as it were, or principle by means of which the form causes the whole composite and, insofar as it is from the matter, is the principle by means of which the material form depends on matter in its own being. For that union is the joining of the two, namely, of the matter and of the form, and, therefore, when the union is such that there is also an inherence, it can at the same time be both the road, so to speak, of the matter to the form and of the form to the matter.

Nor does it matter that the causality of the form ought to be from the form and, therefore, ought to presuppose that the form is prior by the order of nature. For, as we said above, this is not a priority *in which*, but a priority *from which*. But it is no contradiction that the same union is both from the form as informing matter and is, as such, the joining of the form with the matter in order that by means of it the form is sustained by the matter. And thus the very same union, insofar as it is from the form, is the medium or principle by means of which the form actualizes the matter and constitutes the composite, and in this way it is said to be the causality of the form. But, insofar as through it the form adheres to matter and is sustained by it, it is a dependence of the same form upon matter. For the connection between such form and the union is so intrinsic that they mutually depend upon each other for diverse reasons.[26]

To the confirmation I respond that "union" sometimes is taken as the action which, in order to do away with any equivocation, is usually called unification. But sometimes and more properly "union" is taken to mean the mode of union or inherence which remains between matter and form in the being which has been produced, and at times it is taken also to mean the consequent relation, as is extensively explained in my *Commentaries and Questions on the Third Part of the Summa Theologiae* q. 2, a. 8.[27] When, therefore, we say that the union is the causality of the form, we are not speaking about the relation, as is self-evident. For, if this relation is taken as something distinct from the other elements, it is either nothing or is something subsequent to them.

Nor are we speaking about the action from which the previously stated confirmation arises. For we admit that the form, especially the form which is educed from the potency of matter, cannot properly be the formal cause of that action by which it is educed, as we have shown in the place mentioned, because it is its terminus. Hence, that action is in some way actively related to the form itself and, therefore, cannot truly and properly be caused by the form. We are speaking, therefore, about the mode of union, which has a very different nature, because it is not actively related to the form, but is the *quasi* formal joining of the form and the matter. Therefore, it can have some dependence upon both, as has been said.

11. But at this point there immediately arises a difficulty as to why this mode of union is attributed more to the form than the matter. But this difficulty has been be satisfied in *MD* XIII, sect. 6, and nothing else needs to be said here in addition to what was said there.

Notes

[1] The principle of causing of a thing is that which enables it to cause. It remains such a principle even if it is not exerting this causality. Thus a person's vocal chords are the causal principle of her singing and remain so even when she is not singing. Her actual singing is her causal principle of singing in second act, i.e., as it actually exerts itself.

[2] Some causal principles are distinct from the entities they reside in. Thus a person is the *remote* causal principle of her singing, but the proximate causal principle of her singing is her vocal chords. The causal principle of the substantial form, however, is the form itself according to Suarez.

[3] *MD* XIII 8,3.

[4] Though a form is not distinct from its causal principle, it is distinct from its *causality* because it can exist when not exercising its causality; that is, it can exist even when it is not actualizing matter, at least by the divine power.

[5] E.g. Soncinas, q. 28, Javelli, qu. 7, Scotus, qu. 4, and Antonius Andreas, qu. 7.

[6] Reference not found.

[7] That is, they are both substances, albeit *incomplete* ones.

[8] For Suarez's view of this see *MD* XXXI. Suarez held that the essence and existence of created things are really identical but conceptually distinct. That is, he held they refer to the same reality but according to different aspects. The *basis* of this distinction in the thing itself is the contingent nature of created essence which, since it is created, does not necessarily exist and so can be conceived without the property of existence.

[9] Suarez is, perhaps, referring to sect. 8, para. 20.

[10] Cf. *MD* XIII 8,2.

[11] For example, in order for a soul to naturally inform matter, the matter must be properly disposed for it by means of the vital organs. A soul could not naturally inform, e.g., a rock.

[12] *MD* XL, sect. 2.

[13] That is, necessary absent a miracle, and so not *logically* necessary.

[14] *MD* XIV sect. 3.

[15] The *causality* of the form is distinct from the form but not its causal *principle*, which is identical with it.

[16] This doesn't mean that forms other than the rational soul could naturally exist without matter. But since form has some entity of its own, God could conserve it without its natural dependence upon matter in the same way as He could conserve the life of an animal without the oxygen it naturally depends on. The general

principle here is that any causality of a finite entity, no matter how necessary according to the natural order, could be made up for by God in virtue of His infinite causal power, unless doing so would imply a contradiction. According to the doctrine of transubstantiation, which was first declared to be a matter of faith by the Fourth Lateran Council (1215), God transforms, in the sacrament of the Eucharist, the bread and the wine into the body and blood of Christ and miraculously sustains in existence the quantity of the bread and the wine without any sustaining subject or substratum and hence without a mode of inhering in any substratum or subject.

[17]The reason is that a real effect must always be really distinct from the causality that brings it about.

[18]The form cannot include matter because the form, far from containing or producing it, presupposes it in order to exert its proper causality upon it.

[19]*MD* XVIII 10,5-7.

[20]A thing in second act is a thing as exerting its causal principle. So speaking is the vocal chords in second act. First act is simply the *actual* existence of a thing, which actualizes it outside its causes and outside of mere possibility.

[21]The soul is merely united to matter but does not inhere in it because the rational soul doesn't need matter to exist but to be complete.

[22]*Commentaria in IV lib. Sententiarum* (Venice, 1483, 1484).

[23]*In IV libros Sententiarum* (Venice, 1507-1509).

[24]The reason for this is that such forms cannot be made at all except as joined to matter. That is why Suarez argued above that the eduction of such forms and their union with matter are not two acts (sect. 4,3-4).

[25]That is, if the form is the effect of its union to matter, it seems the union could hardly also be the form's causality.

[26]The argument here is that, even if form cannot exist except as united to matter, that does not prevent it from actualizing matter by its very union to it. For example, a color could not exist except as inhering in a surface, but that does not prevent the color from coloring the surface by its very inherence. Thus one and the same thing can be both cause and effect but in different respects. So the union of form to matter is the cause of form with respect to material causality, but it is the very causality of the form with respect to formal causality.

[27]*Opera omnia*, Vol. 17, pp. 325-326. This commentary concerns the nature of the hypostatic union between Christ's divine and human natures.

Section VII
What the Effect of the Formal Cause Is

1. There are only two effects which can be attributed to the form, namely, the composite and the matter, for it has already been said that the generation or union cannot properly be the effect of it.[1] But with regard to the union as already constituted in being, it is clear from what has been said that it cannot be said properly to be the effect of form,[2] except perhaps in the way action is said to be the effect of an agent insofar as the action comes from the agent,[3] although it would more properly be said to be the *way to* the effect.

The First Effect of the Form is Explained

2. **The primary effect of the form is the composite**. With regard to the composite, then, it is quite clear from what has been said that it is the proper and primary effect of the form. For the composite is intrinsically and essentially constituted by the form and has from the form its species and its beauty, so to speak. For the form completes the essential nature and intelligible structure of the composite, as can be inferred from the definition of Aristotle which was given above. Moreover, matter is a cause of the composite, as was shown above, therefore, *a fortiori*, form is, because it contributes more to the being of the composite.[4] Therefore, conversely, the composite is the effect of the form since it depends most of all on form for its being.

3. **Form causes both matter and the composite by a single union**. But some object to this. For, if the composite is the proper and primary effect of the form, then, the proper causality of the form will be to constitute the composite. This cannot, however, be true because the form, by nature, actualizes the matter before the composite. For, since it is essentially the act of matter, it is first directed to matter and through matter to the composite. Therefore, the composite is not the primary effect of the form, but matter as actualized or informed by it is. From this effect the composite results as a subsequent effect.

I respond to these arguments that they do not show two causalities as two effects of form, but show only one effect under diverse relations. For there is only a single union of the form with the matter, and if that is given and every other thing or real mode is removed, matter remains informed by the form, and the composite results from both, although in the form one can consider diverse relations with respect to the matter or with respect to the composite. Again, the matter's being actualized by the form is not an effect really distinct from the composite, because by "matter as informed" we understand only matter with a sort of extrinsic denomination.

For this concept either is no concept at all or is not a concept of a real effect, but of a denomination which the intellect can invent from a concomitance or relation of the form as present. But by "informed matter" we understand matter as intrinsically affected by form. Informed matter, then, includes matter itself, form, and their union. But the composite includes these three and nothing else. These, therefore, are not really distinct; therefore, there are not two effects but one which is conceived and explained by us in different ways.[5]

4. And this is confirmed and explained by an argument by analogy. For in the case of an accidental form it is not one thing to inform a subject and another to constitute with it an accidental composite; for example, in the case of whiteness to whiten snow and to constitute this white thing as such are one and the same. Therefore, the same is true analogously in the case of substantial form. Some respond that the two cases are not alike because from a subject and whiteness there comes to be only something accidentally one which is not something distinct from the components taken together and united. From matter and form, however, there comes to be something essentially one, and there must be something else besides those three, even taken together, so that it can be more perfectly one thing.[6]

But this response supposes a false doctrine. For it is impossible that a substantial composite really include something besides those three things taken together. I shall show this below in the disputation on the essence of material substance.[7] Nor does the difference between accidental and essential unities consist in that, but in the fact that the union and the terms of the union are all of the same order in a being which is essentially one, but not so in a being which is accidentally one. Hence it also turns out that in a being essentially one the union is more intimate and arises from a greater proportion between the elements to be united.[8]

It can be shown that the difference is found in this alone and not in something else because both a being which is essentially one, insofar as we are now dealing with it, and a being which is accidentally one are not something one by a unity of simplicity[9] but by a unity of composition or union. Therefore, the greater unity of a being which is a composite essence consists in a nobler union and in a greater proportion of the parts to be united and not in the addition of a third intelligible entity. If this entity is simple and if, taken by itself, it would be said to be essentially one, it would not be one by composition, and thus that which is constituted by the form will not be a composite.[10] But if that third entity is a unity intrinsically including matter, form, and their union, it is not necessary to add anything to these to make it essentially one. On the contrary, this unity would rather be diminished because of it, for more elements would have been gathered in that composite without any necessity.[11]

The argument given, therefore, retains its force because, if in the case of an accidental form the subject's being actualized and an accidental composite's being constituted, for example, something white, are in reality one and the same, in the case of substantial form the matter's being actualized by the form and the composite's being constituted are also one and the same. Nor does essential unity prevent this, but rather demands it all the more.

5. With regard to the argument for the contrary, therefore, the consequence must be granted, namely, that the substantial composite essence is the primary effect of the form in its genus and that, consequently, the chief causality of the form is to constitute the same composite, not in just any sense—for this is, if said without qualification, common to it and matter—but as perfecting and completing the essence. For matter begins the essence, but form completes it. But when it is added that the form by nature actualizes matter before it constitutes the composite, the assumption is denied because those are not two things, but one in reality. Hence, there is no causality between them and, consequently, no order of nature between them, but at most there can be only an order of reason according to inadequate concepts.

Nor is it a problem that form is essentially the act of matter, for it is just as essentially a part of the composite. In fact, if a comparison has to be made between these, it is more essentially a part of the composite than it is an act of matter since form is not for the sake of matter but for the sake of the composite. But in the form these are not really two, but one thing grounding two relations. From this the argument is rather turned back on itself. For, just as form by one and the same aptitude is a part of the composite and is the act of matter, so by one and the same offering it gives its whole self to the matter and the composite, but to the latter as to a whole and to the former as to a another part.[12] Therefore, even in the effect it is one and the same thing,[13] and it is entirely simultaneous that matter is informed by form and the composite is constituted. The composite, therefore, is the proper and primary effect of the substantial form and is perhaps the only effect in the genus of the formal cause.[14] But we shall have to speak of this last point in the following section.

Whether the Form is More Perfect than the Composite

6. But we must first resolve an objection which arises. For the cause ought to be nobler than its effect, as the Commentator attests in his *Commentary on the Physics* book II, c. 4,[15] but the form is not nobler than the composite;[16] therefore, the composite cannot be the proper effect of the form. Some respond to this objection by denying the minor premise, for Aristotle, in *Metaphysics* book VII, text. 7 and 8 [1028a31], prefers the form to the composite,

saying that it is more a being and is prior to it.[17] The Commentator also holds this at that passage, and Zimara absolutely defends this view in *Theorems* 10, referring to Robert Grosseteste. And he proves this view because whatever perfection there is in the composite is in the form alone and the matter adds no perfection, and all that perfection is, on the other hand, in the form as in a cause, and the form is what bestows along with itself the being which does not belong to the composite except by reason of the form.[18] Therefore, the form is simply more perfect than the composite.

But this response rests on a false foundation. For without a doubt the composite is more perfect than its form. And this is the clear view of Aristotle, for in *On the Soul* book II [1028a31], at the beginning and wherever he distinguishes substance into matter, form, and the composite, he prefers the composite to the form and the form to the matter. In fact, below, when treating of substance, we shall show that "substance" is said of these analogously.[19] And the Commentator explains it this way, in his *Commentary on the Soul,* book II, com. 3. And for this reason Aristotle said that in the category of substance first substance is most of all substance, where, although he compares first substance to second substance, he still prefers first and complete substance to parts and incomplete substances [*Categories*, 2a11-18]. Hence the Commentator also, in his *Commentary on the Metaphysics*, book XII, com. 15, says that the composite has greater nobility than matter or form, and Alexander of Aphrodisias is reported as holding the same opinion. And Simplicius also holds this view in his *Commentary on the Physics* book I, text 70, and in book II, text. 4.[20]

7. The reason for this view is that the composite includes whatever perfection is in the form and adds something; therefore, it is more perfect. The antecedent is proved by some, because the composite includes being,[21] which the form does not include. But this reason is of no account because either existence is distinguished in reality from actual essence or not. If it is not distinguished, then, just as the composite essence includes its own adequate being, so the form includes its own proper being. But if it is distinguished, then, first of all, this argument does not have any place in a human because being first accrues to the soul rather than to the human.[22] Then, in order that the comparison might be correctly made, it should be made precisely between the essence of the form and the essence of the composite, and in that case this argument will not work.[23] If, on the other hand, the comparison is made between the form and a composite as it includes being, the form also should be taken as including being in its own way. For being is as such [*per se*] and primarily owed to form as to the first root of being which also exists through the composite, although the denomination of existing is attributed to the composite in the most absolute sense because of its mode of subsisting.

The proof of the antecedent, therefore, is that the composite includes the perfection of the form and, besides, includes the perfection of the matter. Zimara responds to this that no perfection is derived from matter but rather all imperfection. He is, however, mistaken because, as we showed above, matter includes true reality and a partial essence.[24] Hence, it is necessary that it has some perfection in the range of being and a greater perfection than the accidents. Likewise, subsistence is a perfection, but the material substance has this especially by reason of matter.[25] Furthermore, matter brings with it its own partial being. All these points will be shown below when we treat more at length of subsistence and existence.[26] If the previous argument is applied in this sense, it is efficacious because the composite has complete being, but the being of the form is incomplete. Finally, the union of the form to the matter has some perfection; otherwise, why would form naturally desire it?[27] The composite, however, includes this perfection, while the form does not.

Zimara responds in another way that, although the composite formally includes some perfection besides the form, it does not follow that it is more perfect than the form because all that perfection is from the form and is virtually contained in the form. In the same way, he says, God and the world together are not something more perfect than God alone is. But in the first place, his assertion at least will be false that form is more perfect than the composite, just as God alone is not more perfect than God and the world together. Second, it is false that the form contains eminently or virtually[28] the whole perfection of the composite since it does not virtually have the perfection of matter, nor can it in any way supply the causality of matter,[29] especially since it itself depends upon matter. Finally, form is for the sake of the composite as for the sake of its proper and principal end; an end of this sort, however, is more perfect than that which is ordered to the end, as Aristotle says in *Physics* book II, text. 31 [194a28-31].

An Explanation of a Passage of Book VII of Aristotle's Metaphysics

8. **The first explanation.** To the testimony drawn from Aristotle in *Metaphysics* VII [1029a21], I respond that the passage is explained in various ways. The first explanation is that in text 7 Aristotle is not speaking about the priority of perfection, but about the priority of causality. The philosopher virtually argues in this way: Form is prior to matter, and matter is prior to the composite; therefore, the form is prior to the composite. But if he were speaking about the priority of perfection, the minor would be false; therefore, he is speaking about priority of causality. Thus Albert the Great and Scotus interpret this passage, and St. Thomas points this out too.

But this interpretation is not satisfactory. First, because that way of arguing is not valid, since it changes the genus of cause. Second, because it would conclude better and more briefly that form is prior to the composite because it is the cause of it. Third, it is shown that Aristotle not only says that form is prior, but also that it is more of a being. It is true that in the conclusion Aristotle does not repeat that the form is more of a being, but only that it is prior. Hence Chrysostom Javelli in his commentary on that passage, q. 4,[30] says that form is compared to matter both in priority and in perfection but to the composite in priority only. But this is contrary to the interpretation of everyone. For it is clear from the manner of reasoning and arguing used by the Philosopher either that, for the sake of brevity, he omitted in the consequent that expression which was implied in the antecedent, or at least that by the word "priority" he meant to include the priority of perfection.

The second interpretation of this passage is that form is prior and more perfect not absolutely, but in some respect so that the Philosopher virtually argues in this way: Form is prior to and more perfect than matter because the former is act, the latter potency; therefore, form is also more perfect than the composite and is prior to it, at least in some respect, namely, because form is a simple act not including any potentiality, but the composite includes the potentiality of matter. St. Thomas and Alexander of Hales hold this in their commentaries on this passage, as well as Soncinas, in his *Commentary on the Metaphysics*, book VII, q. 28.

But there are two problems with this interpretation. One is that on account of the excess of perfection Aristotle ought to have affirmed and concluded this point simply, not in some respect, especially since in the antecedent the comparison was absolute, because form is simply more perfect than matter. The other problem is that the composite does not seem even in some respect less perfect than the form. For to include the potentiality of matter is not an imperfection in the composite in comparison with an informing form, but only in comparison with a complete immaterial substance.[31] In the same way a thing's being more simple is not always a greater perfection, even in some respect, when such a thing is ordered to complete something which is simply more perfect.[32]

9. Therefore, I do not think Aristotle in any way prefers the form to the composite but either makes no comparison between them or rather prefers the composite to the form, as Simplicius noted, in the place cited, and this is clear from Argyropoulos' version which reads: "If form is prior to matter and is more a being, that which is composed from both will also be prior for the same reason."[33] Hence the ancient version misled the commentators because in place of the nominative "ipsum" it has the ablative "ipso."[34]

And as for the context, this reading is also more in agreement with the intention of Aristotle. For he especially intended to show in opposition to the ancient philosophers that matter is not most of all substance, but is less perfect than others. Hence, later, in text 8 [1029a27], he refers to the ancient philosophers as saying that matter is substance most of all, but he teaches that this is impossible and concludes: "On this account form and that which is composed from both seem more to be substance than matter."[35] Hence, in the first comparison, when he concludes that the composite is prior for the same reason, he formally and immediately seems only to compare the composite to matter, but he also implicitly prefers it to form, when he reasons this way: Form is prior to matter; therefore, the composite is also, for the same reason, as I add, namely, because it includes the form. And consequently, the composite is prior in perfection and in nobility to the form since it is compared to the form as a whole is to a part.

10. **Not every cause is nobler than its effect.** To the objection given at the beginning, I respond by simply denying the major. For it is not necessary that every cause be nobler than its effect, but only in the case of some efficient and final causes. But it is not the case in the material cause, as all agree, nor even in the formal cause for almost the same reason, namely, that these intrinsic causes are causes in such a way that they are also parts, and neither by itself gives to the effect its whole entity or perfection, but constitutes it by giving to it whatever entity it has. But since the effect arises from many elements, it turns out to be more perfect than each of them. Hence, it can also be added that the effect does not surpass its cause with respect to what it has from that cause; it can, however, surpass its cause with respect to what it has from another cause.[36] Concerning this point we will say more below in *MD* XXVI, sect. 1.

Notes

[1]Neither of these can be the proper effect of the form because they are, respectively, the causality of the matter and of the form which *mediate* between them and their proper effects.

[2]See above, sect. VI, para. 7.

[3]The causality of a cause depends upon the cause as its effect does, but as the causality is intended as a *means* to the effect, it is not primarily speaking the effect of the cause.

[4]Form contributes more to the being of the composite because matter is so destitute of being and definition that it was regularly described by the scholastics as nearly nothing. Hence, the greater part of the essential being of a thing comes from its form, which is why it was regularly said that "form gives being," even though matter also contributes to the essence of the composite.

[5]For Suarez the chief mark of a conceptual distinction is that the entities distinguished by it are so linked that neither can exist without the other (see *MD* VII 2,28). Some conceptual distinctions are merely verbal, that is, not founded at all on any sort of relation or aspect within the object, but merely on different names, e.g., "Kleenex is facial tissue," where "Kleenex" is being used generically. Other

conceptual distinctions, however, are based upon diverse aspects or relations of a thing, which are denoted by our using different concepts. Of *this sort* is the distinction between Bill Clinton understood as President of the United States and Bill Clinton understood as the husband of Hilary. "The President of the United States in 1999," and "The husband of Hilary," are in fact identical, but they are not the same in concept, while "Kleenex" and "facial tissue" are the same in concept, when "Kleenex" is used generically.

[6]The Thomists explain this third thing as the *existence* of the composite which they regard as singular and common to both the form and the matter. In this way they attempt to explain the way a composite substance can be composite and yet have a single substantial being. Cf. John of St. Thomas, *Cursus philosophicus thomisticus: naturalis philosophiae* (Turin: Marietti, 1930-37), I pars, Q. VII, a. V.

[7]*MD* XXXVI, sect. 3.

[8]On essential and accidental unities see *MD* IV, sect. 3. Suarez's basic notion is that in an essential unity the parts come together to form a complete substance, where neither part is a complete substance on its own. Thus matter, for instance, though substantial, is not a complete substance because it lacks the operational capacities which are necessary features of a complete substance and which accrue to it by form.

[9]"A unity of simplicity" is the unity characteristic of a simple thing which is not composed of other things. If such a unity is in itself complete, it is an essential unity. Examples of simple essential unities are the angels and God. Some simple unities are not themselves complete substances, for example, form and matter.

[10]Suarez's argument is based upon his view that essence is in proportion to existence. Thus, that which has a simple existence will have a simple essence and will not be a composite being.

[11]That is, if existence is really a third thing distinct from matter and form, as the Thomists assert it is, it will make the composite being it helps to constitute more, not less, complex and will thus in no way help to render the composite essentially one.

[12]In other words, it is related to the composite as a part is to the whole it helps to constitute and to matter as to another part which with it constitutes the whole.

[13]That is, the same in reality but not in concept. Thus it is the same thing in reality for Chelsea Clinton to be born and for Hilary to become a mother in the sense that these two facts are constituted by a single act having various relations.

[14]The other possible formal effect of the form is to constitute the being of matter. In the following section Suarez denies, contrary to the Thomists, that this is an effect of form.

[15]*Aristotelis Opera cum Averrois commentariis*, Vol. IV (Venice: apud Junctas, 1562).

[16]Because the composite includes something the form does not, viz., matter.

[17]The basis of this view seems to have been a Platonic strain in certain Aristotelians, and even in Aristotle himself, which holds that matter does not add any perfection to form but merely *limits* it to being the form of this particular thing e.g., the matter of a tree on this view would limit the abstract form of "treeness" to being the form of "this particular tree". For a contemporary defense of this notion, see Watkins, *A Philosophy of Form*, (New York: Sheed and Ward, 1935), part I, chapter I.

[18]This is the Thomistic position that matter has no being of its own and is channeled being, so to speak, through form.

[19]*MD* XXXIII, sect. 1.

[20]*Commentary on Aristotle's Physics I* (Stillwater: Oklahoma State University, 1985)

[21]This is what Thomists, such as Soncinas, held.

[22]The argument here is that, since according to the Thomists the human soul, as a spiritual substance, has an existence of its own which it communicates to the body, they cannot hold that, in the case of human beings, the composite includes an existence not possessed by the form of the human being (cf. *ST* 1, Q. 75, a. 2).

[23]The point seems to be that in comparing the relative perfection of two beings one should stay in the same ontological order.

[24]*MD* XIII 4,8-11.

[25]Cf. *MD* XXXIV 5,14-15. The notion seems to be that matter must subsist because it is a sustaining subject which is not sustained in any more ultimate subject.

[26]In *MD* XXXI (on existence) and *MD* XXXIV (on subsistence).

[27]In other words, form would not be naturally ordered to matter if it received no added perfection by being joined to matter. Suarez' argument, based on final causality, echoes Aquinas' argument, against Origen and other Neoplatonists, that the soul must obtain some perfection by being incarnated (cf. *ST* I, Q. 76, a. 5).

[28]An entity X virtually contains an entity Y *iff* X is not of the same nature as Y, but X has all the perfections of Y in a higher way. Thus God contains virtually the perfections of a lion, not because God is a lion, but because He has all the perfections of a lion in a higher way. For example, God doesn't know things the way a lion does, but in His own way He knows all that the lion does in an infinitely more perfect way than the lion.

[29]For example, form cannot sustain itself as a subject in the way matter sustains it, nor can form function as the continuant in generation, nor can it root the accident of quantity.

[30]*In omnibus Metaphysicae libros quaesita textualia* (Lyon: Apud Gasparem a Portonariis 1559).

[31]For example, an angel, which is not only simple, but in itself a complete substance, unlike matter or an informing form, both of which need the other to be complete.

[32]As an accident might in itself be simple, e.g., a thought, but still imperfect in relation to the substance it perfects.

[33]Johannes Argyropulos (1415-1487), was a Byzantine philosopher who traveled widely in Europe after the fall of Constantinople. He lectured on Aristotle in Florence and Rome and translated several works of Aristotle into Latin. (*Cambridge History of Renaissance Philosophy*, p. 808).

[34]In other words, an older version of the text read: "If form is prior to matter, and has more being than matter, *that by which* both are composed, will be prior for the same reason." Thus, since form is "that by which" the composite exists, the older version of the text preferred the form to the composite, which is "that which" exists. Richard Hope's translation of the *Metaphysics* (Ann Arbor: University of Michigan Press, 1978) renders this passage as: "Consequently, if shape be prior to the material and more strictly speaking a being, it will also, for the same reason, be prior to the product of both."

[35]Hope's translation reads: "Therefore form, or else the product of both form and material, would seem to be primary rather than the material itself."

[36]As, for example, the composite cannot be more perfect than the form constituting it in virtue of what it receives from the form, but it can be in virtue of what it receives from matter in addition to what form gives it.

Section VIII
Whether the Substantial Form Is a True Cause of Matter and Matter Is Its Effect

1. The reasons which give rise to the difficulties on both sides. We are not now dealing with matter as informed, for we spoke of that in the preceding section, but with matter with regard to its entity or with regard to its being.[1] And the reason for doubting is that the whole entity of matter is presupposed for the eduction or introduction of the form;[2] therefore, that entity cannot be caused by the form, especially since matter receives its being through creation[3] toward which the form cannot cooperate by being a co-cause.[4] But it counts to the contrary that it is not contradictory that form is a cause of matter since causes are causes of one another, as Aristotle says in *Physics* book II, text. 30 [195a4-14] and in *Metaphysics* book V, text. 2 [1013b9]. Likewise, if form were not the cause of matter, matter would be able to exist naturally without form since, if there is no causality, there is no reason why there is dependence.

A Review of the Opinions

2. On this question there are various opinions in accord with the various views about the being of matter. For those who think that matter of itself does not have any existential being say that form is properly the cause of matter, because that which gives being to a thing is its cause. This seems to be the opinion of St. Thomas in *Summa Theologiae* I, q. 66, a. I, and in *On the Power of God*, q. 4, a. 1. All the Thomists hold this view: Capreolus in his *Commentary on the Sentences* II, dist. 13, q. 1; Cajetan in *The Commentary on Being and Essence*, c. 5 under q. 9;[5] Sylvester of Farrara in book III of his *Commentary on the Summa Contra Gentiles*, c. 4;[6] Soncinas and Chrysostom Javelli, in their Commentaries on the *Metaphysics*, book 8, q. 1. Durand of St. Pourcain holds the same in his *Commentary on the Sentences* II, dist. 12, q. 2, and Argentius in q. 1.[7]

The way of explaining this formal causality according to the opinion which really distinguishes existence from the actual essence of the creature ought to be that the partial entity of matter's essence is of itself incapable of existence until it is informed by the substantial form. But the form itself, according to its own essential entity, is essentially first united to matter and with it constitutes one whole essence, and this is the primary formal effect of the form. It further follows from this that the form communicates the existential being which it brings with itself first through itself to the composite and through participation to the matter, whether that being flows from the form actively, that is, as a consequence, or only formally. The latter can merely consist in the fact that to such a form or to a thing informed by it such being is owed by natural necessity, even if it is bestowed only by the extrinsic cause by which the form comes to be.

Cajetan pointed out this latter explanation in the place cited in his *Commentary on Being and Essence*, and it does not seem that a more suitable explanation can be given based on the principles of this view. For, if existence is an entity distinct from form, the first effect of form cannot be existential being itself, but only essential being, which is something distinct. For the first effect of form is essential to the thing, because form as form is of the essence of a thing. But existence is outside the essence according to this opinion. It does not, therefore, pertain to the first formal effect.

3. Hence, according to the principles of this view, the rational soul in the human Christ has a proper and primary formal effect. For it cannot be deprived of that if it actually informs, and yet, according to this opinion, it does not have a proper created existence. Therefore, form can only give existence formally in a secondary manner, that is, because it is either itself a proper receptacle for substantial existence or constitutes such a receptacle, or—what amounts to the same thing—because substantial being is intrinsically owed to an essence completed by such a form, and not to something else.[8]

Explained in this way this opinion is proven in the first place because matter is pure potency; therefore, it does not have act from itself but through form.[9] Hence, since existence is a certain act, it cannot belong to matter except through a form. Second, because existence is a later act if it is compared to essence; therefore, it presupposes an essential act, but this act is the form. Third, because substantial being is complete and perfect being. Therefore, it is not owed as such [*per se*] except to a complete and formal nature. Therefore, it is owed only to the form or by reason of the form.

4. Durand of St. Pourcain adds that, even if existence is not said to be really distinguished from essence, one must, nevertheless, assert that form is the formal cause of the actual existence of matter. For, although essence is its own existence, this must, nevertheless, be understood proportionally. For, essence in potency will be existence in potency, and actual essence will be actual existence. Therefore, form alone will be actual existence as it formally is in matter. And it follows from this opinion explained in both ways that matter naturally depends upon form in its whole entity so that it cannot remain without it because it cannot remain without existence. But it does not have existence except from the form or through the form upon which existence itself depends. Therefore [form gives existence to matter]. From this it also turns out that, if the form is changed, the matter changes its existence, though under

diverse forms and existences the same essence of matter is preserved. We shall, however, discuss in the following section whether this dependence is so great that God cannot supply it without form.

5. The second and entirely contrary opinion is that form does not give being to matter and is not a proper cause of its being. Henry of Ghent holds this in *Quodlibetal Question* I, q. 14, and Avicenna is cited as holding that view in his *Metaphysics* book IV; Scotus also holds it in his *Commentary on the Sentences* II, dist. 12, q. 2, at the end, and Gregory of Rimini in his *Commentary on the Sentences* q. 1, a. 2, ad. 1,[10] commenting on the argument of Peter Auriol, and also in the same work, q. 2, a. 3. The basis for this opinion is that matter has its own proper being which it does not formally receive from any cause since it is simple[11] and partial and distinct from the being which form gives. And matter has this proper being of its own only from God as an efficient cause. And with respect to that being matter is absolutely and simply presupposed by form by the order of nature; therefore, that being is in no way caused by form, but is completed or actualized by form.

6. **The way in which matter can exist naturally without form according to some.** But if against this view you claim that matter can naturally exist without form, since form is not the cause of it, some respond by granting the inference, which is what Marsilius of Inghen seems to have held in his *Commentary on the Sentences* II, q. 9, a. 2,[12] when he claims that in the beginning God created the matter of generable things without any substantial form and after some time formed it. Gabriel Biel also holds this in his *Commentary on the Sentences* II, dist. 12, q. 1 and 2;[13] and Augustine seems at times to hold it in *On Genesis Against the Manicheans* book I, c. 5, and 7[14] and in book 12 of *The Confessions*, c. 8. If, however, God did this in the creation of the world, it should not be thought to be beyond the natures of things because, as Augustine notes at the beginning of his exposition of *Genesis*, God did not then act as a worker of miracles, but as the author of nature. Nor does Henry of Ghent seem to dissent from this opinion when he says that matter cannot be stripped of all form according to the common course of nature because the corruption of one thing does not occur without the consequent generation of another. If, therefore, corruption could naturally occur without the generation of another thing, matter would naturally remain without form, insofar as matter itself was concerned. In his *Commentary on the Sentences* III, q. 3, a. 1, and q. 13, a.1, Marsilius held that this in fact happened in the death of Christ, and Henry thinks, in *Quodlibetal Question* I, q. 4, that it is probable, and even true, to the extent that in this case there was the separation of one form without the introduction of another. However, he holds in *Quodlibetal Question* II, q. 2, that this was a singular and preternatural occurrence in Christ. Scotus, on the contrary, thinks that this is something natural in the death of any

human, especially in a violent death, and even in the deaths of other animals, as is plain from his *Commentary on the Sentences* IV, dist. II, q. 3.

These authors, however, do not say that in that case matter remains absolutely without any form, but without a specific form and with the form of corporeity which they posit.[15] Others make use of a distinction: Something is said to be natural either with respect to a particular nature or with respect to universal nature. For with respect to its particular nature it is not natural for water to rise, and yet for filling a vacuum this is natural to it in accord with the inclination of universal nature. In this way, these authors say that it is not contradictory for matter, with respect to its particular nature, to be conserved without form if it is deprived of form. But as a result of the due order of universal nature this cannot happen, because, if it is impossible that there be a vacuum in a certain space, this is much more the case in the capacity and potency of matter.

Others, finally, say that matter cannot be without form even according to the particular condition of its nature, although form is not the proper cause of it, unless every condition necessary for existing is called a cause. And this way of speaking seems to come closer to the truth.

Resolution of the Question

7. In the first place, therefore, I say: Form is not the proper cause of matter, giving to it formally the proper being by which matter exists. The proof is that form does not give to matter that partial essential entity which it has in itself, as was shown above,[16] and which it retains under all forms. But that entity includes its own partial existence distinct from any existence coming formally from the form;[17] therefore [matter does not have its proper existence from form].

The major premise is evident, both because that entity of matter, in terms of its proper and partial essential being, is simple and distinct from form, and because it is presupposed in relation to form and remains unchanged in terms of that being under any form whatsoever.[18] Hence, the authors of the first opinion say form constitutes one complete essence with matter, but does not give to it its own proper essential being, which it rather presupposes. Therefore, form cannot be the formal, proper and intrinsic cause of that being of matter. I say, "proper and intrinsic," however, because extrinsically by way of a terminus this being of matter can be said to be derived from form because the essence of matter consists in an aptitude for form. But this is not a relation to form as informing in act, but by aptitude. Hence, the same specification would remain in matter even if it were without form.

The minor premise is proven because, if real essential being is actual, that is, outside its efficient cause, it is intrinsically existential being, as will be proven at length below in treating of being and essence.[19] But matter as pre-supposed by form in terms of its proper being of a partial essence has actual being insofar as it is distinguished from potential objective being.[20] For with-out such being it could not be a true and real subject of change and of form; therefore it does not have such being from form. The explanation and confir-mation of this is as follows: God by the same action by which he created and conserved matter under first form conserves it under all forms which later take its place. Therefore, that action of God is terminated in some being of matter which remains the same under all forms. For creation and the conser-vation corresponding to it are terminated in some being, and an action can-not remain the same unless its terminus is the same. Hence, that being is not given formally by form, for the being which form gives varies when the form is varied.[21] But that being is existential being, because it is temporal and ac-tual being outside of its efficient cause. Therefore, it is not given by form.

8. On this issue Durand of St. Pourçain is not speaking logically when he says that, even if being is not distinguished from essence, matter has its being from the information of the form. He labors under an equivocation when he says that matter only has essence in potency and, therefore, has an essence only in potency and, therefore, has from itself only being in potency. For matter in itself has in potency the essence of the form or composite, but does not have the essence of matter in potency, but in act by the very fact that it was created. For it is one thing for matter to be essentially potency, and it is another for it to be a only an essence in potency.[22] The first, after all, is univer-sally true, even of matter actually existing, because by it nothing else is meant than that matter is essentially a subject or a receptive potency.[23] But the sec-ond is false concerning actually created matter, even insofar as it is considered prior to form. For, although the essence of matter in itself, that is, apart from any efficient causality, is only in potency, something which is common to every created essence, yet, through its creation it becomes an essence in act, though subjectively a partial and potential one.[24] Therefore, as such, it has its own proportionate existential being; this, therefore, does not formally flow from form. But we will say more below concerning this point, that is, con-cerning the existence of matter.

9. **Matter depends on form and cannot exist naturally without it.** I say, secondly, that matter, nonetheless, depends in some way on form in its being, insofar as it cannot naturally exist without it, not only because of the order of universal nature, but also because of a requirement and a need of its proper and peculiar nature. The first part is more frequently accepted by philoso-phers and theologians who for this reason say that there is a mutual and nec-essary connection between matter and material form, as can be seen in the authors cited, and in Avicenna in his *Metaphysics* book II, c. 2 and 3 and in

his *Physics* book I, 56 and book II, 13; Themistius, in his *Commentary on the Physics* book I, the final digression;[25] Plotinus, *Enneads* III, book VI, c. 14;[26] and Paul Soncinas in his *Commentary on the Metaphysics* book V, q. 1.

The proof from reason is that the entity of matter would be useless in the nature of things if it remained without form. For it could not perform any operation. This, however, is abhorrent to nature. Therefore, it is contrary to the order of nature that matter should exist without form.[27] Such an argument is used by many, but it does not seem efficacious. For, although that which is not suited for some function of nature would exist to no purpose in nature, that which of itself is suited for exercising some function for which it was established by nature, even if at times it does not carry out that function, does not exist to no purpose, nor it is simply useless. Thus, even if matter were sometimes to remain without form, it would not be useless in nature, because of itself it would be suited to receive form if an agent were present to introduce it. And it would happen by accident that it lacked form due to the fact that an agent which was disposing the matter to introduce a form took away the disposition necessary for conserving the other form before it was able to introduce the new form. This is what Scotus thinks happens in the death of a human or another animal, and for that reason the cadaver does not remain as useless, nor would matter remain so, especially because little by little it could be disposed to receive another form.

10. Hence, the argument which is usually drawn from the continous succession of generation and corruption also does not seem efficacious, both because it is not certain that every corruption is immediately and in the same instant followed by a generation, as is clear from the opinion of Scotus which was stated. For, although nature does not as such [*per se*] intend corruption, but generation, it can, nonetheless, happen that one thing is corrupted before another thing is generated. Hence, Aristotle's statement, namely, "The generation of one is the corruption of the other" [*De gen. et cor.*, 318a23-25] is perhaps not convertible, or it will have to be understood that he was speaking *per se*, although it could by accident fail to be the case.

11. Another argument is commonly given that what is not suited to operate on its own without another is not suited to exist on its own without that other. Matter, however, by its nature cannot perform any operation without form; therefore, by its nature it needs form in order to exist and cannot exist without it. But I ask whether "operation" is being taken in the proper sense which implies a relation to an efficient principle. And if it is taken in this way, it is beside the point since neither with form nor without form can matter have an operation.[28] Or "operation" is taken broadly for any sort of causality, and in this way, the assumption is false. For one thing often needs the aid of another in order to cause even if not to exist, as the agent intellect needs the

aid of the imagination for abstracting species and, nevertheless, remains in existence without the imagination and is not thought useless even if then, in that state, it does not exercise its own operation.[29] The rational soul also needs the aid of the body for exercising formal causality but not for existing, and the same holds for other causes. In that way, then, matter can need the aid of form in order to exhibit material causality[30] even if it does not require form to exist. And the reason is that causality entails a transcendental relation or reference and, hence, can require the aid of another. The thing from which the causality comes[31] can, however, be more absolute and can require the company of another, not actually, but only by aptitude.

12. From this the other common argument, which is judged to be most *a priori,* is also seen to be weak, namely, that matter is pure potency and thus by its nature ought to depend on the act of form.[32] For the fact that it is said to be pure potency does not exclude the actual entity of matter, but only says that that entity is such that it is essentially potency and established entirely for the task of receiving and sustaining form.[33] It does not, however, pertain to the nature of potency, generally speaking, that it always is under its own act.[34] How, therefore, is it shown that this pertains to the nature of this potency? For from the fact that it is a substantial potency it cannot be inferred, because from this it would rather be considered to be a subsisting potency, although partially and incompletely, and thus able to exist by itself, even if it would not actually exercise its causality, just as the rational soul remains because it is subsistent, even though it is not actually informing matter.

13. **The argument proving that matter cannot naturally remain without form**. It seems, therefore, difficult to give an argument which proves this natural dependence of matter upon form. For at this time, especially in Italy, many think that matter is never separated from form on account of the necessary order of natural agents, both lower and celestial, which always introduce one form when another recedes, but not on account of any intrinsic dependence of matter. For they say that matter would not have to be reduced to nothing if, when one form was removed, another did not take its place, but would naturally continue with its own entity and existence.

One should not, nevertheless, depart from the ancient and common opinion which we can explain and confirm in the following ways. First, it is not likely that this lower matter is more independent of the form of any generable thing, considered in general, than any matter of the heaven is independent of its form, since the lower matter is less perfect. But every bit of the matter of the heaven depends naturally upon its form; therefore, every bit of lower matter depends upon its form. Second, it is not likely that this matter depends more upon accidental forms than upon substantial form, since it is essentially [*per se*], primarily, and principally ordered to substantial form. But this matter depends upon accidental forms so that it cannot naturally exist without any, as is clear, at least, in the case of quantity.

14. **Augustine finally stated that formless matter never came first by any real duration.** Third, the best physical conjecture is that this matter was instituted in order that it would always exist under some substantial form and would never be separated from it. This is a sign, therefore, that matter was created such is that by its very nature it requires the aid of a form in order to be able to exist. The antecedent is clear from induction because matter from the beginning was in its creation constituted under forms. Nor is the contrary view likely, for scripture does not say that in the beginning God created matter, but heaven and earth. It was shown that the words "heaven and earth" cannot be explained as referring to matter.[35] And although Augustine occasionally seemed to be in doubt about this, in book 12 of *The Confessions*, c. 17 and 29, he, nonetheless, rejected the previous opinion and concluded that matter did not precede its formation by time, but only by nature. Hence, in book 13 of *The Confessions*, c. 34, he concludes as follows: "Although the matter of heaven and earth is one thing and its appearance another, you made the matter from nothing at all, but the appearance from informed matter; you, nevertheless, made both at the same time so that form followed upon matter without any interval of delay." He holds the same in book 1 of his *Commentary on Genesis*, c. 19, and book 4, c. 22 and following,[36] and in book 1 of *The City of God*, c. 7.[37]

But after that first creation matter has never lacked all form, and natural causes were so arranged by the Author of nature that one form never abandons matter without another being introduced. That axiom of Aristotle, therefore, in book 1 of *On Generation and Corruption*, text 17 [318a23-25], "The generation of one is the corruption of another," is universally true, nor can it be true of generation that the corruption always follows upon it unless generation always follows upon the corruption of another. For, if something were corrupted and no generation took place, something else could later be generated from the same matter without a new corruption. And since it is true that there is no form of corporeity, or no merely generic form, in matter, as was shown above and as we shall show below,[38] it is necessary that form always follows upon form in matter unless we would want to say that, as a matter of fact, matter often remains without any substantial form and only with accidental forms. This would be absurd and paradoxical in philosophy.

15. Matter was, therefore, made so that it would always be under form; therefore, it is probable that it was made such that it needs form to exist. The proof of the consequence is that it is not absurd to think that prime matter is such that it has this need, a point which that argument correctly proves, because, namely, it is pure potency, that is, imperfect in its entity and incom-

plete and potential. For that need and dependence does not conflict with
these imperfections, but rather squares well with them. Nor does it matter
that it is partially subsistent, for subsistence excludes dependence on a subject,[39] but not on an act or form. Nor should matter be compared in this
respect to the subsistent soul because the soul is much more perfect and more
actual than matter and is absolutely immaterial. Therefore, this mode of dependence is not only compatible with matter, but is also most suited to the
entity of matter and to its imperfection and function; hence, it is more probable that such is the nature of matter.

Second, it is probable in physical things that that which always occurs in
the same way and never in another is naturally necessary.[40] But it naturally
always happens in this way that matter is under some form; therefore, it comes
from a necessity of nature and not from a necessity of the form that, when
one form perishes from a defect of the dispositions, there is no necessity on
the part of another form to introduce a new form. Again, this necessity could
not be attributed to a proximate extrinsic agent alone because there is often
no particular agent from which such a form could come to be; therefore, this
necessity is founded upon an intrinsic need of matter itself.

Nor is it enough to say that this effect is natural from the order of the
universe or from universal nature or that the necessity arises from the universal agent causes which always are ready to introduce a form when the particular causes are lacking; for this universal institution of nature is founded on a
proper need of matter. For, since it pertains to the universal good that no
portion of matter should ever fail or be reduced to nothing, nature, therefore,
provides that matter could never be deprived of all form, but that, when one
withdraws, another always takes its place, because this was necessary in order
that matter could be perpetually conserved in a natural way. Otherwise, why
would nature have been so provident over such a succession of forms, especially when the form which follows was not, as such, necessary to expel the
other form which withdrew due to a defect of the necessary dispositions or
organization?[41]

16. Nor is the claim which was made about the rising of water to fill a
vacuum similar. For universal nature avoids a vacuum on account of the perfect unity and wholeness of the universe and on account of the necessity of
action and influence, and not on account of the advantage of any particular
being. But the fact that matter would be, as it were, devoid of any form would
not constitute any loss to universal nature, if matter could, nonetheless, be
conserved and be acted upon and disposed for generation, and could concur
with that in its own way. Therefore, the universal reason is nothing other than
the conservation of matter.

I confess that this whole discussion presupposes that in fact matter never remains without substantial form and from that infers that this comes about from a need of matter, and I think this inference has been sufficiently proven. But I doubt whether the antecedent has been satisfactorily demonstrated. For we do not experience substantial form except from its effects or accidents. Often, however, there is no effect which clearly shows the introduction of a new form after the withdrawal of the previous form, as in the death of a human being.[42] And for this reason Scotus and others deny that a new form is introduced in this case, although, in order to avoid admitting that matter remains without any form, they posited that the form of corporeity or of composition remains. If we set aside this form, we do not prove by another argument that a new form is introduced in every death or corruption except that otherwise matter would remain without form. And thus we seem to reason in a circle in these arguments. But, although it is true that this is not clearly demonstrated from effects, this axiom is, nevertheless, so in agreement with the natures of things and with the end and with the use and the imperfection of matter that it has been accepted as certain and indubitable by the unanimous consent of nearly all the ancient and more recent philosophers, which is sufficient for establishing a philosophical conclusion.[43]

The Nature of the Dependence of Matter on Form

17. **Two modes of dependence. Arguments which prove that matter depends on form only as a condition.** But it remains to be explained what sort of dependence this is. For it can be understood in two ways, that is, either as dependence upon a proper cause or as dependence upon a condition so necessary that without it being is not due to such a thing.[44] I explained these two modes of dependence at length in Vol. I tome II, part 3, dist. VIII, sect. 1,[45] and Fonseca seems to refer to these in the fifth book of his *Commentary on the Metaphysics of Aristotle*, c. 2, q. 3, sect. 1, when he says that matter can be understood to depend upon form either as upon a true cause or as upon a certain concomitant entity. In sect. 3 he seems to make mention of them when he says that accidents conserve the substance, not *a priori*, but *a posteriori*.

One can doubt, therefore, in which of these ways matter depends upon form. But it seems that it can be reasonably defended that the dependence is only *a posteriori* and as a necessary condition. First, because this sort of dependence is possible. For substantial form or its union with matter and, thus, the whole composite, depends in this way upon certain accidental forms as upon dispositions necessary by way of conservation, as they say, not because they are proper and direct causes of such conservation, but because they are dispositions so natural that they are even necessary. Therefore, for even greater reason matter can have such a dependence on form as upon a necessary and primary disposition. Likewise, matter depends in this way on quantity; therefore, it is can also depend upon form in such a way.

Second, this mode is sufficient for preserving everything which has been said about the dependence of matter upon form, and all the arguments given prove nothing more. This mode is also easy and clear, for according to it the two conclusions[46] stated can be easily reconciled. It is also correctly understood how in turn form depends upon matter and matter upon form, for one is said to depend *a priori* and the other *a posteriori*; one, indeed, as on a true cause, and the other as on a concomitant condition.[47]

18. But according to the other way it is difficult to understand this mutual dependence. For, since matter is absolutely presupposed by form in order that the form can be educed from the potency of matter, it is scarcely understood how matter could depend upon form *a priori*. And that difficulty is further explained and increased because matter comes to be through true creation and is conserved through the same action which continues.[48] Therefore, it does not depend in its own coming to be upon form as upon a true cause because no created cause can naturally concur in creation.[49]

Some respond that this is true concerning the efficient cause, but not concerning the other kinds of cause. For a creature cannot be an efficient cause of creation, but it can, nevertheless, be a final cause, as is self-evident.[50] And for the same reason, a creature can be a formal cause and even a material cause. For, when the whole is created, the parts concur in its being and coming to be in the genus of material cause. But, if the final cause is omitted—for its causality has a peculiar nature because it is not exercised through a real and proper motion distinct from the action of the efficient cause, and thus does not presuppose real being in the thing which exercises such causality[51]—it seems with regard to the material cause that its direct concurrence is incompatible with creation, taken as proper and true creation.

This is easily seen from what was said above concerning the eduction of form from the potency of matter[52] and will be shown more at length below in the disputation devoted to creation.[53] I speak, however, concerning creation in the proper sense. For in the sense of concreation creation can be dependence on a material cause, as was explained above in dealing with the matter of the heaven,[54] because concreation as such supposes creation by the order of nature and thus can have some dependence. For the same reason, therefore, creation as such cannot have a dependence on a formal cause because the formal cause presupposes the material cause, although concreation can have a dependence on form, as was explained above in the place cited. But the matter of generable things is truly and properly created and is not properly concreated, that is, it is not produced through one and the same action by which the whole is created. Therefore, the form cannot concur in its creation as a true cause.

19. This is explained and confirmed in the following way from what was said. For the creation of this matter of generable things and the introduction of form are distinct actions, both now in the conservation of matter and the generation of things and in the first production of sublunar things. But the action introducing the form cannot be the true cause of the action creating matter; much less, therefore, can the form which is introduced through that action be the true cause of the creation of matter.[55] The minor is evident, first because the introduction of form absolutely supposes the creation of matter or created matter. Nor can it be understood that the introduction of form or its union with matter is presupposed in any genus of cause for the creation of matter because the introduction of form as such involves a transcendental relation to a matter that has already been created. Hence, just as a relation cannot be supposed as prior to a term in any genus of cause, so neither can the introduction of the form be supposed as prior to the creation of matter. Second, because otherwise the creation or conservation of matter would essentially [*per se*] depend upon the eduction of form; therefore, it would also depend upon the agent educing the form. And thus natural agents as true efficient causes would conserve matter.[56]

Hence it would also happen that, as often as the form is changed in matter, that action would be changed by which matter is conserved by God, because, if the dependence of an action is changed, the action is changed, since it is itself essentially the dependence, as we will explain below.[57] The consequence, however, is false. For, as matter is the first subject of generation, it is something ingenerable and incorruptible, because it is supposed by generation and corruption. Therefore, for the same reason, it is something unchangeable in terms of that action through which it comes to be and is conserved, because it is presupposed as produced and conserved. Otherwise by every generation of a natural being matter would be concreated, or it would be the same as if it were concreated, because it would begin to be conserved by a new action terminating in the whole, and this is clearly impossible for the action of natural agents.[58] Otherwise, it could for the same reason be said that by such an action new matter is always co-produced. Therefore, the creation or conservation of matter does not depend on the eduction of form as on a proper cause or true [*per se*] action; therefore, much less can it depend on form as on a true cause since form is in every genus of cause posterior to the action through which it is educed from the potency of matter. Hence, from first to last, matter itself cannot depend upon form as upon a true cause, but only as upon a concomitant cause or condition and one which well disposes and actualizes the matter.

20. **Reasons which urge that matter depends upon a form as on a proper cause.** There are, nevertheless, not lacking arguments which seem to show that matter can depend upon form as upon a proper cause which by its act of informing contains matter in its being. And this is so, especially because material substantial form depends upon matter as upon a proper and true [*per se*] cause in its own genus; therefore, matter depends in turn upon form as upon a true cause because, although it does not sustain it as a subject, it is able to contain it as an act. For, just as the efficient act holds the effect in being through its own causality, so the informing act can in a way proportionate to it contain its own subject in being; therefore, substantial form is related to matter in this way.

The consequence is proven, first, because material form is more perfect and more actual than matter; therefore, matter depends more on form than form on matter. Second, because it is not contradictory that there is such a mutual nexus between matter and form as between causes which are causes of each other. This is evident both from that general principle that between causes in diverse genera there can be a mutual priority and also because in the heaven there seems to be this mutual connection between matter and form.[59] For both in coming to be and in being they depend upon each other mutually and essentially [*per se*], as was said above, so that concreation of one depends essentially on the concreation of the other, and conversely.

From this example a third reason can be derived, because the matter of the heaven depends on its own determinate form as on a true [*per se*] cause; therefore, the matter of these lower things will also depend in the same way upon a generable form, although upon an indefinite one. The consequence is evident because the matter of the heaven is more perfect; therefore, if it is dependent, much more so will the other be.

21. **Judgment is rendered concerning the question and concerning the reasons proposed for either view.** These reasons are in fact probable, and thus both sides can be maintained with probability from what has been said. To me, nevertheless, to speak the truth, the first opinion seems more intelligible and easier to accept, and if one attentively weighs the arguments given, the latter arguments can more easily be refuted. I leave this task to the reader, because the matter seems easy. For, below, in explaining how causes are causes of one another,[60] it must be thoroughly explained what mutual priority can come into play between two of them and what cannot, and upon an understanding of this the resolution of the present question depends very much.

Notes

[1]That is, the question is not what being does form give to matter in *addition* to matter's own being, but what being, *if any*, does form give to matter itself.

[2]That is, form could not inform matter if matter had no being of its own for form to act upon.

[3]Matter is simple and so cannot itself be constituted out of pre-existing parts, nor is there any more ultimate subject it could be produced in; hence, its origin could only be by true creation *ex nihilo*.

[4]Since it is finite and only an infinite being can create in the proper sense (cf. *MD* XX, sect. 2)

[5]*In "De ente et essentia" D. Thomae Aquinatis commentaria*, ed. M.H. Laurent (Turin: Marietti, 1934).

[6]*S. Thomae contra Gentiles cum commentariis* (Venice: apud Junctas, 1524).

[7]Reference not found.

[8]The notion here is that form channels existence insofar as, in completing matter, it constitutes something that is *fit* to receive existence. Such existence is *actively* conferred only by the efficient cause of the essence.

[9]In other words, matter is in itself too indeterminate and incomplete to exist on its own, but must be determined through form first.

[10]*Quaestiones super primum sententiarum ingeniossissimi magistri Gregorii de Arimino* (Valentia, 1500; Bibliotecca Nacional de Madrid Incunable 2308).

[11]And as simple, its being could not be intrinsically constituted by anything really distinct from itself.

[12]*Quaestiones Marsilii super quattuor libros sententiarum* (Strasbourg, 1501; rep. Frankfurt-Main: Minerva, 1966).

[13]*Epitome et collectorium ex Occamo circa quatuor sententiarum libros* (Tubigen, 1501; rep. Frankfurt-Main: Minerva, 1965).

[14]*De Genesi contra Manichaeos* in *Patrologia Latina*, Vol. XXXIV, Migne, ed. (1865), pp. 173 ff.

[15]On this see sect. 10,7-15.

[16]*MD* XIII, sect. 4. It should be noted that many of the arguments Suarez gives for the independent existence of matter in XIII depend, as he himself notes, upon the view he takes of the relation between the essence and existence of finite things in *MD* XXXI.

[17]By a "partial existence" Suarez means to refer to the entity or being of something which is naturally ordered to being a part of something else. He does not mean to refer to something half way between being and non-being. For Suarez everything which is, including modes, exists by an intrinsic being of its own, and nothing literally shares in the very being of something else, except in the sense that it depends, according to a certain sort of causality, on something else.

[18]That is, the whole reason for positing prime matter to begin with was to provide a continuant for substantial changes. But this implies, according to Suarez, that a piece of matter constituting a fetus retains the same being *qua* matter that it had when it constituted a spermatozoon.

[19]*MD* XXXI.

[20]Potential objective being is the being mere logical possibilities have, e.g., a unicorn or the Antichrist. Suarez here is saying that matter is not a pure potency in the sense of being a mere logical possibility.

[21]That is, if form gave matter being, the being of matter would vary as the form varied. But Suarez holds that this can't be the case if matter is a true continuant mediating between various substantial changes. Hence, form does not give matter its own proper being.

[22]On this, see *MD* XIII 5,11.

[23]Suarez views the potency of matter as consisting in a real but imperfect actuality which is naturally ordered to being completed by the further actuality and perfection form brings to matter. Thus, for Suarez, real potency is just the actuality of a thing taken according to a relation it has to that which will further perfect and actualize it. There is, in his universe, no shadowy potential being half way between actual being and non-being. For potential being, finite perfectible being suffices.

[24]A subjective potency is a real existing subject which is capable of further actualization and perfection. In this way wood is a subjective potency for a table.

[25]*Themistii peripatetici lucidissimi, Paraphrasis in Aristotelis Posteriora et Physica...*(Venice, 1559).

[26]*Enneads*, trans. A. H. Armstrong (Cambridge: Harvard University Press, 1988).

[27]This argument, of course, would only be used by those who, like Suarez, posit a proper being intrinsic to matter.

[28]The reason is that all principles of efficient operation come from form. Cf. *MD* XVIII, sect. 2,1-4.

[29]According to Aquinas, whom Suarez follows here, the intellect depends upon the images generated by the "fantasy" or "imagination," which resides, as it were, in the brain, to abstract universal concepts. Thus, from seeing many trees a composite image of a tree is generated from which the intellect abstracts the universal concept "tree." The intellect depends upon the fantasy and, hence, the brain only as an *extrinsic condition*, in the way the eyes depend upon light to see. Therefore, the intellect can go on existing even after death when it is no longer attached to the brain which supplies it with images. In this state it will not be able to abstract universals, but it will not be useless because it will be able to continue to perform its function when reunited with the body at the resurrection. Cf. *ST*, Pt. 1, Q. 75, a. 3.

[30]This is true, of course, because matter's causality is properly to sustain form, not to produce it, and so it could not sustain form if form did not exist.

[31]That is, the causal principle. Thus the eye, for example, needs light to see and so has a necessary relation to light even when it is not seeing.

[32]This is the argument used by the Thomists.

[33]For more on this see MD XIII, sect. 5.

[34]As the eye, for example, is not always actualized by sight.

[35]Sect. 3, 7-15.

[36]*De Genesi ad Litteram libri XII* in *Patrologia Latina*, Vol. XXXIV, Migne, ed. (1865), pp. 215 ff.

[37]*De Civitate Dei* in *Patrologia Latina*, Vol. XLI, Migne, ed. (1864), coll. 13ff.

[38]On this, see below, sect. 10, 7-15.

[39]That is, matter does not depend upon any more ultimate receptacle in which it inheres.

[40]This principle seems to have been first explicitly stated by Scotus. By using it, certain scholastics attempted to give a defense of the validity of inductive reasoning. By "natural necessity" the scholastics meant to refer to the laws inherent in the *natures* of created essences. Such a necessity could, of course, be overcome by the power of God, which was usually thought to be limited only by logical necessity or metaphysical necessity. On this see *De cognitione humana*, a. II in *Duns Scotus: Philosophical Writings*, trans. by Allan Wolter (Indianapolis: Hackett, 1987), p. 109.

[41]According to scholastic physics the destruction of the form is caused by the introduction of certain accidents incompatible with that form and the consequent ejection of dispositions necessary for the existence of the form. Thus, intense heat in wood expels the form of wood and disposes the matter in the wood for receiving the form of cinders.

[42]Since the scholastics had no microscope, it seemed to them that at death the soul of a human being simply receded without any new form being introduced in its place. This lead Scotus and others to posit a form of corporeality which they said remained when a person died.

[43]This is a good example of the "empirical" aspect of classical scholastic thought, which did not demand *a priori* deductions of all philosophical conclusions but was often satisfied with probabilities. This empirical or inductive aspect of Suarez's thought separates him from later Protestant scholastics such as Abraham Calov (1612-1682) in his *Metaphysica divina* (1640) and Clemens Timpler in his *Metaphysicae systema methodicum* (1606) and from Leibniz himself. For information on Protestant scholasticism, see Charles Lohr, "Metaphysics," in *The Cambridge History of Renaissance Philosophy* (Cambridge: Cambridge University Press, 1988), pp. 620-638.

[44]That is, that matter has some entity of its own not intrinsically constituted by form but that it naturally depends on form to exist. Compare this with the way in which oxygen is naturally necessary for a human being to exist and yet the human's substance has an entity of its own distinct from the being of the oxygen such that the oxygen is not an *intrinsic* cause of that entity in the way the human soul and body are.

[45]*Commentarii et disputationes in tertiam partem D. Thomae, De incarnatione, Opera omnia*, vol. 17, pp. 335-337.

[46]These are that 1) "Form is not the proper cause of matter giving to it formally the proper being by which it exists," and 2) "Matter depends in some way on form for its existence in that it cannot naturally exist without form...."

[47]That is, matter is a true cause of form by sustaining it, but form is only a condition naturally necessary for matter to exist.

[48]The scholastics often *defined* conservation as "continuous creation" (cf. Leibniz, *Theodicy*, Part 1, para. 27).

[49]Cf. *MD* XX, sect. 1. The usual reason given for this is that, as there is an infinite distance between being and non-being, creation requires an infinite causal power (*ST* I, Q. 45, a. 5., ad. 3). Suarez questioned the cogency of this argument in *MD* XX.

[50]For example, God might create one sort of thing, say plants, for the sake of another sort of thing, say animals. So animals, which are creatures, could be final causes of the creation of plants.

[51]In *MD* XXIII Suarez defined final causality as "that on account of which something is brought about or done."

[52]Sect. 2,14-13.

[53]*MD* XX, sect. 3.

[54]*MD* XIII, sect. 13.

[55]This supposes, as Suarez argues below in XVIII, that created agents truly educe substantial forms.

[56]The agent would conserve matter on this view because it would, in educing form, produce the composite *ex nihilo*.

[57] *MD* XVIII 10, 5-7. Suarez defends the proposition that action, which is the causality of the efficient cause, is nothing other than the dependency of the effect on such a cause. This dependency is a certain mode of the effect.

[58] Because it would suppose that both the matter and the form of a composite substance are produced when a new form is introduced into the matter. In effect this would mean that the whole composite would be created by created agents, thus doing away with the need to posit matter in the place.

[59] For example, the intellect is prior to the will, according to Aquinas, as presenting the object of the will's deliberations, but the will is prior to the intellect as in some way efficiently causing the intellect to focus on *this* rather than *that* object of thought. Thus each is prior to the other in different orders of causality. *Vide ST* I-II, Q. 9, a. 1.

[60] *MD* XXVII, sect. 2.

Section IX
Whether the Dependence of Matter on Form Is So Great That without Form Matter Could not Be Conserved Even through the Divine Power, nor Form without Matter

1. The rational form can naturally be conserved in separation from matter, while others can be conserved in separation from it only supernaturally. With respect to the dependence of form on matter, there can only be a doubt about the material form.[1] For it is agreed concerning the immaterial form that it can remain without matter not only by the divine power, but even naturally.[2] Concerning other forms, however, Aristotle and other philosophers would perhaps deny that they could in any way subsist as separated from matter, because they thought that dependence upon matter and actual inherence in matter was essential to such forms. We Catholics, however, who believe God conserves an accident without a subject[3] cannot doubt—though certain moderns do doubt it[4]—that God could also conserve a material substantial form without matter, because the dependence of an accident on a subject is greater insofar as an accident has less entity and actuality than a substantial form.[5] Hence, all the teachers who will be cited in the following paragraph agree on this point concerning substantial form although they disagree concerning matter.

The First Opinion Concerning Matter is Treated

2. The first opinion concerning matter is one that denies that God can conserve matter without a substantial form. St. Thomas holds this in the places cited in the preceding section along with his followers cited there, and he holds this especially in *Quodlibetal Question* III, a. 1. And the Master [Peter Lombard] points this out in *The Sentences* II, dist. 12, c. 5, where he merely says that matter was not in the beginning of the creation first without all form because such a bodily something which has no form cannot exist. He does not say, however, whether he is speaking about what God can do or only about what created things can do.[6] Hugh of St. Victor seems to speak in the same way in *On the Sacraments* I, p. I, c. 4.[7] Bonaventure speaks more clearly in his *Commentary on the Sentences* in dist. 12 which was just mentioned, a. 1, ad. 1,[8] and Harvey Nedellec in *Quodlibetal* VI, q. 1.[9] Giles of Rome also holds this at the beginning of his *Commentary on the Creation Story in Genesis*, c. 1 and 2,[10] John of Jandun in his *Commentary on the Physics*, book I, q. 26 and Zimara in *Theorems* no. 15.

The chief foundation for this view is that matter has no existence formally from itself, but receives it formally from form. God, however, cannot give a formal effect without a formal cause, and He is also not able to conserve matter without existence. Therefore, He cannot conserve matter without form. It makes no difference that according to this opinion existential being is not the primary formal effect of form. One reason is that, although the primary effect could on this account remain without this secondary effect through the divine power, the secondary effect, nevertheless, could not conversely be given without the primary effect because the secondary effect essentially depends on the primary effect.[11] The second reason is that it pertains to the primary effect of form to be or to constitute the proximate receptacle of existence, an effect which is never separated from it. For even in the humanity of Christ form has that effect. But God cannot constitute an act outside of its proper receptacle.

The second argument, taken from the Commentator, is that matter is pure potency. Whatever exists, however, is in act. Therefore, it is impossible for matter to exist without act because otherwise it would simultaneously exist in act and not in act. The act, however, of matter is form and, therefore, it is impossible for it to exist without form.

The third argument is that, even if matter has some partial existence, it has that in dependence on form in the genus of formal cause. God, however, cannot by Himself supply the effect of the formal cause;[12] therefore [He cannot conserve matter without form.]

Fourth, this argument is commonly given, namely, that, if matter were conserved without form, there would exist, in the natural order some individual under the genus of substance, but not under some species of that genus.[13] For matter would, for example, be in the genus of body but would not be in any species of body.

Fifth, every accidental being comes from an accidental form, and thus nothing can have such a being without form. Therefore, every substantial being comes from a substantial form and cannot exist without it. Matter, however, has some substantial being. Therefore, matter cannot exist without substantial form.

Other arguments are often multiplied, but they do not produce a new difficulty, and therefore I judge it useless to dwell on them at this point.

The Second View is Treated and Preferred to the First

3. The contrary view is quite common. Henry of Ghent holds it in *Quodlibetal Question* I, q. 10; Scotus in his *Commentary on the Sentences* I, dist. 12, q. 2, and in that place also Francis Lychetus,[14] Francis of Meyronnes,[15] John of Bassoles,[16] and other Scotists. Richard of St. Victor holds the same

opinion in q. 4, Gregory of Rimini in q. 1, Gabriel Biel in q. 1, and Marsilius of Inghen in q. 8. Domingo de Soto inclines to the same view in his *Commentary on the Physics* book I, q. 6.

To me this view seems entirely true because I not only do not find any clear implication of a contradiction, but I do not even find a sufficiently probable reason to persuade me that there is a contradiction. In the first place, even if we held that existence is something really distinct from essence, no sufficient reason could be given why God could not place that act in matter alone. For, although according to the natural order that act would have to be received in the whole nature or entire supposite,[17] it could, nevertheless, through the divine power be constituted in one part. In the same way, accidental existence can only be received in an accidental composite or in a substantial supposite by means of an accidental form, but God can, nevertheless, make it remain separately in a separated accident alone.[18] And for even better reason God could conserve substantial being in the material substantial form alone.[19] Therefore, He could also place the act of existence in the essence of matter alone because, although matter is a potency for form, it is, nevertheless, a certain partial substantial essence.[20] Insofar, therefore, as matter is a certain essence, it will be able to be actualized by existence, for existence is the act of essence.

Nor is there any argument which could prove that the order between substantial form and the act of existence, or the dependence of that existence on form, is so essential that it could not be changed or supplied by God. For form is not the cause of the existence of matter in such a way that it intrinsically constitutes matter, since matter and form are presupposed to be simple distinct entities. The causality of form, however, which does not come through intrinsic composition, but either through emanation or through some similar manner, can be supplied by God, as I shall immediately show.

4. But it cannot be said that matter existing by a really distinct act of existence already has form because every act is a form. This axiom is false, according to this opinion, even about an actualizing act. For the authors of that opinion locate in one substantial supposite a substantial form and a really distinct act of existence, and yet they do not admit two substantial forms. Therefore, substantial existence is not a substantial form. And so, they also say that the existence of the created humanity of Christ can be supplied by the uncreated existence of the Word because existence is not a form.[21] Therefore, if matter were conserved with an act of existence really distinct from its essence without another form, it would be truly conserved without form, and thus it would be in act without an informing act, but not without a terminating act.

Add to this the fact that some scholars[22] who hold that existence is really distinct from essence concede that God can in created things conserve an essence outside of its causes and without existence. Although they are stating an obvious contradiction, they, nevertheless, seem to speak logically, given the false principle they have presupposed. Why, therefore, will they not admit that the essence of matter can also be conserved as a real being outside of its causes without a distinct act of existence? For in order that a thing exist in the nature of reality and outside its causes, essential being is sufficient according to them. But matter, from itself and in itself, formally has a certain essential being, although it is partial and diminished.[23]

5. **A relevant and *a priori* proof of the conclusion.** But these arguments proceed from the principles of others, like *ad hominem*[24] arguments. From my own principles, however, an *a priori* argument for this opinion is that, just as matter has its own incomplete essential entity, it also has its own incomplete existential entity. For the existence of a substance is composed in the same way as the essence of the substance,[25] and thus without any contradiction or repugnance God can conserve matter without form just as He conserves form without matter. For, although the proper receptacle, so to speak, of the complete and entire existence is the complete nature or substantial supposite, a part of the nature, or a partial nature, nevertheless, is capable of a partial existence[26] which is proportionate to it and in which it can, by divine power, subsist alone as a part, just as quantity exists as separate in its proportionate existence by divine power.[27]

For no greater repugnance can be adduced in the partial existence of matter than in the partial existence of form or the accidental existence of quantity. For this partial existence of matter does not flow intrinsically from form, but it only naturally depends on it either as on a condition or an actual disposition naturally due it, or at most as on a cause which informs and through its information concurs of itself and helps toward the being of matter.[28] This mode of dependence, however, can easily be supplied by God without contradiction.[29]

With regard to the first dependence of matter on form, which seemed more probable to us in the last section,[30] the issue is clear because that mode of dependence is very extrinsic and *a posteriori* and consists solely in the fact that being is not naturally due to a thing constituted in such a state or lacking either such a disposition or act. God, however, can confer being even beyond what is naturally due to a thing or apart from the natural order, and thus can conserve form in a matter that lacks natural dispositions and soul in a body that lacks its natural organization.[31]

6. The same thing can be proven with regard to the latter mode of dependence because, although according to that mode form concurs in some way as

a cause for the being of matter, it does not, nevertheless, concur as a cause intrinsically constituting that being or as the proper subject of it,[32] but as a cause that informs or actualizes as an extrinsic cause in the sense that it is wholly distinct from its effect. God can, however, be such a cause by efficient causality, even if the form itself is such a cause by formal causality.[33]

This is proven in the opposite way from the material cause which, like the formal cause, is intrinsic, and thus God cannot supply that causality with respect to that effect which it intrinsically constitutes. He can, nevertheless, supply its causality with respect to the other component, namely, form, even if matter in its own genus influences essentially and as a true cause the being of the form. And in this way God supplies the dependence of an accident on a subject, even though it is in the genus of material cause,[34] and in the same way He can supply the dependence of a substantial corporeal form on matter. For, although the causality is truly essential and material, it is not, nevertheless, entirely intrinsic, that is, such that matter itself would be an intrinsic part of such an effect.[35] The causality, rather, is brought to bear upon a thing entirely distinguished from it by sustaining it. God can, however, by producing a form supply the causality which matter provides by sustaining it; He will, therefore, for the same reason be able to supply the causality of the form, not in the composite,[36] but in the matter, not by informing, but by efficiently causing.

The consequence is evident because there ceases as well the whole reason for the repugnance which consists in the fact that God cannot be united to matter in the manner of a form, something which would be necessary to conserve or constitute a composite, but not to conserve one part of a composite without the other. In this respect the argument concerning the matter is the same as that concerning the form because it is not included in the definition of an actually existing essential part that it is form or has form.[37] For the essence of such a part does not demand this since it consists only in an aptitude for form, but not in an actual union with form, nor does its existence demand this since it only extrinsically depends on form in the way I already explained. And, then, matter would in fact exist in entitative act,[38] that is, in the act of existence and in potency with respect to formal act. And in this there is no repugnance or difficulty, since a receptive potency necessarily includes some entity and entitative actuality, as was explained above.[39]

7. **What new element God ought to supply in order to conserve matter without form.** Moreover, from this one can by the way understand the action by which God could conserve matter without form or what new element He must offer in order to conserve it. But one must speak in different ways in accord with the different modes of matter's dependence upon form, which were touched upon above.[40] For, if matter only depends on form as on an act

or consequent disposition, no new action is necessary on the part of God to conserve matter without form. But if from the beginning He created matter alone without form, the action would be exactly the same as that by which God actually created matter under forms, and the miracle or preternatural act would have consisted solely in the fact that God performed that action without the accompaniment of the other action through which He would introduce the form into such matter. Just as, if God created the substance of a soul without the intellectual power, He would create it through the same action [by which He creates it with that power], and the miracle would only be the prevention of the natural emanation of the faculty from the essence.[41] In fact, the soul of Christ was created without its own subsistence by the same action as that by which other creatures are created, and only in that soul the action or emanation of its proper subsistence was prevented.

And one must speak in an analogous way, if God willed to conserve without form the matter which is already under a form. For, by expelling one form and by not concurring in the introduction of another, it would only be necessary that God continue that very action by which He now conserves the matter because through it He sufficiently conserves the entity of matter in the natures of things and outside of its causes. And the miracle would only consist in the fact that God would continue the action of conserving matter in that state in which being would be naturally due to it and without those conditions which are necessary for its natural mode of existence.

8. But if matter depends on form as on a proper cause that essentially influences its being, it will in that way be necessary that God supply that causality of form by another kind of efficiency and action. For, if that causality of form is essentially necessary in addition to the common influence by which God now conserves matter, matter will not be able to be conserved without the causality of form unless its necessity is supplied by another genus of causality. For example, when God preserves quantity without the concurrence of a subject, it is necessary that He supply by means of a special efficient action that concurrence of a subject, without which quantity could not naturally exist, and for this reason we say that God conserves quantity without a subject in a far different way from the way in which He conserves it in a subject,[42] as I dealt with this at length in *Tome III*, Part III.[43] In the same way, it would be necessary in the present case for an analogous reason. But it is not easy to explain what that new action would be which God would use to conserve matter without form. We say, however, that it would be an action in the manner of an absolute and wholly independent creation and would be distinguished from the action by which matter is now conserved because this takes place in the manner of con-creation. This can easily be understood in the case of celestial matter, if it were to be conserved without form, but it is more

difficult to understand in the case of the matter of generable things. For the action by which generable matter comes to be is truly an absolute creation, as was explained above, and for this reason the prior way of speaking with respect to this matter always seems more probable.[44]

A Response to the Arguments for the First Opinion

9. Almost all the arguments for the contrary opinion[45] have been answered from what has been said. For to the first argument we replied that it makes a false assumption, namely, that all existence comes from form as from an intrinsic and *quasi* essential cause, for this is true of complete, substantial existence,[46] but not of any partial existence whatever. And we replied that the inference is not necessary because, even supposing there were that natural order between form and existence, it would not result from this that it is immutable by the omnipotence of God.[47]

To the second argument Scotus and others respond that an equivocation is committed in the use of the terms "potency" and "act." For matter is called a pure subjective potency which, if it exists in its pure state, will lack an informing act. But when it is said that every existing thing is in act, this is understood of entitative act[48] which is not opposed to a subjective potency, but only to objective potency.[49]

Chrysostom Javelli and others think this response is satisfactorily disposed of by attacking the term "objective potency." But we should not cling to the term "objective potency" concerning which there is perhaps a controversy about the term, as even Javelli admits and as will be dealt with below. Rather we should attend to the reality signified, which is the reality of a possible being, whether it is said to be possible from an objective potency or from an active potency of an agent, for here it makes no difference.[50] A reality in act is opposed to a possible reality taken as such, and in this sense it is true that the existing reality must be in act. This actual being of existence, however, is not opposed to pure subjective potency. And if matter which is already created is called pure potency in this sense, the assumption is false.[51]

With respect to the third argument we have already satisfactorily explained how God could supply the natural dependence on form which matter has in its partial existence.[52]

10. **Matter claims for itself a proper, substantial and stable species.** To the fourth argument we reply that that argument does not apply more in the case of matter without form than in the case of formed matter. For matter does not have another substantial and essential species of its own because it is under a form or under this or that form. I say "substantial and essential" because we are treating of prime matter, not of proximate matter[53] which includes accidental forms or dispositions by reason of which it is said at times

to differ in species. But that diversity does not really lie in a substantial difference of matter, but in the accidents. Form, therefore, does not give a specific
difference to matter, but to the composite.[54] Hence, just as matter remains
numerically the same under different forms, so also it remains the same in
species. If, therefore, matter existing without form were an individual in a
certain genus but contained in no species, it would be such also now, or surely,
if there is not now such an individual—as indeed there is not—there would
not then be one either. Hence, the consequence ought to be simply denied
because it does not pertain to the nature of matter that it be in the species of
man or horse, but in the species of matter. That matter, however, would be in
some ultimate species of matter, whether of heavenly matter or of the matter
of the elements.[55]

Hence, it is one thing to say that in such a case there is a matter which
would not be contained in its own scope of incomplete essence under any
ultimate species proportionate to it, and it is false that this follows. But it is
another thing to say that in such a case there would be a matter from which
no complete individual contained under an ultimate species of complete substance would actually be constituted, and we admit that this follows. This is,
however, no problem; rather it is our very own assertion that it does not
belong to the essence of matter that it actually constitutes such an individual,
but that it is apt to constitute it.

To the fifth argument we reply that there is a difference between substance
and accident because an accident and an accidental form are convertible taken
in their whole extension, since every accident inheres in some way,[56] and for
this reason it is contradictory that there be accidental being without accidental form. Substance, on the other hand, and substantial form are not convertible; for there is a substantial subject which in no way is a form, and for this
reason substance is divided into matter, form, and the composite. Therefore,
it is not necessary that all substantial being be intrinsically and formally form;
for in the scope of substantial being there is absolute and complete being, and
this comes properly and essentially from form in its own genus. There is also
partial being, which does not always come from form, except speaking broadly
insofar as it depends in some way on form, which dependence God can supply, as was demonstrated.

Notes

[1]A material form is not made of matter since it determines matter, but it is a from
    that so requires matter that it cannot perform any operation bereft of corporeal
    organs. As such it is a form which naturally must inform matter in order to exist.
[2]Cf. *De Anima*, book I, cap. 10, *Opera omnia*, Vol. 3, pp. 516-545.
[3]The reference here is to the doctrine of transubstantiation, according to which the
    bread and wine in the Eucharist are destroyed and replaced with the body and
    blood of Christ, the accidents of the bread and wine remaining miraculously con-

served by God without inhering in any substance. Suarez gives philosophic support for this doctrine with his notion that any real essence, including any accidental essence, has an existence of its own which it would seem God could preserve separately as doing so would not involve a contradiction. On this see, *MD* XXXI. ✓ Suarez thought that not even God could conserve modal accidents without their subjects, e.g., not even God could conserve the mode of inherence of the quantity of the bread and the wine in separation from the bread and the wine.

[4]Suarez is referring to certain nominalists who did not distinguish the quantity of a substance from the substance.

[5]God could more easily conserve the substantial form than the accidental because the substantial form is the principle of a more perfect sort of being than an accidental form is, and the more perfect a being is the less dependent it is on something else in order to exist.

[6]Even Suarez would hold that according to the natural order matter never exists without form.

[7]*On the Sacraments of the Christian Faith,* trans. by R. J. Deferrari (Cambridge: Medieval Acadamy of America, 1951).

[8]*Commentary on the Sentences,* Vols. I-IV (Quaracchi, 1934 ff.).

[9]*Quodlibeta Hervei* (Venice, 1513; rep. Ridgewood, New York: Gregg, 1966).

[10]*Commentary on Creation* (=*Hexameron*) (Padua, 1549).

[11]The primary effect of form according to the view Suarez is here considering is to complete an essence *capable* of receiving existence. Its secondary effect is to give existence itself. The notion here is that God could not give existence to matter without giving matter the form which renders it capable of existing.

[12]The formal cause causes by joining its whole being to its proper subject and so actualizes it, as the redness of a rose actualizes the rose's potential to be red by inhering in it. But God, according to the Catholic Faith, is necessarily separate from the world and cannot form an intrinsic part of any created and finite essence.

[13]The reason why formless matter would be in no species of being is that specific being is conferred by form.

[14]Francis Lychetus, O.F.M. (d. 1520). Manuscripts and editions of his work include: *In I-III Sent. Scoti* (Paris: Johannes De Prato, 1519-20; Venice, 1520; Venice: Johannes & Andreas Zenarius, 1589). There are many partial editions of this work which is also present in the Scotus edition of Lucas Wadding (Lyon, 1639; rep. Paris, 1893).

[15]*Illuminati doctoris fratris Francisci de Mayronis in primu[m] sente[n]tiar[um] foecu[n]dissimu[m] scriptu[m]...*(Venice, 1504).

[16]*In Quatuor sententiarum libros* (Paris, 1516-1517).

[17]For Suarez the whole nature of a thing is the entire essence of it constituted by form alone in immaterial substances and by form along with a certain particular matter in material substances. The supposite adds to this a certain mode of subsistence causing the nature to exist in itself and rendering it incommunicable to another. Thus Suarez explained the Incarnation by holding that Christ's human nature is a complete individual constituted by a particular human soul (the form of the human being) and a human body, but that His human nature does not have a mode of subsistence of its own since it shares in the subsistence of the Divine Word.

[18]See note 3 above.

[19]This would be easier since a part of a substance, as substantial, has more being than an accident and hence is less dependent upon another finite being than an accident is.

[20]On this see *MD* XIII, sect. 5, and above sect. 8, para. 7.

[21]According to the Thomists the human nature of Christ has no existence of its own, but it is supplied by the Divine Word. Suarez holds, consistently with his denial of a real distinction between essence and existence, that the human nature of Christ has an *existence* of its own, but not a *substantial mode* of its own (cf. *MD* XXXIV, sect. 2).

[22]For example, Giles of Rome.

[23]On this see *MD* XIII, sect. 5.

[24]For Suarez an *ad hominem* argument is not the fallacy we mean to designate by the term. It is rather an argument which turns certain principles of an opponent against him. It is thus similar to what Aristotle called a dialectical argument as opposed to a demonstration.

[25]Cf. *MD* XXXI.

[26]By referring to a "partial existence" Suarez does not mean to refer to an existence midway between being and non-being. He means simply to refer to the existence proper to a *part* of a complete entity, e.g., the existence of a foot of a person as opposed to the existence of the person.

[27]That is, in the Eucharist; see note 3, above.

[28]See above, sect. 8, para. 17.

[29]On the grounds that God can effect *immediately* what He normally effects through the agency of secondary causes, in this case what He normally effects *through* form, though it should be noted that God produces form's effect through His infinite efficient causality and not through proper formal causality.

[30]VIII, para. 17

[31]Suarez thus thinks that the natural necessity that makes matter need form is like the natural necessity that makes form need certain dispositions in matter in order to inform it, as the soul naturally needs matter disposed by vital organs to inform it.

[32]See 8, para. 20. Note that for Suarez no real, simple essence can intrinsically constitute another real, simple essence. An entity Y can only really and intrinsically constitute another entity X, if Y is a partial entity which constitutes X along with another partial entity Z.

[33]See note 29 above. For the difference between formal and efficient causation see above sect. VI, para. 7.

[34]That is, an entity M is the material cause of an entity Z *iff* M is the subject and support for Z in the way that a substance is the subject and support for its accidents. God cannot materially cause anything since His absolute perfection and completeness makes it impossible for Him to be the subject or support for any entities inhering in Him.

[35]If an entity X is an intrinsic part of an entity Z, then not even God could preserve Z without X because it would be contradictory. Thus matter is an intrinsic part of a rabbit and so not even God could preserve a rabbit without its matter, though He could preserve the rabbit's *form* without its matter, and *vice versa*.

[36]God cannot supply the causality of the form with respect to the composite because, of course, there can be no composite without form.

[37]This may appear false since a form must certainly be a form. But Suarez draws a real, though modal, distinction between a form and its causation, though not be-

tween a form and its principle of causing. Hence, he can hold that a form can exist without *informing*, and it is only as informing, i.e., as uniting itself to matter and so actualizing it, that a form is properly called a form.

[38]Suarez distinguishes formal from entitative act. A thing is a formal act *iff* it actualizes or informs something else. A thing is an entitative act *iff* it really exists outside its causes. Thus matter is an entitative act because it is, in itself, a real and positive entity, but it is not a formal act because it does not inform or actualize anything (cf. *MD* XIII 5,8).

[39]*MD* XIII 5,8-9.

[40]That is, it depends upon whether one sees form as providing a naturally necessary *condition* rendering matter naturally apt to exist, or whether one sees form as in some way actually *giving* being to matter.

[41]It is clear that on this view of form's relation to matter, which is Suarez's own view, form is simply an ornament naturally completing matter and so making it naturally apt to exist in the way five fingers naturally complete the human being and make her naturally apt to exist.

[42]Suarez relies on the voluntarist axiom that God can supply immediately through His efficient causality all effects which He normally produces remotely through any secondary cause, whether these latter themselves cause efficiently or in some other way. Thomists simply deny this because they think that form's action on matter is more intimate and less extrinsic than what Suarez thinks and so they deem its causality could *not* be supplied by *any* sort of efficient causality, divine or otherwise. Compare this with the idea that not even God could make a material object bereft of all shape or size.

[43]*Commentaria ac disputationes in tertiam partem D. Thomae, de sacramento eucharistiae, et de missae sacrificio*, Q. LXXVII, a. II, *Opera omnia*, Vol. 21, pp. 271-287.

[44]The notion here is that, as generable matter is created from nothing, it is hard to see how God could conserve it *without form* in a way that differs from the way in which He conserves it *with form*. Suarez thinks this is a further reason to prefer the view which holds that form is not a true cause of the being of matter but merely a condition making it apt to exist.

[45]See above, para. 2.

[46]That is, form *does intrinsically* cause a *composite* substance in that it is one of the parts necessary for making up the composite.

[47]See above, para. 3.

[48]See note 38.

[49]X is a subjective potency *iff* X exists and X is a possible subject for some form F. X is an objective potency *iff* X does not exist and X is capable of being produced and is thus the object of some agent's power. Objective potencies are, therefore, mere logical possibilities.

[50]That is, some might say that a non-actual possible being is possible based upon the power of some cause to produce it, and others might say that it is possible based upon the fact that it is not internally contradictory, like a round square. For interesting reflections on the relations between these ways of viewing possibility, see Immanuel Kant, *The One Possible Basis for a Demonstration of the Existence of God*, trans. by Gordon Treash (Lincoln: University of Nebraska Press, 1979) Part I, observation 2, pp. 67-69.

[51]That is, matter is not in potency as a mere possibility that has no actual being, but is in potency for a substantial form in the way wood is in potency for a desk.

[52]Paras. 7-8.

[53]Proximate matter is matter already informed by some form. So the human body is the proximate matter of the soul as it is already disposed for the soul by certain accidental forms.

[54]For Suarez the being that form confers on matter is accidental to *matter* as such, but not to the *composite substance* made from matter and form.

[55]The matter of the heavens was held by the schoolmen to be inseparable from the forms it was created under, and so Suarez held that it is different in species from the matter of generable things (see *MD* XIII, sect. 11).

[56]That is, every accident naturally exists in and actualizes a substance. As such, every accident is a form ordered to perfecting and actualizing a substance in a particular way. On the other hand, not every substance is an informing form since both matter and the composite are in the category of substance and neither is an informing form.

Section X
Whether There Is Only One Formal Cause
for One Substance

1. **Many partial homogeneous forms are found in the same composite.**
Now that the causality of form has been explained, it is necessary to explain
its oneness or plurality in the same effect or composite. In doing this it will
become clear at the same time whether within this genus of cause there is
some subordination or dependence of causes with respect to the same effect.
That there are many forms in one substance can, however, be understood in
two ways, namely, either in diverse parts of the matter or in the same [part of]
matter. We are not discussing the first way here because, even if there are
diverse forms in diverse parts of matter,[1] each one of them, nevertheless, has
only one proper effect in its own matter. And, if from all these substances one
substance is composed as from parts making up the whole, it is necessary that
those forms not be total, but partial, making up one whole form. And so that
plurality of parts does not prevent there being one adequate formal cause of
one total effect.[2]

And, indeed, if such partial forms are the same in nature, there is no doubt
that they can be multiplied in material forms in proportion to the diversity of
the parts of matter and can be unified to constitute one substance. But whether
even forms diverse in nature can be partial and united among themselves to
constitute one substance and how great that union can be, that is, whether,
they can be united through true mathematical continuity or through some
lesser physical conjunction, all these are not questions pertinent to the present
subject, but to the science of the soul. For all those questions are usually asked
especially on account of the heterogeneous parts of living beings and especially on account of blood and other humors existing in an animal. And I
have dealt with some of these things in Tome I, part II, disp. XV, sec. 5, 6 and
7, of my *De Anima*.[3]

2. The present question, therefore, concerns the formal cause with respect
to entirely the same matter, namely, whether in one single matter there can be
only one substantial form. Many questions are included in this question in
accord with the variety of opinions which must be briefly discussed. That
there are many forms in the same matter can be thought of in three ways. In
the first way, it can be thought of with a proper [*per se*] and essential subordination in the manner of a higher and lower form, of which, though the first
form is act with respect to matter, it is, nonetheless, compared to the further
form in the manner of potency. In the second way it can be thought of with a

subordination which is not indeed essential, but in the manner of a disposition for the form principally intended by generation. Finally, it can be thought of merely as accidental and without any order among the forms. All the opinions which exist or can exist on this matter can be classified under these three headings, and there is a variety of opinions on each of them.

3. To the first heading pertains the opinion we dealt with above in disputation XIII[4] concerning the form of corporeity which is essentially [*per se*] necessary for the introduction of ultimate forms. It will not be necessary to repeat this view and attack it again here.

The Opinion Asserting a Multiplication of Forms According to Essential Predicates Is Rejected

4. The opinion which affirms that substantial forms are really multiplied in the composite according to essential predicates was also treated in the same place and cursorily attacked. This opinion is taken from Avicebron in the book *The Font of Life*,[5] and John of Ghent held it in his *Commentary on the Metaphysics* 2, q. 10 and in his *Commentary on De Anima*, 1, q. 8.[6] Paul of Venice also held the same view in his *Commentary on the Metaphysics* 7.[7]

This opinion, nevertheless, is now out of date and rejected as totally improbable.[8] For, besides the general arguments which we will produce below for the unity of form, this argument proves the falsity of that opinion, namely, that it multiplies forms without foundation or necessity. It was, after all, shown above that universals are not really distinguished from particulars, nor the genera from the species.[9] Therefore, since these predicates are multiplied only through the abstraction and precision of our intellects, it is vain to think that really distinct forms correspond to them in reality. Otherwise, forms which are really distinct and subordinated among themselves would be multiplied even in separate substances and in accidental forms according to the multitude of essential predicates which our reason also distinguishes in these things.[10]

In fact, it would also be necessary that matters would be really distinguished and multiplied in material substances, because diverse essential predicates can be derived from them, such as "to be a material thing," which is common to celestial and inferior bodies, and "to be a generable thing," or something similar. Finally, a great many of these predicates can be abstracted according to various aspects of things.[11] Hence, it is impossible that forms really be multiplied in accord with the number of these predicates. I omit other arguments which we produced above in disp. 13, sect. 3.

5. **How the parts of a thing ought to correspond to the parts of its definition. The order of inference which essential predicates and substantial forms preserve.** But you will object that Aristotle, in *Metaphysics,* book VII, c. 10 [1034b20], says that the parts of the definition correspond to the parts of the

thing; the parts of the definition, however, are the genus and difference; there-fore, really distinct things correspond to what is defined in these parts of the definition, which are not just matter and form. For, "animal," for example, does not signify only matter, but the composite of matter and the sensitive soul. Likewise, Aristotle in *Metaphysics*, book II, c. 2 [944a3], proves that there is no regress to infinity in formal causes because there is no such regress in quidditative predicates. Also, because the properties which come together according to these predicates are distinct in the thing itself, as, for example, to sense, to understand, to move, etc.; therefore, the forms from which these predicates are derived are also distinct.

To the first testimony of Aristotle I respond that either he is not speaking generally concerning every definition, but concerning that definition which is given in a physical way and by physical parts,[12] as when it is said that a human is a being composed of a soul and a body or that, if he is speaking universally, it is not necessary that he be understood to be speaking of parts which are really distinct, but of parts which are really or rationally distinct, as can be inferred from St. Thomas on that passage and more clearly from Alex-ander of Hales who calls the parts real or rational.[13]

But to the second testimony, I respond that from a denial of many or infi-nite essential predicates a denial of many or infinite forms can be correctly inferred because from any form at least one quidditative predicate can be derived; if, therefore, there are not infinite quidditative predicates, neither can there be infinite forms. But on the contrary, from a multitude of quidditative predicates a multitude of forms cannot be inferred because from the same form more predicates can be derived according to various similari-ties and differences it has with other forms.[14] Hence, this is not similar to what is drawn from Aristotle.

6. From this one does very well to infer that, just as from the unity of a form it cannot be deduced that quidditative predicates are not many, but only one, so it also cannot be deduced that they are not infinite or that there cannot be a regress to infinity of predicates, because with the unity of the form remaining, these predicates can be multiplied. But we will discuss in the following section whether there is an end to these predicates for some other reason and how Aristotle proved that there is.[15]

To the final argument I respond by denying the consequence. For, just as from the same cause many effects can arise, so also from the same form many powers can arise, as is known from experience. For at times many powers are found together in the same thing, not only according to the same physical form, but even according to the same specific difference, as in the human being intellect, will, and risibility arise from rationality. But at times these powers arise from the same form according to various grades of it, which are often distinguished by us by the their order to powers or actions, even though in reality the grades themselves are not distinct in the substantial forms.[16] Concerning this matter we said enough in the tract on universals.[17]

A Refutation of the Opinion of Scotus Concerning the Form of Corporeity

7. Thirdly, under this heading belongs the opinion of Scotus and Henry of Ghent which we treated above in disp. XIII.[18] They both posit a form of corporeity[19] or of the compound as essentially [*per se*] necessary between matter and certain substantial forms, although not in the same way. For Scotus thinks that the form of corporeity intervenes between matter and every soul, but not between matter and the forms of non-living things.[20] Henry, on the other hand, requires that form only in a human being.

The foundation of Scotus' opinion, if it is explained *a priori*, seems to have been that the soul, as a form transcending the common level of body, requires in matter a certain disposition and variety of organs which other forms do not require. Therefore, the soul as such does not give the being of the body, but presupposes it through another form, by reason of which matter is supposed to be capable of the organization and disposition necessary for the soul.[21] In inanimate things, however, this necessity ceases.

And this can be confirmed from the usual way of speaking, since we say that a living being consists of soul and body, but we do not say that water or air consist of body and such a form, but of matter and such a form. This is a sign, therefore, that the body, which in living beings is said to be one part of the composite, includes besides matter a certain substantial form which is intermediate between matter and the soul. Further, that definition of the soul is best understood with regard to this body: it is the act of an organic physical body, potentially having life.[22] For, though that body which is distinguished from the soul is a physical part, it does not, however, include the soul itself, even as giving a higher level, because otherwise the composition from these would not be physical but metaphysical. Nor does it indicate matter alone or mere matter, because in this way it is common to all natural things, or matter with accidents, because these do not pertain to the essence of the substance.[23] Therefore, the body includes a special substantial form distinct from the soul.

Scotus was moved secondly and principally by the *a posteriori* argument that in the death of an animal the soul withdraws and a new form is not immediately introduced.[24] One should not, however, say that matter remains without form; therefore, one should say that it remains under the form of corporeity which was previously in the animal. The major is proven because, if a form were introduced, it would be diverse in accord with the diversity of the dispositions. We see, however, that this is not the case, but that in the death of a human being the same corpse remains whether the person dies from an excess of heat or of cold.[25] It also happens that there is often no agent by which such a form might be educed.

Thirdly, Scotus uses a theological argument which especially persuaded Henry. For the body of a dead person cannot always be said to be specifically or numerically distinct from the body of the living person; therefore, it is necessary to admit that the numerically same form of the body remains without a new form, because, if the form is changed, the individual is changed, in fact, the species also is. The antecedent is evident because otherwise there would not have been in Christ's tomb the numerically same body which was in the living Christ. And if a host had been consecrated before the death of Christ and kept during the three days,[26] the numerically same body would not have remained in the host, which seems contrary to the words of the saints.

8. **Two principles of Aristotle are corroborated which are destroyed if the form of corporeity is posited**. But this opinion also multiplies forms without a sufficient foundation, and it can be attacked by the same arguments which we have used against Avicenna in disputation XIII,[27] as was mentioned. Furthermore, Scotus supposes in his view two things which contradict Aristotle. One is that occasionally a substantial corruption occurs without a subsequent generation, in opposition to what Aristotle says in *On Generation and Corruption*, book I, chapter 3 [317a32]. The other is that a substantial corruption occurs while there remains a complete sensible substance composed from matter and form, which is against what the same philosopher says in *On Generation and Corruption*, book I, chapter 4 [319a5]. To these the Scotists respond that Aristotle is speaking of the occurrence of a complete corruption; when, however, an animal dies a complete corruption does not occur until there is such a great change in the matter that even the form of corporeity is cast out. But this same distinction between complete and partial substantial corruption is alien to the doctrine of Aristotle who always defines substantial generation and corruption to be the beginning and ending of the entire substance without qualification.[28] And besides, it follows thirdly that there exists in reality an individual thing in the genus of the category of substance which is not constituted under any species of body, a thing no less impossible to understand than that some animal exists in reality in no species of animal.[29]

9. One could answer on behalf of Scotus that that composite of matter and that form is not, as Avicenna thought, an individual contained under the genus of body in the category of substance; for such an individual ought to be a complete substance really including some specific form which the word "body" in the category of substance expresses confusedly. For this reason this

word is predicated directly of its inferiors. That body, however, consisting of matter and of the form of corporeity alone is only an incomplete and partial substance. For it is part of a certain substantial composite. Hence, just as matter, because it is a part, can reductively fall under the genus of body and not be in a species, so also can that body which is a part of the composite.

10. But this response is not sufficient, first, because in order that some individual should be directly contained in some species it is enough that it actually contain the whole actual essence of that species, and it is not necessary that it contain actually whatever the species contains in potency, as is self-evident. "Body," however, taken as a category of substance is a subalternate species contained under the genus of substance, and the only thing that pertains to its essence is that it be a substance composed of matter and substantial form or that it be a substance existing in itself [*per se*] and capable of quantity. But this complete actual essence pertains to that incomplete individual; therefore [any being which is a body is in some specific species of body conferred by some specific form].[30]

This response is not sufficient, second, because, although part of a substance can be reductively under the genus and not under the species, nevertheless, if genera and species are directly and proportionally assigned to it, it is impossible that it be under a genus without being in some species of that genus, just as we above said that matter, even if conserved by the absolute power of God without form, cannot fail to be in some ultimate species of matter.[31] In that way, then, that form which constitutes that body or corpse cannot be under the common genus of substantial form without being in some ultimate species of the substantial form. Therefore, the composite of such a form and matter will also be in some ultimate species of composite substance; therefore, it will not only be reductively in the genus of body. And this argument, as I was saying above, also proves that that composite is not able to be more fully actualized by any further substantial difference or by a form from which such a difference is derived and that for this reason it is not a part or a potency essentially ordered to a further substantial act, but is a complete substance constituted in ultimate act.[32] For a substance is so complete in act only because it has some substantial form constituted in some ultimate species of such a form.

11. Third, there is an *ad hominem*[33] argument against Scotus that, if he does not think that it is problematic that this body which he says is a part of a substance remains without any further form, there is no reason why he should judge it problematic that matter remain without a form. Therefore, to avoid this problem he should not have introduced this form of corporeity. The antecedent is evident because, just as matter is potency essentially ordered to form, so that body is potency essentially ordered to the soul. And just as

matter under that form of corporeity has some actuality, so it alone has by itself a proper entitative actuality which is enough for it to exist. Therefore, there is no reason why the entity of matter depends on that form of corporeity more than the form of corporeity depends on a further form, that is, on the soul. If, then, the form of corporeity can remain without the soul, matter can also remain without the form of corporeity. That form is, therefore, useless.

Fourth, it follows from the opinion of Scotus that two really distinct forms are often introduced in substantial generation; since, then, changes are multiplied from their terms, there will be two substantial generations for constituting one substantial composite.[34]

12. Fifth, it can happen that a body numerically the same consisting of the numerically same matter and form first lives with a life of a human being and then with the life of an animal. For, when a worm is generated from the corpse,[35] there is no reason why the form of corporeity should change. For, if it remains in the corpse without the dispositions of a human being, it will better be able to remain under the form of any living being. In fact, it seems further to follow from this that this form is limited to living beings without a reason, but ought at least to be extended to all compounds, even inanimate ones. For as Scotus himself even says, it is the form of a compound arising from a mixture of the elements; therefore, whenever there is this mixture, there will be in the matter a disposition sufficient for this form; it will, therefore, be in all inanimate compounds.[36]

Otherwise, it is necessary that Scotus explain what change produced in the matter of a corpse is sufficient to expel this form. Surely none will be able to be assigned with reason except perhaps a resolution into the first simple elements; for such a form seems to be indifferent to all other dispositions which arise from the mixture of the elements since it is said to remain in wood, bones, and flesh, etc. But if this consequent is admitted, a reasonable difference will scarcely be able to be assigned why such a form is not in matter with the form of gold or another homogeneous compound, etc. Hence, if the form of corporeity must be posited, he would speak more logically who posited it in all natural entities along with Avicenna than only in certain ones, as others do. And these arguments are sufficient also against Henry of Ghent's opinion, since what was said concerning living beings in general can be easily applied to the human being alone.

13. **The arguments for the form of corporeity are rendered powerless.** In addition, the arguments which moved these authors to introduce the form of corporeity are very weak.[37] To the first argument[38] I answer that, although the soul is a higher form than the forms of inanimate things and requires an organization of the members in matter, the form of corporeity is not on this account necessary. For the soul is of itself sufficient for immediately actualiz-

ing the matter and for conserving it in being or terminating its dependence. And, consequently, the soul is also sufficient for the composite made of such matter and form to be capable of three dimensions, that is, to be a body in the category of substance.[39] Finally, the soul is sufficient for such a form [i.e., a form of corporeity] to require in diverse parts of matter diverse accidental dispositions by which the different organs are completed, whether because the soul itself, if it is divisible, has diverse parts of distinct partial natures to which those dispositions correspond, or because, if the soul is indivisible, it virtually contains in its eminent and perfect entity all that variety of parts. But whether these accidental dispositions come first in matter by the order of nature or absolutely follow upon the soul as the last and ultimate level, the argument is the same concerning heterogeneous dispositions as it is concerning homogenous dispositions. Thus it is not necessary for this reason to introduce a particular form in living beings, but one ought to philosophize concerning this according to what was said in the previous disputation about quantity and accidents in prime matter.[40]

14. **In what sense a living being is said to be constituted by body and soul.** In confirmation, insofar as it pertains to the issue, when a living being is said to be constituted by body and soul,[41] if by "body" a physical part is to be understood, it includes nothing essentially apart from matter. For, if the form of corporeity is taken away, no other essential element can remain in the body insofar as it is a physical part, as the argument produced there correctly proves. Hence Aristotle, in *Metaphysics,* book VII, text 39 [1037a5], says, "It is manifest that the soul is in fact the first substance, but the body is matter, and a human being or an animal is what results from both." And although in such matter organic dispositions are required as ultimate dispositions and necessary conditions, they do not, nevertheless, pertain to the substantial composition.[42] And, consequently, they are not essentially included in the essential physical part. Yet there is nothing which forces us to understand by the word "body" the mere physical part which is matter, but [we can understand it] as it stands under some metaphysical level of form or—what is the same—as it expresses the composite of matter and the soul, for example, not insofar as it is soul, but insofar as it gives the level of corporeity.[43]

For, to explain the proper nature of the soul and the singular level of perfection which it adds in addition to the common level of corporeity, we distinguish particularly in living beings the soul from the body, and we signify the body in the manner of a physical part, not because the form included in it is a physical part compared to the soul, but because we conceive it in that way and abstract it as if it were a distinct form. On this topic more things could be said, but I omit them here because I wrote of them in tome III, part. II, disputation 51, sect. 4.[44]

15. **In the death of any living being the form of the corpse is introduced into the matter.—Of what species it is and by what agent it is introduced.** To the second argument I reply that the assumption is false.[45] For in the death of a human being or of any animal the form of the corpse is introduced in order that the matter may not remain without a form. This is not the place for speaking about this form and about the unity or the distinction of it and about the efficient cause of it, and it matters little to the subject with which we are dealing. It is probable, therefore, that in living beings which differ in species the form of the corpse which is introduced in the place of the soul is distinct in species, as is clear in the case of plants and also of animals. But whether with respect to the same living being there succeeds a form of the same species,[46] both sides can be stated with probability, as Cajetan argues in opposition to Scotus in his *Commentary on the Summa Theologica*, I, q. 79, a. 4. Concerning the efficient cause, however, one should say that it is produced by some proximate balance along with the concurrence of some universal cause,[47] just as one should say in general concerning these things which are generated accidentally from putrefaction.[48]

To the third argument[49] one should say that the dead body is different in species and, consequently, is numerically distinct with regard to its substantial form. Nor does it matter what is alleged concerning the body of Christ, for that is said to be either numerically the same in relation to the senses both dead and alive because of the identity of the matter, of the quantity, and of the sensible accidents, or it is as a supposite the same because of the identity of the supposite.[50] I spoke on this in tome III in the place cited,[51] and more extensively in tome II, disputation XXXVIII, sect. 3,[52] where I also explained whether the form of the corpse which was in the body of Christ during the three days was hypostatically united to the Word.[53] Henry of Ghent also touches on this question in the place cited above.

It is not necessary, therefore, on account of theological expressions which can have an easy interpretation to invent a new form in human beings without philosophical foundation, contrary to the true nature of substantial and essential composition, as was shown in part above and as we shall show more fully in what follows. A special physical argument[54] which can in a human being be derived from the fact that the human soul is spiritual will be discussed in following points.

The View Concerning the Multiplication of Forms According to the Levels of Things Is Considered

16. The final way of speaking under this first heading can be that in each thing substantial forms which are essentially subordinate are multiplied according to the levels of natural things and according to the number of levels

which are participated in by one and the same substance.[55] There are, however, four levels of material substances, namely, the inanimate, the vegetative, the sensitive, and the rational. Again, certain natural entities participate in only one level, and in these there is only one form, and these are inanimate bodies. But plants participate in two levels; hence, they are constituted by two forms, animals by three, and humans by four.

I do not find this view fully explained in this way. The authors, nevertheless, who taught that there are in a human being three really distinct souls must, if they speak logically, embrace the whole theory just explained. After all, for the same reason they distinguish in a human being three souls, they must also distinguish two in animals, and for the same reason they separate souls from one other, they must distinguish the level of soul from the common level of the corporeal form. For there is the same proportion in all these things. Nor can any other reason for the distinction be given except the subordination and distinction of levels. The following, however, hold that opinion about the distinction of the three souls: John Philoponus in his *Commentary on the De Anima,* book I, text 91,[56] whom John of Jandun follows in his *Commentary on the De Anima,* q. 12,[57] and Paul of Venice in *The Summa on the Soul,* c. 5.[58] I will not in this place report the foundations of the view of these philosophers because it almost coincides with those which were dealt with in reporting the opinions of the others.[59]

17. Only in a human being does it seem that there is found a particular necessity for many souls, at least for two, on account of two chief principles proper to a human being. One is that the rational soul is completely spiritual and indivisible and most distant from the imperfection of matter, and, on this account, extremes so distant do not seem to be able immediately to be united. And, therefore, some form is necessary by means of which they may be united. And this argument particularly supports the view of Henry of Ghent treated above. For, since the rational soul is incorporeal, it cannot give corporeal being. Therefore, neither can it be the form of corporeity. And for the same reason it cannot formally be the vegetative form or the sensitive form, because forms of this sort are material and corruptible. On account of these, therefore, there is required in a human being some material form besides the soul, whether it is one or many.[60]

18. **The Manichaeans posited two souls**. The other reason is that in a human being there are contrary operations. For "the flesh desires what is opposed to the spirit and the spirit what is opposed to the flesh."[61] Contrary operations, however, cannot arise from the same principle, but rather from contrary principles. This argument is used by Ockham, who teaches this view in *Quodlibetal Questions* II, q. 10, and in q. 11 he also adds that these souls are distinct from the form of corporeity, and in animals he also makes such a

form distinct from their sensitive soul.[62] But with regard to the sensitive and vegetative soul he denies that they are distinct. In this he certainly does not speak consistently, nor does he say whether in plants the soul is distinguished from the form of corporeity.

The Manichaeans also claimed that there are two souls in a human being, one spiritual which is given by the good God, but the other an animal soul which is contrary to the former soul and which comes from a contrary principle, namely, an evil god whom they invent, as Augustine reported in the book, *On the Two Souls Against the Manichaeans*,[63] and in his *Literal Commentary on Genesis,* book 10, c. 13 and in the book, *On the True Religion*, c. 9.[64] And Jerome testifies in Letter 150 to Hedibio, q. 12,[65] that many Catholic teachers followed this view concerning two souls in humans, a spiritual soul and a sensual soul, where Jerome was speaking of that passage which moved them to think this in Thessalonians 1, chapter 5 "May the God of peace sanctify you so that your entire spirit and soul and body may be preserved without reproach for the coming of our Lord, Jesus Christ." To this testimony they add that of Daniel 3. "O bless the Lord, you spirits and souls of the just." Philo held the same in the book, *That the Worse is Wont to Attack the Better*.[66]

19. **The refutation of the view presented along with explanations of it**. This view is not only improbable in terms of philosophical reason, but is hardly safe in terms of our faith with respect to that part in which it posits many souls in a human being.[67] And, of course, that general reason for distinguishing many substantial forms from the levels of things, is correctly refuted *a posteriori* from the fact that from that principle it follows that in a human being many really distinct souls are necessary, something which is foreign to sound doctrine. Finally, all the arguments by which we proved that in living beings the soul is not distinguished from the form of the body prove for even better reasons that the addition of a new level is not sufficient for really distinguishing forms.

20. If fact, the arguments given against the first view by which it was shown that forms are not really distinguished on account of different quidditative predicates which are subordinated one to another, prove the same thing, even if one predicate adds a new level to the other.[68] For, when those two levels are conjoined in one and the same thing, the one is compared to the other as a specific difference to its generic difference, and in that way from both of them one substantial species is constituted as from a universal and a particular. Therefore, in reality those levels or differences are not really distinguished as united in such a species. Hence, neither are the forms which are the principles of such degrees and differences really distinguished in such a substance.

This, finally, is explained by applying with proportion the argument given above.[69] For, if there is in a horse, for example, a vegetative soul, it is necessary that it be limited by some specific difference since the vegetative soul as such only indicates a generic nature which is distinguished by various species, as is most evident in trees and plants. There cannot, however, be in a horse an individual and real soul constituted under the genus of the vegetative soul and not under some species of that genus. Therefore, it is necessary that it is limited and constituted by some specific difference.[70]

Either, then, that difference is contained within the vegetative level itself, as the specific difference of a certain tree, for example, of a pear tree, remains within the scope of the vegetative level, or it is itself the difference elevating that soul to the sensitive level. The first alternative cannot be held because otherwise the soul as such would constitute a certain ultimate and lowest species of a plant which would not be capable of any further difference and, consequently, of any further soul.[71] Nor would that level be compared to a subsequent degree as a genus to species, but they would be opposed as two ultimate and distinct species. Therefore, it is necessary to hold the second alternative, namely, that the vegetative soul according to its own generic nature is limited in the soul of the horse by the specific level itself. From this the conclusion is obviously drawn that the vegetative soul in a horse is not really distinct from the sensitive soul, because nothing can be really distinguished by the difference by which it is essentially constituted.[72]

21. And this argument has the same force in case of the rational soul and can be applied in the same way. For, if the sensitive soul, for example, were in a human being really distinct from the rational soul, it would be specifically limited within the sensitive level. Hence, there would be a certain irrational and bestial soul which, with the rational soul excluded either by the intellect or at least by the Divine Power,[73] would truly constitute a certain irrational animal as whole and complete in the species of animal as the horse is. In that way, Augustine rightly says in the book, *Eighty Three Questions*, q. 8,[74] that, when Apollinaris maintained that the Word assumed a sensitive soul without a rational soul, he really said that the Word assumed a mere animal.[75] How, therefore, could the composite constituted by such as soul be further informed by a rational soul?

22. Moreover, there is the best argument which applies, in fact, to all beings, but which is seen more clearly in human beings and is derived from the subordination and dependence of all human powers and faculties. For from excessive attention to the action of one faculty, for example, to the intellective faculty, the operation of the senses is impeded, in fact even nutrition itself. And from the operation of one power, for example, from the operation of the imagination, the heart is moved, and other natural faculties are aroused. From

this experience we proved above[76] that there is a substantial form distinct from the accidental faculties in order that there may be one principle in which all the faculties are rooted and from which there proceeds that sympathy of actions.

23. Besides, theological arguments could be added here, such as the one which is drawn from those words of Genesis 2,7: "God formed man from the slime of the earth and breathed into his face the breath of life, and man became a living soul." That breath which God breathed in was the rational soul, and through it the man was made alive and, consequently, also sentient.

Another theological argument is taken from the Eighth General Council, that is, the Fourth Council of Constantinople, canon 11, which runs as follows: "It appears that some have fallen into such great impiety that they teach that human beings have two souls; since, therefore, the Old and New Testament and all the fathers of the Church assert that a human being has one rational soul, the holy and universal Council declares anathema such inventors of impiety and those who think the same." Hence, in the book *On Church Teachings*, c. 15, this is also handed down as a certain teaching. But because Ockham says that this passage is speaking of two rational souls, in order to show that his interpretation is false, I shall quote the words of the text: "Nor do we say that there are two souls in one human being, as James and other of the Syrians write, one an animal soul by which the body lives and which is mixed in with the blood, and the other a spiritual soul which provides us with reason. But we say that there is one and the same soul in a human being which vivifies the body by its presence and which governs itself by its own reason."

Augustine holds something similar in *On the Spirit and the Soul*, c. 3,[77] and John of Damascus also does in book II of *On the Orthodox Faith*, c. 12.[78] In addition, otherwise, when a human being died, a soul would cease to exist, and when Christ died, he would simply have lost some substance united to the Word. Hence, in order to avoid this problem, Ockham says that the sensitive soul of Christ was conserved in Christ, either with the rational soul or with the body. But if he understands that it remains united to the body, it is heresy; otherwise, that body would not have remained dead, but would have sensation.[79] But if he understands that it remains as separate, he implies an unheard of miracle that a material form was conserved without matter.[80] Likewise, it is unheard of in the Church that the two souls of Christ were separated during the three days. Hence, it would be rash, not to say erroneous, to maintain that.[81]

24. Hence, when the spirit and the soul of a human being are distinctly mentioned in Scripture, they are not distinguished by their substance, but by their function and office, as Jerome indicates above and as we declared exten-

sively in I tom. III part, q. 6, com. a. 2,[82] and disputation XVII, sect. 4.[83] But insofar as the soul absolutely vivifies the body, it is often called by the name "spirit," as in Ecclesiastes 12,7: "And the spirit returns to the Lord," etc.; elsewhere this immortal spirit is called the soul, for example, in Matthew 10,28: "Do not fear those who kill the body, but cannot kill the soul." And of Christ the Lord it is said in Matthew 27 that he gave up his spirit, that is, his soul. Hence, Clement V in his *On the Highest Trinity*[84] said that Christ assumed the parts of our nature as united, namely, the body and the rational soul.

25. **The rational soul, although unextended, is the form of a material body**. Nor are the arguments given for the contrary view difficult to solve. With regard to the first argument[85] I deny the minor since, although the soul is indivisible and spiritual, it can be immediately united to matter because it is essentially its act. It does not matter that there is a vast difference in the perfection of being between matter and the rational soul, since for union one need not pay attention to distance or nearness in the perfection of being, but rather to proportion and suitability in the mutual relation of act and potency,[86] and this proportion between matter and the soul is found to be sufficient. In fact, it is perhaps greater and more perfect than between matter and any other form.[87]

In the other case, even if one imagines that matter is already informed by some form or extended, material soul, the rational soul will not have the proportion to be united with it because, insofar as extension is concerned, that form is as extended as matter.[88] Therefore, if a disproportion arises from this, it is not removed, but increased for other reasons.

The first reason is that, since that sensitive soul is a substantial and specific act, as was proven, it is more distant from the rational soul with respect to the proportion required for union than matter is from the soul,[89] and in this way it impedes rather than aids the union.

The second reason is that, if the sensitive soul were to intervene, the intellectual soul would only be a mere principle of understanding; however, a mere principle of understanding is not suited for informing the body, as we shall show at length below when we treat of the separate intelligences.[90] Therefore, in order for the rational soul to be the true form of the body, it is necessary that it be the principle not only of acts of understanding, but also of operations which are exercised through the body. Therefore, it must most of all be the principle of the operations of the senses, which are nearer to acts of the understanding.

And this is so necessary because some have doubted whether the soul itself, insofar as it is intellective, informs the body. But there is no reason for their doubt since the rational soul is essentially the form of the body according to its totality and according to all its levels which, although they are distinguished conceptually by us, are really the same thing in the soul. Hence, although the intellectual powers which are received into the body do not flow from the essence of this soul, nevertheless, the same sensitive powers and even the vegetative powers flow from it with a certain singular perfection proper to the rational soul, and they flow with a proportion enabling them to serve the actions of the mind.[91] This is also an argument that the sensitive soul is the same as the rational in the human.

26. **How the rational soul is the form of corporeity**. From this it is also understood how the rational soul, although it is incorporeal, is able to be the form of corporeity. For to be the act or form of corporeity is not the same thing as to be corporeal or extended, but to be a form constituting with matter one composite substance capable of quantity.[92] Hence, as I said above in disputation XIII,[93] to be the form of corporeity is absolutely the same as to be the substantial form of matter, because, precisely insofar as it is the substantial act of matter, a whole, material, and corporeal substance is constituted from both of them. Therefore, since, even if the rational soul is indivisible, it is the true substantial form of the body, and has whatever is necessary to be the form of corporeity. From this one can also conclude that the soul also sufficiently contains the intermediate levels, namely, the vegetative and the sensitive, so that it can formally confer them on the composite since it cannot contain the extreme levels without these intermediate ones.

It is, however, frequently said that the rational soul contains these levels only virtually or eminently.[94] Certain others, nevertheless, do not think this suffices for the formal cause, although it is sufficient for the efficient cause. And so one should undoubtedly say that, as it does not belong to the nature of the form of corporeity that it is formally corporeal, so it does not belong to the nature of the vegetative and sensitive souls that they are material and extended, but that they are the formal principles of the vegetative and sensitive actions and that they formally constitute the living being according to those levels of life which the rational soul truly and formally has. It is said, nevertheless, to contain these eminently when a comparison is made to the forms which do not transcend the perfections of those levels, because it contains their perfections in a higher way. Hence, speaking in general, one should not say that it belongs to the nature of every vegetative or sensitive form that it be corruptible or educed from the potency of matter, but one should add that this belongs to the nature of the vegetative soul alone or of the sensitive soul alone. In a human being, however, there is no form which is either a vegetative or sensitive soul alone. Hence, there is in a human being no form educed from the potency of matter. Nor does this pose an obstacle, as some claim, to the natural generation of a human being, since for this it is not necessary that the form come to be through eduction.[95] Otherwise, even if there were in a human being a sensitive soul educed from the potency of matter, there would not be generated a human being, but an irrational animal constituted by such a soul. For natural generation, therefore, it is sufficient that the union of the soul with the body take place in a natural way through a natural disposition and action.

27. **Contrary operations in the human being**. To the last argument of Ockham,[96] I reply that, in the first place, the diversity or opposition of operations indicates a diversity of proximate faculties, but not of forms, as was said above.[97] Second, that there are contrary operations in a human being can be understood in two ways, namely, either at the same time or at diverse times. The latter can happen not only in the same soul but even in the same potency, as is self-evident. The prior, however, is not true if understood with regard to proper contrariety. For, when the will and the appetite are simultaneously moved by contrary loves, they tend toward objects under diverse aspects and also in a diverse way. For, if the love of one is efficacious, the other is inefficacious. From this one rather infers that these appetites are rooted in the same soul, since the act of one retards the act of the other, if it is in some way resistant to the other. If, however, the two agree with each other, the act takes place more easily and promptly. And this concludes our discussion of the first heading or way of imagining that there are many substantial forms in the same matter.

Concerning Heterogeneous Parts and their Forms

28. The second way of thinking about a plurality of forms can be that two forms happen to remain in the same matter or the same part of it when one is imperfect and compared to the other as a disposition preparing the matter and not as a generic form compared to a specific form. In this respect there is a great difference between this way and the preceding way, because in that way each form is essential to the composite, and the predicates taken from each particular form are essentially and quidditatively predicated of each other, as "man is animal," etc. This would be clearly contradictory if the forms were distinct. But according to this second way the form which is a disposition to the other does not belong to the essence of the substance composed from matter and the other form, just as such accidental dispositions do not belong to the essence, but are, in some way, extrinsic causes.[98]

29. I find, however, two opinions which seem to pertain to this second heading. One is that which posits only in living beings individual specifically distinct partial forms in individual dissimilar parts which dispose the matter for the complete form which is one form really distinct from all those partial forms. Antonius Andreas holds this in his *Commentary on the Metaphysics* of

Aristotle, book VII, q. 17, and Paul of Venice in *The Summa on the Soul*, c. 5; Augustine Niphus in his *Commentary on Generation and Corruption*, book I, text. 78;[99] and this view is commonly attributed to the Commentator because in his *Commentary on the Physics*, book VI, commentary 59 he says that the heart, head, and other like parts differ specifically, and in his *Commentary on the Metaphysics*, book II, text 17, he says that the animal and its parts agree in the form of the whole but differ in their proper forms. And some understand Aristotle to be speaking of these parts when he says, in *On the Generation of Animals*, book II, c. 3 [736a33], that a human being first lives with the life of a plant, then with the life of an animal, and finally with that of a human being.[100]

The arguments [for this view] are especially that in these parts there are dispositions which are not only diverse but even contrary, and from these there arise operations of a diverse nature. Therefore, these parts also have partial forms of a diverse nature.[101] Likewise, a heterogeneous part after being cut off retains the same nature of flesh or bone, and yet the form of the whole does not remain. Therefore, the partial form remains. Third, these parts are specifically diverse, for they are said to be heterogeneous or dissimilar for this reason. But they do not differ with respect to the form of the whole; therefore, they differ with respect to their partial forms.[102]

30. This opinion, of course, is deservedly rejected by all who deny that there is a plurality of forms; I shall mention them later. Chrysostom Javelli especially attacks this in his *Commentary on the Metaphysics*, book VII, q. 16. And besides the general reasons which prove the oneness of the substantial form, this view is attacked in the following way. We speak of living beings either as having an indivisible soul or as having a divisible one which is coextensive with matter. If the discussion is about the latter, it can be easily conceded that in diverse, heterogeneous parts of such beings there are diverse, heterogeneous parts of the form.[103] For in a tree that part of the form which is in the branch is really not of the same nature as that which is in the fruit, etc. Those forms are, nonetheless, partial and suited to be united to one another and joined together, and in that way they constitute one complete form of the whole.[104] Hence, it is false to imagine that there is another form of the whole which is added to these partial forms and which also informs all those parts. After all, what purpose does such a form serve, and by what probable evidence is it proven? For whatever is in the whole and the individual parts, as far as accidents and operations are concerned, is sufficiently preserved with only those partial forms or—what is the same—with only the complete form composed from those parts.

Besides, I ask whether the form of the whole is indivisible or extended. The first alternative cannot be affirmed concerning these material forms, and if it is held concerning certain others, that pertains to the second alternative proposed above. That form will, therefore, be extended and composed of parts. Concerning it I again ask whether its parts, which correspond to the diverse heterogeneous parts of the body, are entirely alike and of the same nature as one another or are in some way diverse and unlike. The first, i.e., that they are entirely alike, cannot be accepted, especially if one speaks consistently according to this view. For the arguments upon which it rests run counter to it. That is, how would the form which is in itself of a uniform nature require diverse and contrary dispositions in diverse parts, especially since the form is not whole in the individual parts, but is whole according to the diverse parts which are entirely like to one another? Likewise, how would that form have diverse actions in diverse parts? If this is attributed to diverse dispositions, diverse accidental dispositions, then, will suffice for that diversity of actions, since the actions are themselves also accidental. Therefore, it is superfluous to invent for the individual parts two substantial forms, namely, a partial one and a complete one, of which the one is a disposition for the other. And besides, what we shall say in the following paragraph will count for even better reasons against this way of multiplying forms.

31. **The forms of all irrational animals are divisible.** In those living beings, then, which have indivisible forms there seems to be some greater reason for doubting, but a doubt really has a place only in the composition of a human being. For, though there is some controversy concerning the souls of perfect animals, I presuppose, nonetheless, that it is more probable that no material form is truly and properly indivisible.[105] For a form can be indivisible in two ways: in one way, because, although it consists of parts, they cannot, nevertheless, be naturally separated, as in the case of heavenly forms, or they cannot be separated so that they are conserved as separate, but are corrupted as soon as they are divided. And in this way perhaps the souls of perfect animals are indivisible. This indivisibility, nevertheless, has nothing to do with the issue with which we are dealing, because it is enough that the soul itself consists of heterogeneous parts and that the whole arises from the inseparable union of them,[106] so that it is useless to invent other partial forms in the individual parts,[107] as the argument given above proves. For the argument will work equally whether the form is divisible or indivisible in the sense mentioned, as is self-evident. In an other way a form is, therefore, said to be indivisible properly and in the strict sense, because it does not consist of any parts.[108] Such a form is necessarily whole in the whole and whole in each part, and we think that only the rational soul is indivisible in this way.

32. **In the heterogeneous parts of the human body there is a single form.** That, therefore, such a form does not require diverse partial forms in the parts of its organic body is proven, in the first place, from the eminence and

perfection of such a form. Since it is in itself an indivisible act, it is primarily and essentially [*per se*] ordered, as to its adequate receptacle, to the whole which consists of all those parts partially disposed in different ways so that from them there arises the whole disposition befitting the perfection of such a form. Therefore, in such a composite such partial forms are also superfluous. The consequence is evident, first, because the indivisible form itself is sufficient for completely and perfectly actualizing any part of that matter, even if it is variously disposed. Then, also, because those partial forms would not negate the fact that the indivisible form itself is ordered to all those various parts as composing its adequate receptacle, nor would they negate the fact that the same form is the root principle and source of all actions which are performed through those various members. And in this genus it is also a sufficient principle of them. Therefore, those other partial forms are superfluous.[109]

33. Second, it is impossible that one substantial form be the proximate and permanent disposition for another substantial form. One form can, of course, be the remote and, so to speak, passing disposition for another. In this way the form of the blood is a disposition and, as it were, a path to the form of the flesh, but it is, nevertheless, a remote and passing disposition, because the forms of blood and flesh do not remain together, but the flesh comes to be from the blood as from a passing matter.[110] Similarly the form of the embryo is a disposition for the form of a human being, and in this sense one should interpret what we cited from Aristotle above,[111] namely, that a human being first lives with the life of a plant, then with the life of an animal, etc. For in this statement he indicated the process of generation from the imperfect to the perfect through various dispositions until the introduction of the final form is arrived at. The more imperfect form, nonetheless, always withdraws at the arrival of the more perfect.

But that one substantial form is the ultimate disposition for another, and at the same time remains with the other form, is impossible, because any substantial form gives being absolutely and constitutes a complete essence in the category of substance.[112] Therefore, one form cannot be such a disposition for another.

Nor does it matter if someone says that this is true of whole forms, but not of partial forms.[113] For, if in all the parts of the human body there were such forms besides the soul, out of all these partial forms there would arise one whole form distinct from the rational soul. For, just as all parts of the matter are united to one another and constitute one whole body, so also all those partial forms would be united to one another just as the parts of matter which they inform are. They would, therefore, constitute one whole form in its own proper genus and species. Therefore, a partial form cannot be a disposition for another whole form of the same matter.

34. From this I come to the third argument. For either that form composed from those partial forms is the vegetative or the sensitive soul, or it is a form of something inanimate. The last alternative cannot be correctly asserted, because otherwise those partial forms would not serve the proper vital functions of the individual members, even though these forms are said to be posited chiefly for this reason.[114] And besides, everything which was said above concerning the form of the compound or of corporeity counts against such a form.[115]

And, in a similar way, if such a form is said to be a soul, everything which was adduced above against those who posit two or three souls in a human being counts against this view.[116] Nor does it matter if someone contends that one form is not composed from these partial forms, for then the same argument will apply to any form taken by itself, for instance, the form of flesh or of bone.[117] For in this consideration any of these forms is really called partial in name only, since it is not a true part of any complete form. In itself, therefore, each form will be complete, and it will be possible to ask about it whether it is a soul or not, and the argument given above will apply.

35. And similarly, one could ask whether these partial forms or the whole form composed from them remains in the body or perishes when the rational soul withdraws.[118] If the first is affirmed, it first follows quite logically that that body remains alive when the rational soul withdraws. For, as I said, those forms or the form which arises from them ought to be a soul; otherwise, they would not serve for the operations of life. Likewise, it follows that the part cut off and joined to a human body would be univocally flesh or bone, etc., which is contrary to what Aristotle says in *Metaphysics*, book VII, text. 56 [1040b7], and more clearly contrary to what he says in *On the Generation of Animals,* book I, c. 19 [possibly to 722b16-26] and in *On the Soul,* book I, c. 1 [book II, 412b20-25]. But if all such partial forms withdraw when the soul withdraws, they are, first, invented without any proof or necessity. And, second, there follow many theological problems which we pointed out above,[119] namely, that in the death of Christ some substantial form was lost by the Word or remained separate along with the rational soul.

36. **How Plato posited plural forms in a human being and the refutation of his view.** Add that Aristotle in *On the Soul,* book I, text. 91 and following [411b5], expressly attacks the opinion of Plato which posits many souls in diverse parts of the body. The argument is the same, however, concerning many partial forms. It is true that Plato only posited diverse quasi-partial souls in diverse parts of the body, but he did not, indeed, posit one form of the whole in addition to the partial forms.[120] This way of positing many souls

is not germane to the present question because according to it many forms are really not posited in the same part of matter. Nevertheless it is evident that this is entirely false because it follows from it that the rational soul does not inform the human body, but some part of it, and consequently it follows that it is not the principle of all vital acts of the human being. This is opposed to sound doctrine which defines the rational soul to be the true form of the body. And it was also shown above that from the connection of all vital operations one can infer that they are rooted in one principle.[121] Next, there is the argument of Aristotle which is most relevant to the issue. For he argued in this way: Either those souls informing diverse parts are united in one soul, or not. If they are not united, then they do not constitute something essentially [*per se*] one. If, however, they are united in one soul or are contained in one composite by means of one soul as common to all, that one soul suffices, and the other forms are multiplied falsely and superfluously. This argument applies with equal force to any partial forms.

37. The solution to the arguments for the contrary view are clear from what was said. To the first[122] I respond that those various dispositions of the organic parts make up one complete disposition for one whole form, whether divisible or indivisible, as was explained. But with regard to the operations of these parts, if the discussion concerns simply natural and transient actions, for example, to warm or to cool something, and so on, these actions proceed proximately from the first qualities by which these parts are disposed and affected in diverse ways. If, on the other hand, the discussion is about vital operations, such as to inhale, to exhale, to touch, to see, and so on, these proceed proximately from the diverse vital faculties which at times exist in the same part of the body, at other times in diverse parts. But the radical principle of all is one and the same form because it is the universal principle containing all these virtually. Therefore, it is not necessary to multiply partial forms because of these dispositions or operations, especially since, even if they were posited, it would still be necessary to admit that a higher and whole form informs those parts, requires in them those various dispositions, and is able to carry out those various operations through them.

38. **Whether, if a part which has been cut off is reunited, it is reunited substantially**. To the second argument[123] I respond by denying the antecedent. For in a heterogeneous part which was cut off the same form which was present before does not remain, and for this reason a severed hand is equivocally a hand, as Aristotle said. But it is commonly insisted against this that, if such a severed part is reunited after a short period of time to the whole according to the same part from which it was severed, it is truly and substantially united and lives as before. Therefore, it retained the same form; other-

wise, it could not again be informed by that form because there is no return from privation to possession.

But the same difficulty could be raised against every opinion since it cannot be denied that the severed part lost by separation the information of the whole form, for example, of the rational soul. If, therefore, such a part is afterwards reunited and informed by that form, a return is made from privation to possession. If, however, it should be denied that such a part is again informed by the rational soul, we shall for the same reason deny that it is truly reunited with it. Hence Paul Soncinas, in his *Commentary on the Metaphysics*, book VIII, q. 10, ad 7, thinks it more likely that a perfect physical union of such a part is never again produced. But with regard to the experience which is said to show that such a part is again living and sensing, one could respond by maintaining that there is no sensation in that part, but in parts near it, just as in bones or teeth there seems to be a feeling of pain as a result of the nearness of other parts. But with respect to the nourishment and preservation of the balance of the materials within that part, this can be said to be produced by juxtaposition. But because these things are difficult to believe, it is perhaps more probable that that part is again informed by the rational soul, nor is it a problem that from that partial and almost momentary privation there is a return to possession of it, because the form remains whole in itself, and the dispositions which were in the part remained numerically the same and in that short time they were also only slightly diminished. Therefore, it is no problem that the same form should immediately return to that part of matter.[124]

39. **Whether heterogeneous parts differ in substantial species.** To the third argument one can reply by denying the assumption, namely, that heterogeneous parts differ in substantial species. For it is enough that they differ accidentally, and for this reason they are said to be unlike because of a diversity of dispositions. In living beings, nonetheless, which have extended souls I think it more probable that between the parts of the soul which inform diverse organic parts there is a greater diversity than there is between parts of a homogenous form and that for this reason there is in the substance itself a diversity between these parts which can be correctly called partial specific diversity. In the human form, however, there is a special difficulty about how the soul informs these parts and is united with them in a diverse way according to the nature of the dispositions. But this matter pertains to the science of the soul.[125]

40. The second opinion which also pertains to this second heading is that of Avicenna, of the Commentator, and of others, who say that the forms of the elements remain in all compounds. For it does not seem possible to believe that they would remain for another purpose than to be dispositions for the form of the compound. Avicenna holds this in *Sufficientia*, book I, chap-

ter 10, and the Commentator in his *Commentary On Generation and Corruption*, book I, the chapter on the compound,[126] and in his *Commentary On The Heavens,* book III, text. 67.[127]

These people differ because one thinks that the substantial forms of the elements are indivisible and for this reason affirms that they remain substantially whole and perfect in the compound, while another thinks that those forms can become more or less intense, and for this reason he says that they remain in the compound in a less intense state in proportion to their qualities. For he thinks that these forms of the elements are so imperfect that they are, as it were, intermediate between qualities and perfect substantial forms. Perhaps because of this Plato, in the *Timaeus,* [49a-50a] called them qualities, and thus they are like qualities in having various degrees.

Augustine Niphus follows this explanation of this view in his *Commentary on Generation and Corruption,* book I, text 118 and in his *Commentary on the Metaphysics,* book VIII, disp. IV and book XI, the final disputation.[128] Zimara also follows this explanation in *Theorems* 48. Many medical doctors have also followed the same opinion as can be seen in Thomas of Garvo in his *Summary of Medicine,* book I, tract. I, q. 1,[129] and especially Galen in *On Method,* book II, c. 2,[130] and in *The Substance of Natural Faculties,* at the end.[131] Among theologians the same view was held by Peter Auriol in his *Commentary on the Sentences* II, dist. 15, as John Capreolus and Gregory of Rimini report.

41. **Various ways of explaining this view.** This opinion, however, can be understood in various ways. First, it can be understood that the forms of the elements remain in the diverse and smallest parts of matter. And in this way Avicenna claimed that such forms remain in the compound, and he perhaps wanted the form of the compound to inform all those particles and to unite them to one another. Otherwise, he thought a substantial union could not be preserved, but only one by juxtaposition, as is self-evident. For each of these particles would be distinguished by quantity, just as they would be by matter and form; therefore, they would also be distinguished by place, since they could not spatially penetrate each other. Therefore, they would be said to be united only by juxtaposition, as water is with wine, while they remain whole in their own substances. The individual particles, nevertheless, would not be united, and consequently the whole would not be substantially united or essentially [*per se*] one, because the parts would not be essentially connected.[132] Hence, they could be easily separated through mutual action or local motion. Some other form, therefore, is needed which is proper to the mixture and which is different from the forms of the elements, as we shall show again below in opposition to Peter Auriol.[133]

But it is also impossible [that the form of the whole should supervene on the forms of the elements in compounds]. First, because the form of the compound and the forms of the elements require diverse and incompatible dispositions, even if we omit the general arguments against a plurality of forms. Second, because, since all parts of the compound, especially in homogeneous things, have the same balance of the primary qualities, no reason could be given why in one part of the matter of the compound there is the form of fire and in another the form of water,[134] etc. This argument also works in heterogeneous things. For any heterogeneous part is composed and compounded of homogeneous elements.

Third, because, if the diverse forms of the elements remain in parts disposed in the same way, this is a sign that that form in such a part is not a disposition for the form of the compound, since in a similar part the form of the compoud can exist with a contrary form of the substantial compound.[135] It can, therefore, exist equally well or better, even if no form of the element exists in that part of the matter, provided that there is present there a proportionate balance of primary qualities. This balance of primary qualities also cannot depend on a form of such an element, since in another similar part it is said to exist with a contrary form.

From this one also concludes that such a form is irrelevant for every action and conservation of that part of the compound in which it is said to exist. And thus from no effect or natural sign can one infer that the forms of the elements remain in this way in the compound.[136]

42. This opinion can be understood in another way, namely, that all the forms of the elements simultaneously inform each part of the matter of the compound, and then the form of the compound supervenes, also informing that whole matter. And this version has so many absurdities that it seems for that reason not to have been defended by anyone. For, in the first place, it follows that forms which are formally incompatible simultaneously exist in the same part of matter in their whole and perfect being.[137] For the forms of the elements are formally incompatible with one another. For, if their dispositions are formally incompatible,[138] how will their forms not be? Otherwise, how will one element be generated from another? Or why will the generation of one element be the corruption of another, if their forms are not incompatible in matter?

Second, if such forms do not have proper dispositions at the level proper to them and, consequently, lack their proper actions, they can not give anything to the form of the compound; therefore, they cannot be dispositions for it. In fact, it is impossible that the same form requires in the same part of matter dispositions which are entirely incompatible and which exist in perfect being, for example, the highest heat and greatest cold. But the substantial forms of water and fire are no less incompatible with each other, especially in their perfect being. Third, the general arguments customarily made against a plurality of forms apply especially against this view, because it posits in the same part of matter many specific forms which are in themselves sufficient for constituting a supposite having without qualification its own proper being and which require highly incompatible dispositions. For the form of earth demands the greatest density, but the form of fire the greatest rarity. The latter demands intense heat, while the form of water requires intense cold. How, then, is it possible that such whole and perfect forms inform the same part of matter at the same time?

43. **The forms of the elements are perfectly substantial.** This opinion can be understood in a third way, as the Commentator explained it, namely, that all the forms of the elements are in the whole matter of the compound and in all its parts, broken down, nevertheless, as he says, and in a less intense level. And then the whole matter so affected and disposed by those forms is informed by the form of the whole.

In this opinion objectors commonly attack what the Commentator presupposes, namely, that the forms of the elements are not perfectly substantial, but are intermediate between accidental and substantial forms. St. Thomas argues against this in his *Commentary on Generation and Corruption*, book I, text 84, that it is impossible that there be something intermediate between a substance and an accident. His first reason is that there is no intermediate between contradictories, while substance and accident are distinguished by immediate contradiction.[139] His second reason is that something intermediate is found between the extremes of the same genus, but substance and accident are of diverse genera.[140] Finally, we can add that the substantial form of fire and of any element is in itself sufficient to actualize matter so that it constitutes or conserves it in its being and so that it constitutes with matter one supposite which is properly and univocally a substance. Therefore, such a form is as properly and univocally substantial as any other. And this was confirmed above when we showed that substantial forms exist.[141]

44. **Intensification is incompatible with substantial forms.** But perhaps the Commentator does not deny this, but calls them intermediate only because among substantial forms they have the least perfection. And as a result, they have in some properties a similarity with accidental forms. Against this, having set aside the controversy about the manner of speaking, I show in the second place that it is false to attribute to them a similarity with accidental forms in this condition of becoming more or less intense, because this condition is so proper to accidents or qualities that it is directly opposed to substantial form as such. If, therefore, the elemental forms are truly and properly substantial, as was shown, they cannot be similar to accidents in this condition. The antecedent is proven first from the Philosopher in the chapter on substance in the *Categories* [3b35-4a9], where he says that substance does not

admit of more and less.[142] But if the substantial form of water became more or less intense, then, just as water is more or less cold, so it would really be more or less water.

45. Second, St. Thomas argues in I, q. 76, a. 41, ad 4, that the substantial being of anything is indivisible and that every addition or subtraction varies the species, just as in numbers, as is said in *Metaphysics*, book VIII, text. 10 [1043b33]. This argument can be misunderstood, because by a similar argument it could be proven that a quality cannot become more or less intense since even in accidental forms it is true that their essences are indivisible and that their species are like numbers and that, consequently, any subtraction and addition varies the species.[143] But the argument should be understood regarding essential and formal addition, not regarding intensive addition. The same reply, therefore, can be made concerning substantial form.

I answer, nonetheless, that the nature of substantial and accidental form is diverse, for the substantial form is that which first constitutes the essence of the thing absolutely speaking, and for this reason it is necessary that it be entirely indivisible and invariable so long as it remains in the same matter. This is explained *a posteriori* from that effect from which we above infered that there are substantial forms, namely, from the return of water to its original coldness.[144] For, if the substantial form of water were capable of becoming less intense, it certainly would be less intense with the lesser intensity of its coldness because, just as the form depends on its dispositions, so also the intensity of the form depends on the intensity of its dispositions. Therefore, it would be impossible for water to return later to its original state by its intrinsic power because a form, when once having become less intense, cannot intensify itself.[145] Nor does it have another prior principle from which that intensification could flow. In order that water, however much it has been heated, could restore itself to its original state by its intrinsic power, once the extrinsic agents have been removed, it is necessary that it remain in the whole and perfect nature of water and, consequently, that the formal constitutive principle of water remain intact, so to speak, so long as it is not wholly corrupted. And in this sense we say that it belongs to the nature of substantial form that it is invariable and immutable in its entity, as long as it remains essentially the same and in the same matter, because it is the radical principle of all properties and it constitutes the primary essence of a thing.

46. And this point is confirmed because for this reason, as the Philosopher attests in *Physics*, book V [perhaps VI, 236a1-5], and in *On Generation and Corruption,* book I [reference not found], the substantial corruption or generation of the elements does not take place successively along with an alteration, but in a moment at the end of an alteration when the sufficient disposition for it is completed, because, of course, the substantial form does not

become less intense and is not destroyed by parts, but all at once. But if it could become more or less intense, it would certainly be introduced successively and similarly expelled. In fact, as often as water were heated by fire, as many degrees of the form of fire would be introduced as degrees of heat, which is incredible.

Add to this that, if the forms of the elements could become more or less intense, why would the forms of the compounds not also become more or less intense in accord with the greater or lesser intensity of the simple forms, especially since the latter are said to be required as necessary dispositions for the former? For example, if the form of gold requires in its matter six degrees of the form of fire and two of water in order to be in its natural state, then, if through a contrary action those degrees of the form of fire became less intense in the gold and the form of water became more intense, why would the form of the gold not withdraw from its natural perfection and become less in its entity? Certainly no sufficient reason can be given. For it is not enough that it is more perfect; after all, it only follows from this that the degrees of its extension will be more perfect. It should be said, therefore, that it belongs to the nature of the substantial form that it has or constitutes an essence which is indivisible in its intensity, and for this reason such a property accrues to the substantial forms of the elements to the same degree as it does to all other substantial forms.

47. **The forms of all the elements can in no way exist in the same matter.** Third, this opinion must be principally attacked on the basis of the issue with which we are now dealing, for it is impossible that so many substantial forms simultaneously exist in the same matter. For, though they are said to be less intense, each one, nonetheless, if it is substantial, gives being without qualification and constitutes a true substance and a substantial supposite. It is not possible, however, to understand that one supposite is simultaneously in four or five distinct species and that there are many individuals of diverse substantial species constituted from the same matter.[146] We will explain this argument more extensively below.[147] There is also the argument against Averroes that, if the forms of the elements in diminished levels remained simultaneously in the same matter, fulfilling matter's capacity, the potency of matter would be, therefore, sufficiently actualized by them, and the composition would be sufficiently completed by them alone. Therefore, it is both superfluous and impossible that a new composite form could be added to all those forms.

48. **The form of a compound is distinct from the forms of the elements.** Peter Auriol, as Gregory of Rimini reports above,[148] said that the form of the compound is not a simple form, but is only a mixture or aggregation of the forms of the elements in a less intense being. But it is self-evident how absurd this opinion is. For it follows from it that compound substances are not be

true substances which are essentially one. It also follows from it that animals, and even human beings, do not have one simple form. Lastly, it follows from it that no compounds differ substantially and essentially, but only in terms of more and less, and that they do not have properties or actions of a more perfect nature than the qualities and actions of the elements. Those properties and powers of the compounds, therefore, clearly evince proper substantial forms of a nobler nature than the forms of the elements.

49. And from here by turning back the argument we conclude that those forms of the elements joined together in the same matter and, as it were, presupposed for the form of the compound would be superfluous even if, as is impossible, they were not incompatible. For the form of the compound is sufficient, along with the faculties which flow from it and the balance of the primary qualities which disposes the matter, for the being of the matter, for the substantial being of the composite, and for every physical action which can be known by experience concerning such a composite. Although this balance is not some simple quality virtually[149] containing the primary qualities, as Averroes thought, but is formally composed from the first qualities in a diminished being, as the true and common view has it, the view which is extensively treated in *On Generation and Corruption,* it does not, nonetheless, require substantial forms of the elements formally existing there; rather, the form of the compound suffices to which such a balance is natural, and such a form has the power and force for conserving or reclaiming such a balance if the extrinsic impediments are removed.

50. And in this respect the elements are correctly said to remain virtually in terms of their substantial forms in the substantial form of the compound, but formally in terms of their accidental forms, though such accidental forms do not remain whole but as diminished. This was well explained by Scotus in his *Commentary on the Sentences* II, dist. 15, and he was followed by Gabriel Biel and Gregory of Rimini in the same place; Giles of Rome in his *Commentary on Generation and Corruption,* book II[150] and others were undeservedly attacked by Cajetan in his *Commentary on the Summa Theologiae,* I, q. 76, a. 4, at the end. For their view is not opposed to the doctrine of St. Thomas. Nowhere, after all, did St. Thomas deny it, but rather taught it in the sense explained by us in *Opusculum* 33. Nor is there any difficulty in it, because the form of the compound is not said to contain the forms of the elements in the genus of formal cause nor does it contain them eminently according to their whole perfection, as Cajetan seems to have thought, but only according to a certain participation and suitability, as we said.

51. From this, therefore, we conclude with reason that it does not follow from the mixture of the elements that there are many substantial forms in the compound, because the forms of the elements do not remain formally in the

compound, but only virtually.[151] This is the view of Aristotle, as I will show below, and is commonly accepted, as is evident from Alexander of Aphrodisias, John Philoponus, and St. Thomas in his *Commentary on Generation and Corruption*, book I, and from the same St. Thomas in *Summa theologiae* I., q.76, a. 4 and in *On the Power of God* q. 5, a. 7. Other scholastics also held this view in their commentaries on *The Sentences* II, dist. 12, especially John Capreolus and Gregory of Rimini in the place cited and Scotus in q. I; Harvey Nedellec in the treatise *On the Plurality of Forms*, q. 5;[152] Giles of Rome in *Quodlibetal Question IV*, q. II;[153] Paul Soncinas in his *Commentary on the Metaphysics*, book X, q. 27 and book XII, q. 68.

This discussion, however, concerns the substantial forms of the elements; for the accidents formally remain, but that is not relevant to the present question. Hence, the philosophers who denied substantial forms in the elements have consequently said that the elements remain formally in the compound. Galen proceeds in this way; for, as we saw in section I of this disputation, he does not acknowledge substantial forms in the elements, but only primary qualities. Hence, with respect to the question at hand he does not contradict us, but rather favors us. Consult him in *Methods*, book I, c. 2, and the little book *On the Substance of Natural Faculties*, near the beginning, and *Concerning the Teaching of Hippocrates*, book 8.[154]

52. **An objection is raised.** But some raise as an objection to us Aristotle, who in *On Generation and Corruption*, book I, c. 10 [328b25], defines the compound as "the union of altered parts able to be united." When, therefore, the elements are united, they are not corrupted, but only altered. And thus in that whole chapter Aristotle often repeats that the parts which are able to be united are not corrupted. For, if one perished, it could not be united. After all, those things which do not exist, he says, are not received into a union. Second, the same Aristotle in *Metaphysics*, book V, c. 3 [1014a26], defines an element as "that from which something comes to be so that it exists in what comes to be and into which that which comes to be is ultimately broken down." Therefore, if the elements do not remain in the compound, they are not elements, and the compound will also not be broken down into them, something which is false and contrary to experience.

For, when wood is burned, we experience that smoke, vaporous humors, ashes, and fire proceed from it. Nor is it enough to claim that all those are contained in the wood virtually or potentially; otherwise, even water would be called a compound, at least of air and water, both because water has in itself a certain quality of air and also because, when water is heated, an airy vapor is exhaled from it. This is confirmed, because from virtual containment it only follows that elements can be generated from the compound. But this is not enough, since a compound can be generated from any element, and one element can be generated from another. Hence, Aristotle says in *On the Heavens,* book III, c. 3 [302a20], that the elements are contained in wood and flesh because they are clearly separated out of them, but that, on the contrary, flesh and wood are not contained in fire, because they cannot be separated from it. It is one thing, therefore, to be separated and another to be generated; therefore, separation requires formal containment.

Third, Aristotle says, in *On the Heavens,* book I, c. 7 [269a28-29, c.2] that the compound is moved by the motion of the predominant element; therefore, it remains in it. Fourth, in *On the Heavens,* book III, text. 67 [298a30-31], in *On the Parts of Animals,* book II, c. 1 [646a13], and in *Meteorology,* book 4, c. 12 [389b23], he says that the elements are the matter of the compound.

53. **Aristotle's opinion: The elements only virtually remain in the compound. The definition of the compound is explained.** I reply that Aristotle in *On the Heavens,* book III, c. 3 [302a16], asserts that an element remains either in potency or in act in the compound; for, he says, it is uncertain in which of these ways it remains in the compound. The question he there left undecided, he resolves in *On Generation and Corruption,* book I, c. 10 [327b24], when he expressly says that those elements which are taken into the compound exist in one sense and in another sense do not. For they are not, he says, in act, but they remain virtually or potentially, and he locates the difference between the [the generation of the] compound and other changes in this.

And in *On the Parts of Animals,* book II, c. 1 [646a13], he says that the first composition of bodies is "that which is made from the primary bodies which some call 'elements.' I mean: earth, water, air, and fire. But it can perhaps better said to be made from the powers of the elements; for humidity and dryness, heat and cold, are the matter of composite bodies." Therefore, Aristotle's view is sufficiently clear on this matter. When, therefore, Aristotle says that the compound is the union of altered parts able to be united, he says "altered" rather than "corrupted" to show that they do not entirely perish, but remain virtually and according to their qualities. Nor does Aristotle deny in this chapter that in a true compound the parts able to be united are corrupted, and he could not deny it, for, since a new substantial form of the compound is introduced by the union of the elements, it is necessary that a substantial corruption of the parts to be united should occur, because the generation of one thing is always the corruption of another. He says, nonetheless, that the elements do not entirely perish because they remain virtually.

54. **The description of the element is explained.** To the second argument one can reply, first, that that definition of an element does not fit these simple bodies which are commonly called elements, but rather fits the first principles from which a natural thing is composed. Averroes favors this view in his *Commentary on the Metaphysics,* book V, com. 4, when he says that prime

matter is properly an element, but that simple bodies are elements only in the opinion of human beings. For, because the ancient philosophers did not know another matter except such simple bodies, they called them elements. And thus Aristotle in book II of *The Parts of Animals*, c. 1 [646a14], does not call them elements unqualifiedly, but "things which some call elements." He speaks the same way in *On Generation and Corruption*, II, c.1 [328b33], and in other places.

This can be confirmed from that part of the definition of an element which says that it is "that from which something is first composed." But these bodies are not things from which something is first composed, since they are themselves composed from prior entities. Likewise, Aristotle says in the same place that an element ought to be something indivisible. But these bodies are not indivisible, as is clear. According to this view it is easy to reply to the argument that compounds are made from elements by noting that that part of the definition of "element," namely, "that which is present in the compound," does not properly fit these bodies, since they are not properly elements.

Second, so that we do not seem to argue only about the word, we admit that the name and definition of "element" properly fits these bodies; in fact, in his *Commentary on the Metaphysics,* book 5, lect. 4, St. Thomas maintains that they are more properly elements than matter and form. For he thinks it belongs to the nature of an element that it is directly and properly in some species. I do not, nevertheless, see why this pertains to the proper sense of the word and that it is not sufficient that an element be something partial in its species. And so, it seems that in Latin "element" is the same as a principle of something which in its order is first in composition and last in decomposition, and for this reason it also belongs to the nature of an element that it is indivisible, not absolutely and in every way, but in its own order and class. And, likewise, it does not belong to the nature of an element that it is not always present formally nor that it is always present only virtually, but that it is present in a way suited to its composition.

In that way, then, the four elements truly participate in the nature of an element, because in the kind of composition by which one body can be made from many they are first, for they are not composed of other bodies and all others are composed from them. Likewise, they are simple and indivisible because they cannot be resolved into many bodies. Finally, they remain present in the way which is necessary for that kind of composition which pertains to compounds. And thus, in *On the Heavens*, book III, c. 3 [302a16], Aristotle explicitly uses a disjunction in his description of the element as "that which is present either in potency or in act."

55. **The word "element" properly applies to prime matter. At times it was applied to form.** Hence, it is not a problem that prime matter is prior to these

bodies and is formally present or remains in its composite. For this is the only reason that matter can also truly and properly be called an element, although for another and perhaps prior reason, namely, that matter is prior in composition and is simpler than the elements. This is something St. Thomas noted in his *Commentary On the Heavens,* book III, lect. 8, where he seems to retract the view which he held in his *Commentary on the Metaphysics,* book 5, as Paul Soncinas noted in his commentary on the same work, book V, after q. 9, concerning text 4 of Aristotle. Soncinas also adds in book XII of his commentary, q. 27, ad 1, that form can also be called an element, and Aristotle gives it that name in *Metaphysics,* book XII, c. 4 [1070a33ff], and also St. Thomas in the place cited. For, although the word "element" seems chiefly to be assigned to the material principle, as is plain from common use and from the proper sense of that part of its definition: "that from which something is made," yet, speaking more broadly, the name "element" extends to any part, just as a whole is also said to be composed from its parts, both formal and material. In fact, for this reason any part is said to have the nature of matter in relation to its whole, if it is considered absolutely under the common definition of a part. For this reason, therefore, any part can be called an element, if it is primary and indivisible in its own order.

56. From this it follows that we reply to the other part of the argument by saying that it does not belong to the nature of an element that the composite or compound can be resolved into it so that the element can really be conserved as separate from that which is formed from the elements. For not every natural composite can be resolved into matter and form in this way. And for a similar reason it is not necessary that the compound be resolvable into numerically the same elements from which it was perhaps composed, but it is sufficient that it be resolved into similar elements. This will sometimes happen if the efficient causes are suited and available for producing that resolution. But often it does not happen in that way, but the whole compound is changed into a single sort of element, especially into earth. Hence, even if the experience which was presented in the argument were true, it would not prove anything. For it is not necessary that those things which are seen to be produced from wood when it is burned are present in it formally, but only virtually according to some less remote disposition by reason of which all those things are newly generated. They are not, nonetheless, true elements, but imperfect compounds, because smoke is not air, nor are ashes earth.

57. **In the bodies of compounds smaller particles are sometimes taken in**. Add to this also that in the bodies of compounds there are often many substances accidentally mixed in through openings or through the division and interposition of parts. Such substances are later not so much generated anew by the action of some agent as they are separated out,[155] as happens in the

fermentation of wine and in the corruption of blood outside veins. And it perhaps also occurs in that action of fire on wood, though it could also happen that the same substances which were there are not separated out, but others are generated from them in accord with their diverse dispositions. But this mingling of substances does not pertain to the subject with which we are dealing, because, although there are many forms present, they are, nevertheless, in diverse matters and make up diverse composites, though they are joined locally.

58. **How the compound is moved by the predominant element.** And, finally, there does not follow from this what was implied by that argument, namely, that one element is resolved into another or is constituted by another. For, though water comes together with air in humidity, it does not, nevertheless, have humidity from participation in the form of air, but from itself and from its own simple nature. But when a humid vapor is exhaled from water through heating, the water is not resolved into air. For that vapor is not air, but a certain imperfect compound. But when it happens that water is changed into air, there is not a resolution into parts united, but a corruption and generation. Hence, elements exist far differently in a compound from the way one element exists in another, since an element is present in an element only in passive potency, but it is present in a compound not only in this way, but also virtually and by a certain participation in an active potency.[156]

Aristotle should be understood in this way when he says that elements are in a compound in act or in potency. And from this the solution to the third testimony is evident. For, in order for a compound to be moved by the motion of the predominant element, it is sufficient that the compound contain that element virtually and participate in the qualities of that element more than of any other element. Finally, the elements are said to be the matter of the compound which is formally passing, but virtually remaining. Hence, in *On Generation and Corruption,* book II, c. 5 [332a8], Aristotle denies that the elements are the matter of natural things. He says, "For, if air remained, there would not be generation, but alteration." It is clear, therefore, that it never happens that many substantial forms are united in the same part of matter on account of the disposition of one form toward another.

Whether Two Non-Subordinate Forms Can Inform the Same Matter at the same Time

59. **Matter can be informed with two forms by God.** There remains that we should speak of the third way of imagining two substantial forms in the same matter without any relation to each other or without any respect to some third form toward which they dispose the matter, but only through

accidental concomitance, as whiteness and sweetness are found in the same subject. But it is not necessary to spend much time in attacking this position, first, because I find no opinion on this point. For, as far as I know, no philosopher has until now said that two substantial forms could simultaneously and naturally inform the same matter in this way. I say "naturally," however, because with respect to God's absolute power I do not think that it implies a contradiction, whether that matter is posited in diverse places with diverse forms, something I showed elsewhere is possible, or whether it has the same form in the same place. For the unity of place does not add a special incompatibility.[157]

The second reason is that these forms simultaneously existing in the same matter would not really constitute one essence or one substance, because one of these forms would not pertain to the essence of the composite of matter and the other form, nor the converse.[158] Hence, if we suppose that one form is the form of wood and the other the form of gold, the wood would not be the gold, nor the gold the wood, since forms essentially diverse are not predicated of one other, even in the concrete,[159] except by reason of the same supposite in which they come together.[160] Those forms, however, do not come together in the same supposite, but only in the same matter with which, as they constitute diverse natures, they also constitute diverse composites, leaving out of account other miracles.[161] Hence, although matter could be said to be informed by the form of wood and of gold, the wood, nevertheless, would not be gold because wood is not matter, nor is gold matter. And thus, even if this case were admitted, there would not be two formal causes of one effect,[162] which is what we now are inquiring about, but each would constitute its own effect which would have only one formal cause.

60. **Why the same matter cannot naturally be simultaneously actualized by many substantial forms**. From the above, nonetheless, there is understand the natural incompatibility on account of which such forms cannot simultaneously inform such matter, but it is not a problem that one and the same matter with many forms successively constitutes essences which are even specifically distinct; in fact, it naturally occurs because matter is indifferent to any form and can be actualized by any form. But that the same portion of matter simultaneously constitutes diverse essences with diverse forms is contrary to the nature of things for many reasons.

The first is that the potency of matter is sufficiently actualized by one form, and its dependency is sufficiently terminated by that form. The second is that diverse forms require diverse dispositions which are naturally incompatible, and this is a sign that their natural effects are naturally incompatible. The third is that matter serves the form for its natural motions and actions; the same matter cannot, however, simultaneously serve two distinct forms which have distinct natural inclinations. The fourth reason is that, otherwise, if matter could in this way be under distinct forms, then, for the same reason, it could be under any number of them to infinity because accidental beings can be multiplied to infinity. And no greater incompatibility can be found in three rather than in two forms, and so on in any number. This, however, is both in itself absurd, and it is contrary to the end and purpose of matter because in this way it would be useless for the generations and corruptions of things. Hence, the axiom that "the generation of one thing is the corruption of another" satisfactorily shows that matter is incapable of being simultaneously informed by many forms.

The True View is Given along with the Conclusion of the Whole Question

61. There remains, then, the true view which asserts that one substantial composite has only a single formal cause and that in one natural composite there is only one substantial form. This is what St. Thomas holds in I. q. 76, a. 4, and Cajetan holds the same thing in the same place in his *Commentary on the Summa*, as well as all the Thomists. John Capreolus, for example, defends this view at great length in his *Commentary on the Sentences* II, dist. 15; Sylvester of Ferrara in book II of his *Commentary on the Summa Contra Gentiles*, c. 58, and Paul Soncinas in his *Commentary on the Metaphysics* q. 7. Gregory of Rimini as well holds this view in his *Commentary on the Sentences*, book II, dist. 17, q. 2; Giles of Rome holds this in his *Commentary on the De Anima*, book II, q. 6[163] and in *The Treatise on the Plurality of Forms*.[164] Harvey Nedellec also treats it at length in *On the Plurality of Forms*, and Marsilius of Inghen in his *Commentary on Generation and Corruption*, book I, q. 6.[165]

From Aristotle, however, we have nothing explicit on this matter. But this view is clearly inferred from his principles. For he never attributes more than one form to a natural composite, and in this sense he assigns three principles of a natural thing, namely, matter, privation, and form. For this reason, after all, he often says that, as often as one thing is generated, another is corrupted, and the converse. Besides, he says that the substantial form is the proper, essential [*per se*] and immediate act of matter and that for this reason something essentially one comes to be from them, as is derived from *On the Soul*, book II, text 7 [412b5] and *Metaphysics*, book VII, text 49 [1039a3].

62. Arguments for this view, however, can easily be taken from what was said against the other views. The first is taken from a sufficient enumeration of the parts, because there cannot be in matter many forms essentially subordinated as act and potency or ordered as disposition and form or even simply by concomitance without any order between them. But besides these ways no

other can be thought of. Therefore, many substantial formal causes can in no way concur toward the same effect.

63. The second argument is taken from the sufficiency of any substantial form. Any substantial form is necessarily such that it is by itself alone sufficient for constituting one substantial supposite complete in some ultimate species of substance. It, therefore, not only does not require another form which with it causes that effect, but cannot even admit it. The antecedent is clear from what was said. For it was proven that every substantial form necessarily must be constituted in some ultimate species of substantial form and that, consequently, it belongs to its nature that it give being absolutely and completely up to the ultimate nature in the genus of substance. The proof of the consequence is that either a second form would come to the composite as already constituted by the prior form and would immediately actualize it, or it would come to the matter simultaneously and as if concomitantly with the prior form. The first way is incompatible with the nature of substantial form which is by itself ordered to substantial potency. But a complete substance is no longer in substantial potency, but only in accidental potency. For what Aristotle said above is most of all true of it, namely, that what comes to a being in act does not come to it essentially, but accidentally.

The second way, however, is incompatible both with the substantial forms themselves and with the capacity of matter. For the forms are incompatible with one another according to their specific differences since, from the fact that every substantial form constitutes a complete substantial nature, it determines for itself the matter which it informs and, as it were, draws it to its own being so that it does not admit in matter another substantial form even of the same order.

Matter likewise has a limited capacity and, as it were, power of causing so that it cannot sustain more than one substantial form simultaneously nor can it concur in causing form except as ordered to constituting one essence. Even in the heavenly bodies this can be seen, and it is no less necessary in this lower matter which is the principle of corruption, insofar as it is subject to one form so that it necessarily abandons it, if it receives another.

64. The third principal argument can be produced from what we said above to prove that there are substantial forms in natural things. The strongest arguments by which substantial form is proven rely on the fact that for the complete constitution of a natural being it is necessary that all the faculties and operations of the same being be rooted in one essential principle.[166] That they are so connected and rooted is also proven by the natural effects of a being, as we demonstrated there. Therefore, a plurality of forms is entirely foreign to the constitution of a nature. Nor is there any evidence in all of nature for maintaining such a plurality, and the subordination of essential predicates is

not evidence for it, as we said. Therefore, Aristotle said in *On the Soul,* book II, text. 31 [414b27], that the later form contains the prior ones, because the form which gives the final difference also gives the previous forms.[167]

The multitude of actions, faculties, or organs is also not only no evidence for a plurality of forms, but rather especially requires the oneness of the form. Finally, the change or succession of generations and corruptions indicates and requires the same oneness. Therefore, there is nothing to cause us to doubt that one formal cause is sufficient to each natural effect. Nor do any new objections present themselves against this truth which it is necessary to satisfy.

From What Has Been Said It Is Concluded That There Is no Regress to Infinity in Formal Causes

65. And from this we can, in passing, resolve that question which is often raised concerning the formal cause, namely, whether in such a genus of cause there can be a regress to infinity. For, if we are speaking of a proper, physical formal cause, it is clear from what has been said that there is no place for this question. Since it can only be asked when many causes can concur for the same effect. For how can there be a regress of causes when there is only one cause? It has been shown, however, that there can only be one formal cause; therefore, the question about a regress to infinity has no place with regard to this cause.

Second, this regress is usually found either in causes which are intrinsically [*per se*] and essentially subordinated or in causes which are subordinated accidentally. It was, however, shown that no substantial forms are essentially [*per se*] subordinated. Hence, those who distinguish them according to the order of essential predicates can suffer some difficulty on this point. For it is perhaps not impossible that there be a regress to infinity in these predicates, as we will touch on in a following section.[168] But according to our view it makes no difference, because we hold that, in whatever number these predicates are multiplied, they not only do not require distinct forms which are essentially subordinated, but even that such predicates can, with respect to the same composite, only be derived from one and the same form. Thus, not only from the natures of things, but even by the absolute power of God, there cannot be substantial forms which are essentially subordinated in this way, because there cannot be a substantial form which is not constituted in some ultimate species of such a form and, consequently, which does not essentially include all previous levels of such forms.[169]

Nor does it matter that in *Metaphysics,* book II, c. 2 [994a3], Aristotle proves that there is no regress to infinity in these forms from the fact that there is no regress to infinity in quidditative predicates. For, although from the denial of the latter one can very well infer the denial of the former, one cannot infer from the affirmation of the latter the affirmation of the former, as we said above.[170]

Again, there are in this genus of cause no causes which are subordinated accidentally, because it was also shown that many causes cannot concur simultaneously to inform the same matter, even if they do so merely accidentally. But if someone should say that there can be a regress to infinity in forms contained under the same genus or species and should call them formal causes which are accidentally subordinated, he must necessarily notice that they are not the causes of one and the same effect, but that each one has its own distinct effect. But, when the subordination of causes is investigated, it should be understood with respect to one and the same effect; otherwise, there is no subordination, but simply a multiplication of things or effects.

Hence, even if by the absolute power of God forms were multiplied accidentally in the same matter, there would not be in that case a subordination of causes because, as I said above, they would not constitute one and the same effect, but diverse effects.[171] And, besides, they would have no order among themselves, but would be multiplied entirely accidentally. In this genus of cause, therefore, there is no regress of causes, neither to infinity nor in some finite number.

A Regress to Infinity is Excluded from the Material Cause

66. From this one can understand, finally, that it is even less possible for there to be a regress to infinity in matter, because, if it were possible, it could only arise from an infinity of forms. For, as we showed above, there is necessarily one prime matter which is not in another subject.[172] But this prime matter in each composite can only be one, because another matter cannot be received in it since this is contrary to the nature of matter.[173] Nor can many matters to be united in the same composite and informed by the same form unless one of them is united to another so that from both one potency is produced;[174] but this is in no way intelligible. Therefore, in substantial matters not only can there be absolutely no regress to infinity, but there also can be no regress or plurality at all.

67. But if the discussion is not about prime matter, but about proximate matter,[175] proximate matter is either understood substantially and as a potency immediately and essentially [*per se*] receiving form, or proximate matter is understood accidentally, that is, as affected by dispositions suited for form. In the first way prime matter alone by its simple entity is really also the proximate matter for any form, and so there is no regress, and such a regress could only be imagined if between prime matter and the ultimate substantial form there would intervene other substantial forms, some of which would be

related to the others as a proximate potencies to its own acts. Such forms, however, do not exist, as was shown, and even if they did exist, an infinite regress in them would not be intelligible. For an infinite multitude of forms is no less impossible than an infinite number of any beings in act.[176] Also, it is necessary that there should be some first form, that is, one which first informs the matter. For, since matter in itself is immediately potency, it is necessary that it be immediately informed by some determinate form; otherwise, formation would never begin. Again, on the part of the other extreme, it is necessary that there also be some ultimate form; otherwise, the information would never end, and the thing would not be constituted in some certain and determinate species. Between those two extremes, therefore, there cannot intervene an infinite multitude of forms, because for each extreme there necessarily must be some immediate one which would be related as proximate potency and its act. I omit the other arguments which Aristotle gives in the place cited for this because this matter is too clear to need proof.

68. But if we are speaking about matter which is proximate by reason of accidental dispositions, the same arguments prove that there cannot be a regress to infinity in those dispositions. For, if they are not subordinated, one to the other, but are related concomitantly, as the four primary qualities are, then there cannot be such a regress in them, merely because qualities actually infinite in number cannot exist at the same time, and much less can a finite form require them. But if these dispositions are subordinated, one to another, as act and proximate potency, just as quantity and quality are, then the argument produced about substantial forms applies, namely, that in them there must be a primary and ultimate form; otherwise, the disposition would neither be begun nor completed. But between those extremes there cannot be an infinite multitude.

Nor is the argument which could be adduced about the infinite points contained between two extremes similar, because the points are only potentially infinite, that is, they constitute along with the parts one continuous, finite quantity, but a multitude of forms would be infinite in act. Likewise, one point is not immediate to another, and so all the intermediate points between two extremes cannot be counted. But if one form, whether substantial or accidental, is compared to another as potency to act, it must necessarily be proximately related to it. Therefore, there can in no way be a regress to infinity between matter or form.

69. There apply, however, the arguments produced about lasting matter from which a thing comes to be so that the matter is present in it. But in the place mentioned in *Metaphysics,* book II [994a3], Aristotle speaks about transient matter, when he denies that there is a regress to infinity in material causes. For, if earth is generated from water, and grass from earth, and some-

thing else from grass, this does not go on to infinity, but makes a circle. Nevertheless, whether this process occurs or not, it does not pertain to [essential] causality[177] because that process is only accidental, and for this reason nothing would prevent the causality from tending toward infinity. But if it does not tend toward infinity, it is only because there are not infinite species of generable things nor a progression to infinity in the generation of such species, but a circle is always produced and a return to the same species. Some think that this necessarily follows from the fact that each of these species manifests a limited perfection. But this is no argument because at least by the divine power it is not impossible for the species of compounds to be multiplied to infinity, even if any species is finite and there is always, as a matter of fact, a highest and lowest species contained under every genus, though another could, as a possibility, be produced, either more perfect or less perfect than those produced.

Others say that it is shown by experience that there is no progression to infinity in the generation of one species from another, but that there is always produced a return to the same species. About this experience I doubt very much whether it is evident to us, because by the power of the heavens and the concurrence of the elements many things which are hidden from us are perhaps generated anew. Add to this that St. Thomas says in III, q. 10, a. 3, that infinite things are contained in potency in the creature. And he is speaking about substantial things, for he has said about these that the soul of Christ does not see an actual infinity.[178] Hence, in explaining that passage in his work, we said that it can be understood regarding infinite species or infinite individuals.[179]

If, therefore, infinite species of compounds are contained in the potency of a creature, it is not impossible to go on to infinity in the generation of them. And perhaps Aristotle is not opposed to this in the passage we cited, for he only proves that this process is not necessary for the causality of things, because the generation of one is the corruption of the other, and in this process a return is easily made in terms of the species, even if it is not made in terms of the individual.

It seems, nonetheless, more probable, naturally speaking, that there is a stopping point in the generation of things according to species because the powers of natural causes are finite and the modes or aspects and concurrences by which they are applied are determinate and finite. And, for this reason, though infinite things are contained in the absolute power of the creature, if in created things and causes all conditions and combinations were brought about which could absolutely be brought about, they could, nonetheless, as a matter of fact come to be in accord with the order of the universe only in finite ways, and for this reason it is also more likely that there is a stopping point and end in this process.

Notes

[1]For example, the form of the leaf of a tree, which actualizes the matter of the tree in a way that is different from the forms of the matter in other parts of the tree.

[2]So Suarez doesn't think it is a problem that there are many partial forms in, for example, a tree the forms of the roots, branches, leaves, etc.. The question is only whether, in addition to the form of the tree that is made up of all the partial forms, there is another form that is peculiar, as it were, to the whole tree.

[3]*De anima, Opera omnia*, Vol. 3, pp. 589-593.

[4]*MD* XIII 3,21.

[5]*Avencebrolis Fons Vitae ex Arabico in Latinum translatus...*(Münster I. W. , 1892-95).

[6]John of Ghent (= Johannes de Gandavo), a master of theology at Paris c. 1303.

[7]*Summa Naturalium Aristotelis* (Venice, de Colonia: 1476).

[8]The opinion is that there is a different substantial form for every essential predicate of a substance, where "an essential predicate" refers to a necessary property or feature of a substance which cannot be naturally lost as long as the substance endures, e.g., risibility in man. This view, popular among some earlier scholastics, lost currency in the later Middle Ages, due largely to the criticisms Aquinas leveled against it.

[9]*MD* VI, sect. 2. According to Suarez, the animality of David and his rationality refer to the same form in him, but are distinguished by the human mind since animality can be found separately from rationality, e.g., in rabbits, and rationality can be found separately from animality, e.g., in angels.

[10]For example, according to this view, the redness and color of a red rose would be really distinct. For Suarez, the two are the same in the rose, since the rose is colored *in virtue of being red*.

[11]For example "to be a thing capable of shape," or "to be a thing which is necessarily not identical with the Eiffel Tower," etc.

[12]By a physical part Suarez means a real, as opposed to a metaphysical or a logical part; he does *not* mean a corporeal part.

[13]Rational parts in a definition might be, for example, "animality" and "rationality" in the human being.

[14]So the human soul can root both the sensitive and rational powers of the human being. We can distinguish the "rational" from the "sensitive" because the rational and the sensitive powers are distinct. Nevertheless, the soul rooting both sets of powers is one, not two.

[15]XI, para. 19.

[16]Suarez is referring to the grades of perfection in being, for example, "living," "sentient," "rational." He follows St. Thomas in holding that a higher form can give to a substance all the powers a lower form gives. Thus, the rational soul, as more perfect than the purely sensitive soul, can not only bestow rationality on the human being, but it can also bestow the sensitive powers.

[17]*MD* VI, sect. 9.

[18]MD, XIII, sec. 3,21.

[19]This form was held by Scotus to give three-dimensional being to material substances.

[20]That is, for Scotus there is a form of corporeity distinct from the soul of any animate being; this form remains after the being dies. However, there is no form of corporeity in, say, a bit of gold, which is distinct from the form of gold.

[21]The notion is that the soul cannot inform bare matter as such but only matter already possessed of a certain grade of being. But all grades of being come from form; hence, the soul presupposes another form in the matter it informs.

[22]This definition of Aristotle's from the *De anima* was already cited by Suarez in sect. V, where he used it to explain the nature of substantial form in general.

[23]The notion is that the body is included in the definition of the living being and nothing that is in the definition of a substance can be an accident. Hence, if the body cannot be pure matter, then it must be a corporeal substance constituted by a form of its own, not matter along with certain accidents, such as quantity.

[24]Scotus thought that when an animal dies its corpse remains, which corpse previously constituted the body of the animal. This corpse is itself a substance which, therefore, has a form of its own.

[25]That is, a corpse, *qua* body, looks and feels the same as a living body save only that it lacks certain accidents, e.g., heat, and this is true no matter what caused the person's death.

[26]That is, the three days intervening between Christ's death and resurrection.

[27]Sec. 3. Avicenna held that prime matter is not a pure potency but includes in itself a primordial extension. His view was thus somewhat similar to Descartes'.

[28]That is, Aristotle did not think that substantial being admitted of more or less and so, according to him, a substance could not be partially corrupted or generated.

[29]The reason for this is that the form of corporeity would give corporeal being as such, but not corporeal being of a *specific* sort.

[30]The argument here is that the form of corporeity, if it existed, would have to give specific being since in giving substantial existence as such to matter and in making it capable of quantity, it would give that which pertains to the definition of corporeal substance. In a similar way, the form giving sentient being would give to the matter it informs that which pertains to the definition of an animal. But every animal is a *specific* sort of animal; the same, therefore, holds of corporeal substance.

[31]That is, even parts of substances are in some proportionate genus and species of their own.

[32]The idea is that that which is already a complete substantial being cannot be further completed substantially but only accidentally.

[33]By an *ad hominem* argument Suarez means an argument against an opponent based upon the opponent's *own* principles showing that he is inconsistent with those principles.

[34]That is, when a living thing comes to be, both its corporeal form and its soul are produced. This would ground a twofold generation for the production of one substance, which Suarez regards as absurd.

[35]This example is based on the outdated Aristotelian theory of spontaneous generation. Such a theory was the result of Aristotle's inability to detect the presence of the eggs of maggots and other such entities in rotten flesh.

[36]The notion is that a compound presupposes matter existing at a certain grade of being in the way a living thing does. Therefore, if a living thing requires the form of corporeity, so does a compound.

[37]Having attacked Scotus' position by first inferring absurdities from that position, Suarez next attacks the soundness of the arguments Scotus used to support his theory.

[38]See above, para. 7. This is the argument based on the metaphysical distance between the soul and prime matter.

[39]The notion here is that the soul is perfect enough in itself to actualize in matter the very dispositions the soul requires in matter in order to inform it.

[40]MD XIV sec. 3. Suarez agrees with Scotus that 1) accidental dispositions introduced into a certain subject rendering it fit for the introduction of a new substantial form need to be present at the moment that the new form is introduced, and 2) that accidents cannot naturally be transferred from one substance to another. Hence, he agrees that some subject must remain underneath, so to speak, the accidents disposing matter for a new substantial form. However, Suarez thinks that prime matter alone, without the form of corporeity, is a fit subject for such accidents.

[41]See above, para. 7. This is the argument that, since we say that the living are constituted out of body and soul, and since prime matter is not a body, the form of corporeity must be posited.

[42]Suarez is here, in effect, arguing that any perfections necessary in matter for the soul to inform it need only be accidental, not substantial.

[43]That is, though the term "body" does not refer to pure matter stripped of all form, but to a corporeal substance, that does not show that the soul itself could not be the form giving corporeal being to the body of a living thing. For more on this see Aquinas, De ente et essentia, c. 2.

[44]De eucharista, d. 51, a. 4, Opera omnia, Vol. 21, 198-207. .

[45]See above, para. 7. This is the argument that a form of corporeity must be posited since, after the death of an animal, matter does not exist stripped of all form and yet no efficient cause can be assigned to explain the generation of the corpse form.

[46]That is, whether two living beings of the same species have the same specific sort of cadaver form introduced into their matter after death.

[47]That is, the cadaver form is generated by elemental powers remaining in the matter of a living being after death, with the concurrence of causes such as the sun (a "universal cause" according to the schoolmen).

[48]Such as maggots; see above, note 33.

[49]See above, para. 7. This was a theological argument based upon the need to suppose a form of corporeity to explain how the body of Christ, while it was entombed after his death and prior to the resurrection, was numerically the same as His living body.

[50]That is, it is the same body containing the same partial mode of subsistence that it had when Christ was alive.

[51]See above, note 42.

[52]Opera omnia Vol. 19, pp. 624-626 ; the reference should be to question L, De morte Christi.

[53]That is, whether it was personally united to the second person of the Trinity.

[54]That is, a special argument based on the philosophy of nature.

[55]These grades were distinguished by the medievals according to the perfection of the powers characteristic of each grade (cf. ST I, q. 78, a. 1). Coffey discusses whether or not these grades determine various species of corporeal being or only generic grades of them in his Science of Logic (New York: Longmans, Breen and Co., 1912),

79-81. He notes that Clarke and Zigliara affirmed that they *do* determine various species of corporeal being, but he disagrees with them on this point. More recently Mortimer Adler has argued for the view Clarke and Zigliara defended, while Maritain has supported Coffey's view. See Mortimer Adler, *Problems for Thomists; The Problem of Species* (New York: Sheed & Ward, 1940).

[56] *Commentarius Joannis grammatici Philoponi...In Aristotelis Stagiritae libros tres De anima* (Lyon, 1558).

[57] *Quaestiones de Anima* (Venice, 1553, 1583; rep. Minerva, 1966).

[58] *Scriptum super libros de anima* (Venice, 1481).

[59] See above, para. 4.

[60] Laid out formally the argument given here is something as follows:

1) If the rational soul in humans is identical with the forms in them giving them vegetative and sensitive powers, then the rational soul has all the essential properties of vegetative and sensible souls.

2) All vegetative and sensible souls are corruptible and mortal.

3) No rational soul is corruptible and mortal.

4) If (2) and (3) then no rational soul has all the essential properties of vegetative and sensible souls.

---

5) No rational soul has all the essential properties of vegetative and sensible souls.

---

6) The rational soul in humans is not identical with the forms giving them vegetative and sensitive powers.

[61] *Galatians* 5:17.

[62] *Quodlibeta septem* (Paris, 1487).

[63] *De duabus animabus contra Manichaeos liber unus* in *Patrologia Latina*, Vol. XLII, Migne, ed. (1865), coll. 93 ff.

[64] *De vera religione* in *Patrologia Latina,* Vol. XXXIV, Migne, ed. (1865), coll. 121 ff.

[65] *The Letters of St. Jerome* (Westminster: Newman, 1963).

[66] *Philo with an English Translation*, trans. by F. H. Colson and G.H. Whitaker, Loeb Classical Library (Cambridge: Harvard University Press, 1950), pp. 198 ff.

[67] According to Rabade, Suarez is referring here to the Council of Vienne (*De anima ut forma corporis*), as well as to the Lateran Council under Leo X, session 8 (*De anima humana doctrina contra Neo-Aristotelicos*). See Denzinger, *Enchiridion symbolorum*, ed. by Adolfus Schönmetzer (Freiburg: Herder, 1965), p.284 and p. 353. The "Neo-Aristotelians" referred to by the Lateran Council include, for example, Pietro Pomponazzi, who argued, based on his reading of Aristotle, that human reason could not prove the rational soul to be by nature immortal.

[68] See above para. 4.

[69] See above, para. 10.

[70] That is, there is nothing that is just a plant but not a specific sort of plant.

[71] This is in accordance with a general axiom of Suarez that a complete substantial being can only be further perfected by an accidental, not a substantial, form.

[72] In the same way, the very corporeal substantial being of the horse *must* be contracted and it can be contracted by the specific nature of the horse itself. It does not need to be contracted by a difference contained only in the grade of simple corporeal substantial being. Suarez is here focusing on the problem of confusing what is specifically inanimate with what is generically corporeal. Compare with

"animal" taken generically and taken specifically as equivalent to "brute." For more on this see Aquinas, *De ente et essentia*, c. II, 6-7.

[73]That is, if there were a specific animal soul in the human being distinct from her rational soul, God could preserve that soul in existence separately.

[74]*De Diversis Quaestionibus LXXXIII, Corpus Chritianorum, Series Latina*, Vol. 44a (Turnholt: Brepols, 1975).

[75]Apollinaris of Laodicea (d. 390) was a grammarian, priest and bishop. Apollinaris taught that the Word of God assumed only a body and a sensitive soul.

[76]Sect. I, para. 15.

[77]*De Spiritu et Anima* in *Patrologia Latina*, Vol. XL, Migne, ed. (1865), coll. 779 ff.

[78]*Expositio Fidei Orthodoxae, Patrologia Graeca*, Vol 94 (Paris, 1864), coll. 790 ff.

[79]Because it would continue to live the life of an animal in virtue of its sensitive soul.

[80]The reason is that material forms are dependent upon matter for all their operations. Hence, since operation follows being, material forms cannot naturally exist bereft of a matter suited to them.

[81]In saying the view under consideration is "rash" but not "erroneous," Suarez is invoking the distinction between that which is formally heretical and that which is properly subject to theological censure.

[82]*Opera omnia*, Vol. 17, pap. 541-543.

[83]Ibid., pp. 560-563.

[84]*De Summa Trinitate et fide catholica* in *Henrici Denzinger Enchiridion Symbolorum* ed. K. Rahner (Freiburg: Herder, 1955) #480, pp. 221-222.

[85]The reason is that the rational soul is so distant from matter that it cannot be immediately united to the body.

[86]See above, sec. 6, 2 and 9.

[87]The reason is that higher forms are more dominant over their matter than lower forms. Hence, the lower in the animal kingdom one goes, the more form is "lost" in the divisibility and potency of matter and the less strong its unity is. At the higher levels, however, as form becomes more perfect, so the dispositions requisite in matter for the information of the form become also more perfect, allowing for a tighter union between soul and body.

[88]So positing a lower substantial form intermediate between soul and body will not solve the difficulty because a substantial form lower than the rational soul will itself be extended and so, by the reasoning of Suarez's adversaries, will be unfit for the rational soul's information.

[89]The reason for this is that the union of soul and body requires that the two be related as act and potency. But any form is act and so is less suited to be informed by the soul than matter is.

[90]*MD* XXV 3,10-16. Suarez's assertion here depends upon the notion that one substantial form cannot inform another, nor inform what the first substantial form informs. Hence, if one body is informed by a sensitive soul prior to the advent of the rational soul, the rational soul will not be able to inform either the sensitive soul or the body that the sensitive soul informs.

[91]This is in line with the principle that the higher act can perform all the functions of lower acts, but not *vice versa*.

[92]That is, "corporeal form" should be generically defined as any form, whether inanimate, animate, sensitive, or rational which is a principle of corporeal being. This is in opposition to "corporeal form" taken more specifically as the form of an inanimate being.

[93]Sect. 3, para. 21.

[94]The scholastics distinguished between formal or virtual containment this way: X is formally an F, *iff* X is an F. Thus Nefer is a cat and so he is formally a cat. On the other hand X is virtually an F, *iff* X is not an F but X has all the perfections of an F. Thus Nefer is not a plant but he is virtually a plant because he can do all the things a plant can do, such as grow, reproduce, etc.

[95]For more on this see above sect. II, para. 12

[96]The argument is that diverse and opposing kinds of operation must proceed from diverse substantial forms. But human beings perform diverse and even opposing operations; therefore, human beings are constituted by diverse substantial forms.

[97]Para. 24.

[98]This way of conceiving of a plurality of substantial forms in one composite is more empirical than the above way, which could be called logical or metaphysical. It is based upon observing that living beings are generated in stages, and from this it is inferred that the forms of prior stages remain as *dispositions* for later stages. The earlier ways of conceiving of a plurality of forms were not based upon empirical observation but upon generic and specific distinctions within the *concept* of a thing's essence.

[99]*Suessanus, De generatione et corruptione* (Venice, 1526).

[100]The empirical basis of this reason for positing a plurality of substantial forms is here clearly indicated.

[101]So, for example, some parts of the human body produce acids while others produce antacids. Thus, as these parts have contrary properties, they must emanate from specifically distinct forms.

[102]That is, the flesh and bone, for example, of a human being are specifically distinct. Nevertheless, as parts of the human being they share in the form of the whole human being so that their difference can only arise from *partial* substantial forms peculiar to each.

[103]It is important to note here that Suarez did not deny the existence in non-human living beings of partial substantial forms. What he did deny is that, in addition to one composite form composed out of these partial forms, there is a form of the whole informing each partial form. Suarez' chief argument for this view seemed to be that, as a composite substantial form should be understood as arising from the partial forms constituting it, there is no need to posit *another* form of the whole *besides* the composite form made out of these partial forms. But it seems that this view of Suarez opens him up to the charge that his composite substantial forms do not have enough unity to constitute something essentially one.

[104]For a Thomistic response to this argument see John of St. Thomas, *Cursus philosophicus thomisticus*, III Pars, Q. II, a. 1.

[105]See the above work of John of St. Thomas for arguments for the opposing view. A perfect animal is a non-human animal which has all of the sensitive powers, e.g., a cat or a dog.

[106]That is, both the forms of heavenly bodies and of perfect animals are divisible in the sense that they arise from the union of really diverse and partial substantial forms. As such, in neither is it necessary to suppose a form of the whole distinct from the form arising from the union of the partial substantial forms.

[107]That is, such partial substantial forms as the opposing view posits.

[108]In this sense only spiritual forms are indivisible. For Suarez there are two classes of such spiritual forms, the informing and the subsistent. The informing spiritual

form is the human soul which, though it is spiritual, has need of a body to constitute one complete thing. The subsistent form is the angelic substance which does not inform anything and which exists perfectly in separation from any material organism.

[109]Suarez' argument against a plurality of substantial forms in the case of the human being is different from his argument against such a plurality in the case of non-human animals. In non-human animals he thinks it is unnecessary to posit a form of the whole distinct from the composite form arising from the substantial forms informing the heterogeneous parts of such animals. On the other hand, in human beings he thinks that it is unnecessary to posit substantial forms for the distinct parts of a human body because the perfection of the human soul makes it capable of informing all the parts of the human body without needing intermediate substantial forms.

[110]In this sense one form Y is made from another form X only in that Y *succeeds* X in the same matter.

[111]See above, para. 29.

[112]In other words, nothing can, at one and the same time, be two distinct sorts of substance. But, since every substantial form gives substantial being, this means that nothing could be constituted by two distinct kinds of substantial form. Cf. *ST* I, q. 76, a. 3.

[113]The objection is that, even if the complete or whole form of a substance is necessarily singular, this does not mean that there could not be distinct partial substantial forms in a substance in addition to the form of the whole. So even if the human being can only have one soul, viz., the rational, it can still have other partial substantial forms in its parts, for example, the partial substantial forms of its various organs, tissues, etc.

[114]The assumption here seems to be that only a living substantial form could be a disposition for another living substantial form.

[115]Para. 8-13.

[116]Para. 19-20.

[117]That is, if it were the case that no composite form could arise from other partial forms.

[118]The reason for this seems to be that, if they are truly distinct substantial forms from the soul of the whole organism, they should, or at least could, remain after the soul of the whole organism recedes.

[119]Para. 15.

[120]Suarez asserted this because he interpreted Plato as denying that the rational soul truly informs the body. Such an interpretation of Plato was common among the scholastics, see *ST* I, q. 76, a. 3.

[121]Probably a reference to sect. 1, para. 15.

[122]See above, para. 29.

[123]That is, from privation of a previously possessed form to its repossession.

[124]Suarez here simply rejects, as being contrary to experience, the principle that a severed piece of matter cannot regain a form it had lost.

[125]*De anima*, Book I, cap. 14; *Opera omnia*, Vol. 3, pp. 567-572.

[126]*Aristotelis Opera cum Averrois commentariis*, Vol. V (Venice: apud Junctas, 1562-74; rep. Frankfurt am Main: Minerva, 1962).

[127]Ibid..

[128]Reference not found.

[129]Reference not found.

[130]*Galen on the Therapeutic Method (= De Methodo Medendi)*, R. J. Hankinson (Oxford: Clarendon, 1991).

[131]*De substantia facultatum naturalium fragmentum, Opera Omnia*, C. G. Kuhn, Vol. 4, 757-766 (Leipzig, 1821-33).

[132]The reason for this is that, as the substantial form of a thing gives it its substantial and primary being, it must substantially inform every part of it.

[133]Para. 48.

[134]That is, if there is one form of the whole in all the parts of a composite, then each part of it has the same proportion of primary qualities, i.e., hot, cold, moist, and dry. But this means there cannot be distinct elemental forms in different parts of a compound as different elemental forms have different proportions of the primary qualities.

[135]The reason is that, by the hypothesis, it would inform every part of the compound, even parts which, between themselves, have contrary dispositions.

[136]If this is the case, the need to posit the continued existence of elemental forms in compounds disappears.

[137]Because, for example, fire and water would coexist in the same part of matter.

[138]For example, coldness is a disposition for water, while heat is a disposition for fire.

[139]They are contradictories because one exists *in itself*, while the other exists *in another* (i.e., not in itself).

[140]The reason for this is that the only term common to them is being itself and being is not a genus since it is necessarily in every mode of being; hence, being cannot be contracted by specific differences in the way a genus is; cf. *MD* XXXII, sec. 2.

[141]In sect. 1, especially para. 18.

[142]The notion here is that a thing is either, for example, a horse or it is not. There are no degrees in substantial being for, even though one instance of a substantial essence may have a more perfect participation in certain qualities characteristic of such an essence, we would not say it was more or less that *sort* of essence. For example, we would not say that a crippled person is less of a person than any other person.

[143]The notion seems to be that, for example, one shade of blue is in a different species of blue from another shade of blue.

[144]Sect. 1, para. 8-10.

[145]This is in accordance with the general scholastic maxim that nothing can give what it does not have. Cf. *ST* I, q. 2, a. 3.

[146]This argument of Suarez seems to contradict his view that Christ was one supposit subsisting in two distinct natures, viz., a human and a divine nature. Nevertheless, Suarez might insist that this was possible in Christ's case because of the ability of the divine nature to assume a finite nature and that, at any rate, the case of Christ is extraordinary while the cases here talked about are according to the general order of nature.

[147]Para. 67.

[148]Para. 40.

[149]On virtual containment see note 94 above.

[150]*De generatione et corruptione* (Venice, Naples, 1480).

[151]Suarez is following the view of St. Thomas here, which is that when a compound is resolved into the elements from which it was made, it is not resolved into numerically the same elements as before, but only into elements of the same sort. This

happens because compounds, though they do not formally contain the elements, contain their *properties*. Cf. *De mixtione elementorum*, Leonine edition, Vol. XLIII.

[152]Reference not found.

[153]*Quodlibeta* (Louvain, 1646; rep. Frankfurt am Main: Minerva, 1966).

[154]*Galen on the Doctrines of Hippocrates and Plato*, Philip De Lacy, ed. (Berlin: Academie-Verlag, 1978).

[155]They are separated out and not generated because they are not really part of the compounds they are in. They are simply surrounded by the compounds, like a marble in a person's stomach.

[156]That is, in a potency which is able to produce a certain element.

[157]Suarez does not think, that is, that it is a logical contradiction for two things to exist in the same place. This accords with his view that no accident individuates and that place is a modal accident.

[158]In the envisioned case, two forms would inform the same matter to make up two different substances which are in no way related to each other so as to compose a single substance. An analogy might be to two different accidents inhering in one substance which are not, in themselves, related to each other, e.g., a man's skin color and his knowledge of physics.

[159]The scholastics distinguished between abstract and concrete notions or terms. Thus "humanity" is abstract because it represents the form of a certain sort of being in abstraction from the individual entity it is the form *of*. The concrete form of the same notion is "human being" which represents the nature as actually existing *in* a human being; cf. J. Maritain, *Formal Logic*, trans. by Imelda Choquette (New York: Sheed and Ward, 1946), pp. 32-33.

[160]As one might refer to the grammatical philosopher because both the accidents of grammatical and philosophical knowledge exist in the same individual substance, or as one might say that a man was God when referring to Christ.

[161]Perhaps Suarez is obliquely referring to the miracle of the Incarnation. For Christ was one supposite consisting of two distinct natures.

[162]Because the two forms would not be contributing to constitute a single substance.

[163]*Expositio Egidi Romani Super libros De anima cum textu* (Venice, 1496).

[164]Perhaps a reference to *De gradibus formarum*, J. S. MaKaay, ed. (Venice, 1502).

[165]*Marsilii de gen. et corr. Commentaria* (Venice, 1520).

[166]Sect. 1, para. 7. This clearly shows that Suarez leans more heavily on the metaphysical arguments for form than on the physical.

[167]So, whatever gives something a cat form, gives it an animal form, a living form, etc.

[168]Sec. 11, para. 22.

[169]So not even God could make a material thing that is not either living or non living, plant or animal, vertebrate or invertebrate, etc. Perhaps this is the reason Wolff held that the individual is that which is "completely determined."

[170]Para. 5.

[171]Para. 59. Thus a bunch of forms that are not essentially ordered to one formal effect but which inform the same matter would no more constitute one thing than an army, a football team, or a pile of rocks does.

[172]XIII, sec. 1-2.

[173]As matter by its nature is the ultimate subject and so cannot be received into a more ultimate subject.

[174]For example, the matter in the atoms of hydrogen and oxygen merge together, so to speak, to form the proximate matter of a molecule of water.

[175]Proximate matter is matter already informed by a substantial form. Thus the elements are the proximate matter of compounds.

[176]Suarez here leans on Aristotle's doctrine that every actual number is definite and therefore finite; hence, an actual infinity of things is impossible; cf. *Physics* book III, c. 5.

[177]It does not pertain to essential causality because, if from earth water is generated, earth doesn't remain in the generated water. Water can be generated from earth only as from a terminus *from which*.

[178]The reference here is to the human soul of Christ, not to His divine soul, so to speak. The human soul cannot partake of the omniscience of God because no created thing can sustain infinite attributes. In opposition to both the Catholic, Reformed, and Orthodox traditions, the Lutherans taught that Christ's human soul did, in virtue of the hypostatic union, partake of certain of God's infinite attributes, namely, omniscience, omnipotence, and ubiquity, but not *aseity*, infinity of substance, simplicity, immutability, etc.

[179]That is, there are potentially infinitely many species of created things and potentially many individuals in each of those.

Section XI
On the Metaphysical Form, the Matter
That Corresponds to It, and the Causality It Exercises

1. **In any composition there is an element which functions as matter and one which functions as form.** Since the distinction of form into physical[1] and metaphysical is very common, and since everything we have said thus far pertains to physical form, it seems to belong to the task of the metaphysician to say a few things about metaphysical form. Given what we have said, these things can be handled briefly because metaphysical form is called a form only by analogy and by a certain metaphor. From what has been said above[2] one should notice that besides physical composition from matter and form, there is another type which imitates it; this composition in itself abstracts from real matter[3] and is therefore called "metaphysical."

Insofar as the present discussion is concerned, this composition is twofold, one from nature and supposite,[4] the other from genus and difference.[5] I omit the composition which is from essence and existence[6] because it is rather obscure and, in terms of the present question, no special meaning of form is involved in it, as will become clear from what we will say.

Second, one must consider that in every composition, insofar as one thing is understood to emerge from many elements, something is always considered matter and something form. For, in the first place, the composition from matter and form is the primary real composition and one most proper and essential [*per se*], and for this reason every other composition is explained by a certain analogy with it. In the second place, matter is something formless and imperfect and is a certain beginning and, as it were, foundation of a nature, but form is as it were the beauty, the perfection, and consummation of a nature. In every composition, however, there is something *quasi* potential which is the foundation and beginning of the thing and something which is the terminus or consummation of it. And for this reason something is always considered as matter and something is considered as form. This is so true that even in a composition from integral parts which seems to be most material, one part is always considered as material and the other as form. This will be seen more clearly in heterogeneous things; for example, in a human being the head is like the form of the other parts. And in artificial things, the roof, for example, is like the form of the building. In accord with this analogy, theologians also distinguish the matters and forms of the sacraments.

And in homogeneous things, where that diverse relation between parts cannot be distinguished because of their similarity and uniformity, all the parts are said to be the matter of the whole, but the composite is said to be related as form to the individual parts. In all of these examples no special causality is involved,[7] but only a union with an analogy and proportion to matter and form.

2. From these points one can understand that in general that form is called metaphysical which essentially constitutes a thing itself in its metaphysical composition or which completes or actualizes the essence of a thing. Nor can this form, when taken in this general sense, be described in any other way. There is, however, a difference between the two metaphysical compositions mentioned above,[8] namely, that the first between nature and supposit—we are speaking of creatures—is the composition of a thing, that is, a composition from elements which are in some way actually distinguished in the thing itself, as are nature and subsistence, about which we will deal extensively below.[9] But the latter is a composition of reason, because its extremes are not actually distinguished in reality, but only by reason, as has been shown above.[10]

There is also another difference, namely, that in the first composition one extreme is the whole essence of the thing, while the other extreme does not refer intrinsically to the essence, but is a terminus or mode of the essence.[11] In the other composition, however, both extremes are essential, and neither expresses explicitly or actually the whole essence of the thing, although in a confused way either could include it.[12] As a result, the form of the first composition is often said to be the whole, real, and most properly metaphysical form,[13] but the form of the latter is more of a form according to reason, and for this reason it can be called not only metaphysical, but also logical.[14]

The Essence of the Metaphysical Form Is Revealed

3. **The metaphysical form is the whole essence of a thing.** It must, therefore, first be said that the properly metaphysical form which is the form of the whole is nothing else than the whole essence of a substantial thing which we also call the entire nature of a thing. It is not called a form because it specially exercises the proper causality of a form, but because by itself it constitutes the thing essentially. I explain and prove each of these claims. For in a human being, for example, this form of the whole is said to be humanity which, since it consists of matter and the form of a human being, expresses the whole essence of a human being. For that which "human being" adds to "humanity" does not belong to the essence of a human being, as we shall argue below when we deal with subsistence and as is readily seen in the mystery of the Incarnation. For in Christ there is the whole essence of a human being, though there is no human, created subsistence.[15]

Furthermore, this form of the whole is found not only in material things, but even in spiritual ones. In fact, it is found by us not only in created things, but even in God Himself. For we conceive the Deity as the form which essentially constitutes God and each divine supposite[16] insofar as such a supposite is God, although it is proper to God that nothing which pertains to His essence is really distinguished from His essence.[17] In this way God's essence differs from the nature of the form which the essence has in created things, because [to have a distinct mode of subsistence] does not pertain to perfection absolutely, but includes imperfection. Therefore, this form in immaterial things cannot be anything else but their essence.

In material entities, however, this form of the whole differs from the physical and partial form,[18] as is shown from the common use of these words and from the very distinction of physical form from metaphysical form. It does not differ form the physical form, however, except insofar as the form of the whole expresses the whole nature composed of matter and form, while the physical form only expresses the formal part. Therefore, this metaphysical form expresses even in these things their whole essence. We shall show below in the disputation on the essence of material substance,[19] that matter also pertains to the essence of this substance, and so the nature composed of matter and form is the whole essence of it, and in that way the first part of the conclusion is proven.

4. **The metaphysical form is designated by the word "nature."** But that this metaphysical form is often called most properly by the word "nature," is established, first, from usage; for in that way we also attribute to God a divine nature, to the intelligences an angelic nature, to human beings a human nature, and so on with other things. Second, in this way we distinguish nature from supposite, either really in created substances or only by reason, as in the divine. And in this way we say that in God the nature does not generate, but the supposite does, and that the Divine Word assumed a human nature, not a human person.[20] Likewise, each thing has through its nature that it is such a thing and that it is essentially distinguished from others. Finally, as nature is commonly considered, it expresses an order to operation in which it only differs from essence in that the name "essence" was taken from its order to being, while the name "nature" was taken from its order to operation. For nature is said to be that which, as it were, makes something to be born; hence, nature is said not to be idle, and to be the producer of things and to do nothing in vain, and so on. However, the primary and adequate principle of operations in each thing is its essence, a fact which is obvious in the case of immaterial things. But in material things the form seems to be the principle of operation because it is the formal and active principle. Nevertheless, because matter also concurs in some manner in its genus with the form, espe-

cially for natural and intrinsic motions or acts, I have for this reason said that
the primary, radical, and adequate principle of each thing is its essence. Therefore, the essence itself and the form of the whole are the same as the nature of
each thing.

5. **Etymology of the word "nature" and its various meanings.** I am aware
that Aristotle in *Metaphysics*, book V, c. 4 [1014b16-1015a1] assigns various
meanings to the word "nature" and among them mentions in the last place
that meaning by which it signifies the substance or essence of a thing, and he
says that this is a transferred use from another meaning by which "nature"
signifies the form which is the terminus of generation. And in *Physics*, book
II, c. 1 [192b21] he narrows the concept of nature to the first intrinsic principle of motion alone, and for this reason "natural being" is usually said only
of material substances. I think, nevertheless, that these assertions must be
understood of this word "nature" with regard to its imposition, but not with
regard to the thing signified by it.[21] For these are usually quite distinct in
analogous terms, as St. Thomas rightly noted in I, q. 13, a. 6.

With regard to the imposition of the word, it is very likely that this word
first signified the other things which Aristotle lists there, for example, natural
generation and, especially, the origin or birth of living things. For "nature:
natura" is said of a thing "about to be born: *nascitura*," and from this the word
could have been used for signifying the intrinsic principles of a generated
thing, namely, matter and form. Or, as St. Thomas says in I, q. 29, a. 1, ad. 4,
because the birth of living things comes from an intrinsic principle, this word
has for this reason been used to signify the first intrinsic principle of motion
which is matter and form. And because the essence of a thing is completed by
form, that word was finally used to signify the essence of a thing. But because
the ancient philosophers who debated about nature knew only material substances, they for this reason attributed nature to them alone, and because of
this they have especially obtained the name "natural beings."

6. But if we look to the reality signified and speak of this word metaphysi-
cally rather than physically, this word absolutely and principally signifies the
essence without qualification and the entire essence of each thing, as it is
signified in the manner of the whole form. And in immaterial things it is
simple, but in material ones it is composed of matter and form, because neither matter nor form is the whole nature of a thing, but only a part of it. But
the entire nature of a thing is composed of both, and for this reason it is
rightly called the whole form in the metaphysical sense.

Accidents, on the other hand, as they do not have an essence absolutely
speaking,[22] so they also do not have a nature except with qualification, such
as, an accidental nature, and they are more appropriately said to be according
to nature, contrary to nature, or beyond nature.[23] Hence, in accidents, as will

be seen below, this account of the whole form with which we are now dealing has no place, properly speaking. (I am speaking about the real order, whatever the case may be with the possible order in our way of conceiving). And the reason is that an accident is a *quasi* partial and physical form; hence, it is in itself an incomplete nature and one so imperfect that with its subject it does not make something one essentially [*per se*], but only something one accidentally. And from this it happens that from both of them there does not result an entire nature and a form of the whole as does result from matter and substantial form.

7. **Whether the metaphysical form exercises some causality.** Finally, the last part of the conclusion can easily be proven from all that has been said. For, in the first place, since this form of the whole in material things includes the prime matter, it cannot exercise the proper formal causality which consists in actualizing some subject. Likewise, in immaterial things, since the whole essence is simple and abstracts from every receptacle, it cannot be said to be a form on account of proper formal causality. And, if it is permissible to argue from theology, the humanity of Christ is the metaphysical form of the man Christ, and yet it is not the true form of the Divine Word, having true causality upon Him by reason of which it may be said to formally constitute this man.[24]

This argument can be extended to any nature whatsoever with respect to its proper supposite. For nature is related either to subsistence itself or to the composite of nature and subsistence. With relation to subsistence nature does not have formal causality, but rather a *quasi* material causality (I omit active causality which I shall deal with later),[25] because subsistence proper is not related to nature as its subject, but as its terminus. Hence, subsistence is in some way an act of nature rather than the converse. Likewise, because subsistence is a mode of nature as a result of which it modifies and in some way actualizes it, nature does not, therefore, in this relationship exercise formal causality. For this reason, in the example of the mystery of the Incarnation we mentioned, theologians say that the humanity is not only not related to the Word as its form, but rather that the Word acts as form insofar as it in some way perfects and actualizes humanity, although no proper and true causality is exercised.

8. From this it further results that even with respect to the whole composite or supposite, the entire nature is not called the whole form because of a true and proper causality of the form. For this causality is never exercised with respect to the composite unless it is first and immediately exercised on some subject from which, together with the form, the composite results. If, then, the whole nature does not exercise formal causality with regard to the other extreme of this composition, it cannot exercise it over the whole composite.

The result, therefore, is that the integral nature is called a form only because it is the whole quiddity, principle, or essence that intrinsically constitutes the supposite in such a genus or species. And this constitution is not brought about through a causality in some way distinct from the nature, but comes through the intrinsic actuality and entity of the whole nature. And on this account also this form is said to be metaphysical and not physical.

9. Hence, we also understand incidentally that no proper matter corresponds to this form. For, as has been said, it is not called a form because it informs some subject. But, if we speak generally, it is only the supposite that corresponds to this nature as essentially constituted by it. In material things, however, the entire nature can be compared as the whole form to the partial natures[26] from which it is composed. For, although one of these is the form, nevertheless, insofar as both matter and form are of themselves incomplete and imperfect parts, they can be related as matter to the whole composite nature, and this latter can as something whole and completed be related to the parts as form. According to Aristotle in the *Physics,* book II, text 31 [195a19], the whole is related as a form to its parts, although in this passage he is talking especially about the integral whole with respect to its own parts.[27]

10. **In each composite there is only one metaphysical form.** Finally, from what has been said it is understood that this form can only be one with respect to the same thing. This is obvious because it expresses the whole nature of a thing, and in each thing there can be only one nature. Nor does it matter that in terms of reason one can distinguish in the same thing a specific and generic form of the whole, such as, humanity, animality, etc. For, if these are taken with respect to the same thing, there are not many forms in the thing, but only one and the same form conceived of in different ways. And insofar as that form is conceived of as many according to reason, it is not taken with respect to one, but with respect to many, even according to reason.[28] For animality is not the form of the whole human being, but of the animal as such. And thus, in due proportion, the form of the whole is one with respect to the same thing.

11. **Reply to an Objection.** One can only raise one doubt regarding the view set forth. If the form of the whole is the form of the supposite, it includes not only the essential principles, but also the individuating principles which do not belong to the essence of a thing, because the form of the whole and the entire nature of Peter is not only humanity but *this* humanity. Therefore, it is false that this form includes only the whole essence of a thing. Then, it follows that existence is not included in this form because it too does not belong to the essence. The consequent, however, seems false. For, if the form of the whole does not include existence, how does it really constitute a thing?

One must say in response to this that form must be taken in proportion to that which is constituted by it, and thus it always expresses only the entire nature and essence of a thing. For, if it is related to the common species precisely taken, it includes only the essential and specific principles of a thing, and humanity expresses the whole form of the human being. But if it is related to a determinate individual, in that way it includes the essential, individual, and particular principles. Though these do not, absolutely speaking, belong to the essence of a thing, since the word "essence" implies a certain abstraction of the mind, they do, nevertheless, belong to the essence of the individual insofar as it is an individual, as we said above in treating the principle of individuation.[29]

The same thing should be said concerning existence. For, although existence does not absolutely belong to the essence of a thing which is or can be created, it does, nevertheless, belong to its essence as existing or as constituted in the state of an actual entity. And for this reason, although this form includes only the essence of a thing, it, nevertheless, includes existence in order to actually constitute the thing, not only as a necessary extrinsic or concomitant condition, but also as a condition intrinsically constituting the actual entity of the nature itself, by which it formally constitutes such a substance or substantial individual.

What the Logical Form Is

12. I say secondly: the metaphysical form according to reason, which is also called the logical form,[30] is usually said chiefly of the essential difference; it is, nevertheless, attributed in some respect to the genus and also to the definition. Hence, this form does not have a proper and real causality, but only a causality of reason, and a proportionate matter corresponds to it.

This whole assertion is perfectly clear and is established from the common way of speaking, if we suppose what was said above concerning this matter in the treatise on universals, where we said how the genus and the difference are related to each other and whence they are derived.[31] There we said, among other things, with Aristotle, in the *Metaphysics*, book VII, text 42 and 43 [1037b8-1038b1], that from the genus and the difference there arises something essentially [*per se*] one, because they are proximately related to each other as potency and act in the same genus and as essentially ordered to each other.[32] St. Thomas said in lect. 12, part 5, concerning that passage in the *Metaphysics*, that the genus and the difference are not related as a potency and act that are really distinct, but that they express the same essence as determinable or as determined by the difference.[33]

From this one understands that the difference imitates the form in its function of actualizing, terminating, and distinguishing, and that, for this reason, it is that to which the character of metaphysical form primarily pertains, while the genus has the character of matter in relation to it, because it is something potential which can be actualized, and it is indifferent to many things, until it is understood to be contracted and determined by the difference. From this it also follows that the difference in itself is more perfect than the genus, because that which within the same genus functions as act is more perfect than that which functions as potency.

For this reason we also said in the place cited above that the difference is taken from the nobler principle. In this too, then, there is a proportion between the form and the difference, because, just as the form is more perfect than the matter, so the difference is more perfect than the genus.[34] Again, just as matter and the form are really distinguished so that one is not the other and one does not include the other intrinsically, so the genus and the difference are separated by the concepts in terms of which they are distinguished so that the difference is not actually contained in the concept of the genus and the genus is not contained in the concept of the difference. Otherwise, there would not be a proper metaphysical composition, nor would they be related as a proper act and its potency, because it belongs to their essence that they do not include each other. Aristotle taught this in *Metaphysics,* book VII, in the place cited above [1037b8-1038b1], and in book III, text 10 [998b24], and in *Topics,* book VI, c. 3 [144a27-144b10].

13. Because of this it also happens that, just as it necessarily does not belong essentially and necessarily to matter that it should be under this or that determinate form, so the genus also does not essentially and necessarily require any determinate difference, although it necessarily requires some difference in an imprecise way, as matter requires form. Here one should, however, note the difference between matter and form on the one hand and genus and difference on the other because, although matter naturally cannot be without some form, it does not, nevertheless, absolutely imply a contradiction that it be conserved without form. Similarly form can at times be independent of matter, even naturally, and even a form which naturally depends upon matter can be supernaturally conserved without matter.[35] But the genus and the difference are essentially united so that it is absolutely impossible that either the genus subsists without any differences or that the difference subsists outside the genus which it actualizes.[36]

The reason for this is evident because the genus and the difference are not really distinct, but express the same essence as determinable and determining, and for this reason it is no wonder that they cannot be separated in reality in the way mentioned above.[37] It is also evident because there cannot be in reality something which does not have a determinate essence and, consequently, one constituted in some proper and ultimate species in which both common or generic and proper predicates[38] are necessarily included. They cannot, therefore, subsist separately and abstractly in the way they are conceived.

14. **How the genus and the difference are understood to be united.** From this one can further understand another difference between the form and the matter and the genus and the difference, namely, that, even according to the true way of conceiving them, there does not intervene between the genus and the difference an intermediate union distinct from them, as we said above that between matter and form there does intervene a mode of union really distinct from either.[39] For the actual union of these latter two does not belong to their intrinsic nature; in fact, it is separable from them, and for this reason it is necessary that it mediate between them and be distinguished from them.

But the genus and the difference are essentially united—or rather are one in reality, even though distinguished by reason—so that they are absolutely inseparable in reality and, in a way, according to reason. For, although the difference can be understood without the genus by a precisive concept, it cannot, nevertheless, be conceived negatively as existing without the genus or as not actualizing the genus.[40] And for this reason, just as in the case of real modes, which are only modally distinguished from the things they modify, we say that they are not united to things by a distinct union, but by themselves, so for much better reason the difference should be conceived as an essential mode[41] of the species and as by itself contracting and actualizing the genus without another intermediate union.

15. **The difference does not exert any real causality.** Finally, from this it is understood that the difference, insofar as it is said to be a form, does not have proper and real causality because real causality does not exist except between things which are in reality distinct, or at least it is necessary for such a causality that there be some real influx and causality distinct by its very nature from the cause or the effect. Neither of these obtains in this case, however, because the difference is not really distinct from the species or from the genus insofar as it contracted by it. Nor does any causality intervene there distinct from the difference. This, then, is only a certain constitution according to reason and our way of conceiving which by an analogy and proportion to a real cause is called form or formal causality. The same thing should to be said about the genus, insofar as the nature or causality of matter is attributed to it.

Nor does it matter that the reality constituted by these is often a true and real essence, such as a human being or a horse. For, although such an essence is in itself real, it is not, nevertheless, as so composed, a real being, but a being of reason [*ens rationis*], since the composition itself is only a composition of reason.[42]

16. **How the genus is predicated of the whole species.** But someone will object: If the difference is related to the genus as the form, and the genus is

related to the difference as the matter, each of them, therefore, is related to the species or what is defined as a part to the whole. Therefore, neither will be able to be absolutely and directly predicated of the species. For, though a part can be obliquely or denominatively predicated of the whole, it cannot be absolutely and directly predicated of it. For we do not say, "A human being is matter," but "A human being has matter," or "A human being is material." These expressions, "A human being is an animal," and similar ones, will, therefore, be false.

This objection was set forth only to explain the other part of the conclusion in which we said that the genus with respect to the species and the definition with respect to the thing defined are often called metaphysical form. It is, therefore, a common distinction that the genus can be considered in two ways, and the same holds proportionally for the difference: either precisively, as expressing a certain level and of itself, as it were, staying in that level. And in this sense the genus is a part, and as such it is not predicated of the whole, because it conveys the idea, for example, that a human being is an animal taken in the precisive sense and all alone and abstractly, or that a human being is no more than an animal. This idea is plainly false. And in this way the genus is related as matter to the difference, and conversely the difference is related as the form to the genus. This is the sense in which we have been taking these terms up to this point. And in the same sense we concede with regard to the objection everything which is inferred in it, namely, that the genus and difference are parts and that as such they are not predicated of the whole. They are called not only parts, but also elements by Aristotle, especially the highest differences and genera because of their simplicity and because ultimate resolution is made into them in metaphysics, as is clear from *Posterior Analytics,* book II, c. 14 [98a1-12].

But in another way the genus is considered as a whole which is usually called potential or confused, because it confusedly expresses the whole quiddity of the species. In this way it is most correctly predicated of the species or of what is defined, because it is not now predicated as a part, but as a whole. And this is the common sense of this expression, for when it is said that "A human being is an animal," nothing is excluded from the human being, but the same supposite which is a human being is also said to be an animal, or a human being is said to be an animal by the same form or essence by which he is a human being. Both of these assertions are true. The genus, therefore, insofar as it can be predicated of the species, as something superior in relation to the species and as it were containing it, is said in a certain way to have the character of form with respect to it. Conversely, the lower differences, insofar as they are subject to the higher and in some way in themselves sustain them, have a certain character of matter. And for a similar or greater reason the species is compared to the individual as a form, and the individual to the species as matter.[43]

17. And I understand Aristotle in this sense when, in *Metaphysics*, book 5, c. 2 [1014a-10], he refers both parts of the definition to the formal cause. For, with regard to the genus, I think it should not be understood formally as a part, but as a certain whole, as I explained. But because the whole definition explains the whole essence and is the proper account of that which is defined and is most properly predicated of it, it can for this reason be called a metaphysical form, although it is not composite. And in this way it is easy to explain all the similar expressions which consist only in a certain analogy or figure of speech.

18. **The difference between the metaphysical and the physical form**. The only thing left to do is to explain a minor doubt which arises from noting the difference between this metaphysical form and the physical form, because the physical substantial form is not multiplied in the same composite, as we said above, but this form can be multiplied. For the genera of the same thing can be many, and the differences can also. In fact, though the definition seems to contain and explicate the whole essence of the thing, it can, nevertheless, be multiple, as is established from *Posterior Analytics,* book I, c. 7 [reference not found], and book II, c. 8 [93b35-94a5], and book XII, and from *On the Soul,* book II, c. 7 [possibly to 415b8-28].

The reason, however, for this difference is easy to explain because really distinct physical forms are so related that each constitutes a perfect and complete species of substance, and their composition must be real and physical, and for this reason they are incompatible in a substance which is properly and essentially [*per se*] one. But this metaphysical form, namely, the difference, does not produce a real composition, nor is it distinguished from another difference except by the division and abstraction of the mind. Our mind, however, can divide and abstract the same thing in various ways, and for this reason it can conceive many predicates of genus and difference in the same thing. Hence, a plurality of essential differences does not preclude essential unity and composition from genus and difference.[44]

Is There is a Procession to Infinity in Essential Predicates?

19. But from this differenece a difficulty immediately arises. For it follows that there can be a procession to infinity in these formal and material metaphysical causes, that is, in quidditative predicates. The consequence, however, is opposed to what Aristotle says in *Metaphysics,* book II, c. 2 [994a1], where he thinks that there cannot be a procession to infinity in the parts of a definition, which are the genus and the difference, any more than in the forms themselves. And for this reason he proves from the negation of an infinity of

predicates the negation of an infinity of forms. The inference, however, is proven, because it is no more impossible for there to be two differences in things than three or four, and so on to any number whatever. Therefore, it is possible to proceed to infinity in this number.

This is especially so, because this number of predicates does not arise from distinct things or modes which exist in reality in one and the same substance, but arises from our own concepts with some foundation in reality. But we can divide and abstract in an infinite number of ways, and there is a foundation in these things for this to be done by us on account of the various similarities and differences which one thing has with others. And this difficulty is especially pressing if one species is not only related to other species which have been produced, but to all possible species which can be multiplied to infinity and in infinite ways.

20. **Some reasons commonly offered for the conclusion are refuted.** One must, nevertheless, absolutely say along with Aristotle that even in these formal causes there is no procession to infinity. All the interpreters teach this and offer various reasons for it. The first is that, otherwise, a constituted thing would be infinitely perfect because each predicate adds some perfection. But the consequence will perhaps be denied because one finite perfection can be the foundation of infinite concepts which, although they express perfections distinguished by reason, do not increase the perfection of the thing.[45] The second reason is that, if these differences are infinite, the properties which follow upon them will also be infinite.

But we shall respond that really distinct properties do not always arise from the specific and generic differences, as is evident in these predicates: "substantial," "spiritual," "Gabriel," etc., but it is enough that the properties themselves correspond proportionately according to universal or special intelligibilities, as was also touched on above.

21. **The true reason for the conclusion.** The third and most probable reason is that it is necessary that there be a highest genus which would be like the first matter of this composition and a specific and lowest difference would be like the final form. Therefore, the intermediate forms necessarily are finite and determinate in number. The major is proven from Aristotle because in these quidditative predicates one is always prior to the other, that is, more universal and extending to more things. But it is not prior unless it approaches more to that which is first. Therefore, it is necessary that there also be some highest genus. Second, this is evident from experience, by reflecting on all the categories and especially on substance which, as it immediately signifies a complete substance, is a highest genus. For nothing more universal with respect to substances can be thought. I presuppose, however, that being is not a

genus, although, if it were a genus, it would cause no problem since it would be the highest genus.[46] And thus we have what we are after.

Furthermore, it will not be a problem if one contends that this resolution ought to be carried out up to the transcendental predicates[47] because, even if that were true, one would stop in some ultimate predicate. The reason is that in all things or substances there is some first or least essential agreement in terms of which either a transcendental predicate or a highest genus can be abstracted. The minor is proven from the very constitution of the ultimate species, because there cannot be anything which is not constituted in some ultimate species; otherwise, it would not have a determinate essence or an essence different from other determinate species. The ultimate species, however, must be constituted by some ultimate difference. I do not now question whether this ultimate difference is simple or coalesces from many, each of which is commonly held, as Porphyry seems to signify in the chapter "On the difference." And Aristotle strongly favors this idea in *Topics,* book I, c. 3 [103a25], and in book VI [140b30-35], c. 3 and 4, and in *The Posterior Analytics,* book II, c. 14 [possibly 97a11-12, c. 13]. For this is not relevant to the present discussion because one must necessarily come to a stop in differences which are not actualized by others, even if perhaps two or three of these come together to constitute the ultimate species.[48] For now the argument we have given only applies to the subordinate differences.[49] The first consequence, however, seems to be self-evident, because between the first and last extremes there cannot be infinite intermediate differences, just as we said above concerning forms. For the argument given there applies equally here.[50]

22. **Objections to the preceding argument**. But this argument can be attacked in two ways. It can be attacked, first, by saying that, although predicates essentially [*per se*] subordinated in one line in the manner of act and potency are finite, those, nevertheless, not subordinated or in different lines can be multiplied to infinity. For example, one might hold that there are many highest genera: either by holdng that many different predicates not subordinated to one another come together for the constitution of the ultimate species and that these can be multiplied to infinity,[51] or by holding that one and the same genus, whether proximate or remote, can be simultaneously contracted by many differences which are not wholly incompatible with one another nor subordinated one to the other. For example, "animal," according to the ancient philosophers, is contracted through "rational" and through "mortal," which come together in a human being and are separated in others.[52] And "substance" can be immediately divided through "living" and through "corporeal," which in some substances come together and in others are separated.[53] From this it also seems to follow that there is a certain circle in these differences and that they are in turn compared to one another as po-

tency and act. For if "substance" is immediately divided into "living" and "non-living," "living substance" can again be divided into incorporeal and corporeal. If, on the contrary, "substance" is divided into "corporeal" and "incorporeal," "corporeal" will be divided into "living" and "non living."[54] But if this is not a problem because these are reflections of the intellect, that multiplication of predicates to infinity will, for the same reason, not be absurd.

Another way of avoiding this difficulty is that, although there is a highest genus and a lowest species, it is not impossible that between these the intellect can divide or distinguish many predicates to infinity, just as between the extreme points of a line there are infinite parts or points. For, just as these are infinite in potency, so those predicates, as they are in the thing, are said to be many only in potency, because in the thing they are not actually many unless they are distinguished by the intellect. And for this reason, although the intellect can distinguish more and more predicates to infinity, it does not follow that in the thing they are infinite except in potency. From this it also results that those predicates which we actually distinguish are always finite, both because we can only form a finite number of concepts of things and because all similarities and differences of any species to other species which have been made are in a certain and determined number, even if with respect to possible things they could perhaps be multiplied to infinity. And in this way one could interpret Aristotle on the essential differences or predicates which are as a matter of fact abstracted or can be abstracted by human reasoning or thought.

23. **Problems are solved, and the words of Aristotle are explained.** But I, nevertheless, think that the argument given is efficacious and that it is simply impossible that predicates be multiplied to infinity. And I first assert with respect to any thing that there is only one highest genus or predicate and one ultimate difference. And the first part is proven sufficiently both by reason and by usage or experience; with regard to the second part some have doubts, but it seems, nonetheless, equally certain to me. The first reason is that a difference is taken from a form, but every form that is specifically different from an other form has an essential level of being proper to it and not common to others. From this one can infer, therefore, that the difference is entirely proper to it and not common to another.

The second reason is that the ultimate species cannot be constituted by the mere conjunction of two common differences, because each of the differences constitutes a subalternate and generic species, but the ultimate species is not an aggregate of two subalternate species; otherwise, it would not be one proper and specific essence, nor would it be one metaphysical composite constituted from its proper act and proper potency. For example, in the case of the human being, if "rational" and "mortal" were taken as subalternate and common differences, "man" would never be constituted from their aggregation. But "rational" must be taken as proper to a human being, that is, including reasoning or an aptitude for that. In this way, however, "rational" will be the simple proper difference of a human being, but "mortal" will in itself be a subalternate and common difference, not for other beings using reason, since there is no rational or intellectual mortal being other than the human being, but for other sentient or living beings.[55] And it turns out this way in all the species of things. And this is what Aristotle said in *Metaphysics*, book VII, text. 43 [1038a17], that one should proceed in the division of common differences "until one arrives at those without differences," that is, until one comes to the ultimate and completely proper differences, as St. Thomas and all others explain the text. "And then," Aristotle says, "there will be as many species as there are differences. For each individual difference," St. Thomas adds, "constitutes one most specific species."

24. **The intermediate differences fall within a finite number.** If this principle is accepted, it is explained in this way that the intermediate differences can only be finite in number. And, in the first place, if the differentiating levels were distinct in the thing, it is evident that they could only be finite because they would be actually many. Therefore, they are either finite or infinite, but there cannot be infinite levels of perfection in a finite thing; therefore, they will be finite. Especially because of the fact that those levels cannot be understood as having something in common with one another, as proportional parts, but as things completely distinct and indivisible. Nor are they related to the thing as points to a line, for points are so indivisible that they do not increase the quantity of the line, but each difference adds a certain level and a *quasi*-determinate part of the perfection, from the conjunction of which parts there arises the entire perfection of the species which, since it is finite, can only arise from finite *quasi* parts.

Hence, just as in the intensive breadth of a finite quality one can distinguish only finite degrees not sharing in one another, from the conjunction of which there arises the whole finite intension of the quality, so one should philosophize in the same way concerning the differentiating levels within a genus. But although these levels according to the truer view are not actually distinguished in the thing, the argument given, nonetheless, has the same force in relation to the distinction and conception of our minds, because, even as distinguished by reason, they are conceived as not having something in common with one another if the levels are themselves taken precisely and formally, as they ought to be taken. For one subalternate difference does not include another because the lower does not pertain to the concept of the higher, nor is the converse true.

There are, therefore, differentiating, intermediate levels which are wholly distinct from one another and which do not have anything in common with one another. Hence, on the one hand, the distinction of these levels, even if it is only according to reason, cannot go on to infinity, nor can it be compared with the division of the parts of a continuum. And on the other hand, each of those levels is truly indivisible in terms of its concept. For each difference, whether generic or specific, is indivisible and is indivisible in such a way that it essentially increases the perfection of the thing in relation to the concept of the mind. Therefore, even in relation to the concept of the mind a finite essence cannot be divided or constituted save by a finite number of such differences. And since these differences are indivisible, one cannot proceed in the division of them to infinity.[56]

25. And thus the inference made in the third argument retains its force, and the objection implied in the second attempt to evade it ceases. For a finite thing cannot contain an infinity, even in potency, of things not sharing anything in common and increasing the perfection or quantity of the essence. Hence, if all the differences which are founded in the essence of things were once conceived and distinguished by reason, the number of them could not be increased, whether in relation to existing or in relation to possible things. For through those differences the essence is alike or different from all things which exist or can exist.

26. And by this the prior objection is easily excluded. After all, by whatever reason differences are multiplied, whether they are mutually subordinate or not, they cannot exist except in a finite number for the reason already given, namely, that a finite perfection cannot be divided, even mentally, into more than a finite number of *quasi* parts which do not have something in common. It is, however, more probable that all differences which come together to form one essence are in some way subordinated one to another, as potency and act; otherwise, they could not constitute something essentially one. And it is also not likely that a circle is produced in this case, since act and potency are related to each other as opposites.

27. Hence, although the same genus is divided by us in various ways, it is, nevertheless, not always divided by proper and immediate differences by which it is proximately contracted and actualized. And for this reason it can sometimes happen that two differences are related to each other as act and potency. For instance, in the example given, although substances can be divided by "corporeal" and "incorporeal," "living" and "non-living," the first division is always immediate and proximate. The sign of this is that the first division is taken, as it were, from the intrinsic principles and the absolute entity of the thing, but the second is taken from the order of operation. And for this reason the difference "living," as it is found in corporeal things, is always related

as act and not as potency to the bodily level. And although that difference is also found in incorporeal things, it is, nevertheless, found in a far different way because an incorporeal substance is, so to speak, wholly living; that is, it lives by reason of its whole substance, while a corporeal substance lives by reason of a part of it.[57] And it seems to be taken in this special way when "living" is used as a difference of a body. And although we may grant that it is possible that there is a common difference of "living" which abstracts from those two modes, there at least results from this that some genera not set down as subalternates have a common difference, which is perhaps not a problem. For Aristotle thought this in *Topics,* book VI [144b20-30], about which we will speak in another place.

28. **Another argument of Aristotle for the conclusion.** In this way, then, our third argument has been satisfactorily explained and confirmed, and the first argument also has been corroborated by the preceding discussion. But if the second argument is not understood with regard to properties in the strict sense, as they refer to faculties of operating or some other reality distinct from the substance, but with regard to any mode of being or operating, it can be defended,[58] because we distinguish these genera and differences especially through their order to some property of this sort.

Finally, Aristotle adds another argument, namely, that, if there were a regress to infinity in these differences, we could never know or define a thing sufficiently distinctly, because completely distinct knowledge or definition begins from the highest genus and comes by the addition of all the differences to the last difference. But this could not be done if the differences were infinite. This is especially the case in human cognition which proceeds little by little from one thing to another, just as it is impossible to go to infinity successively by counting, as is established from the *Physics,* book III, c. 7 [207a33-b21], and is quite self-evident.

Notes

[1] By "physical form" Suarez does not mean "corporeal form." Rather, he means a form that informs a matter which is really, i.e., physically, distinct from it. In this sense the human soul is a physical form even though it is an immaterial and immortal substance.

[2] *MD* VI 8,7.

[3] That is, it is not a composition which necessarily includes matter. The reason is that even immaterial substances can have metaphysical forms. Thus angels are constituted out of a form which is identical to their immaterial essence and a mode of subsistence.

[4] By "supposite" Suarez means to refer to the individual essence of a thing along with a real mode of subsistence which makes it exist in itself as a full substance, incommunicable to another. On this see *MD* XXXIV 2,20.

[5]For example, the composition of the definition of the human being from "animal" (the genus) and "rational" (the difference). In this composition "animal" functions as matter and "rational" as form, since "rational" determines "animal," which is, in itself, indifferent to any number of different species of animal. Cf. *MD* VI 8,7 and St. Thomas, *De ente et essentia*, c. III.

[6]Suarez dealt at length with this composition in *MD* XXXI.

[7]No special causality is involved because there is not in these cases any substantial form, properly speaking, binding the parts into a true substantial unity.

[8]That is, the compositions from nature and supposite and from genus and difference.

[9]*MD* XXXIV, sect. 2.

[10]*MD* VI, sect. 8. By a composition of reason the scholastics meant a composition the mind produces. Thus, since Suarez holds that no universals actually exist (*MD* V, sect. 1), the composition of genus and difference is not a real one *in things* but is merely an invented or imagined composition the mind produces when noting the similarities and differences between things. For Suarez's doctrine on "beings of reason," see *MD* LIV.

[11]For Suarez subsistence is a "mode" making an essence exist *in itself* rather than *in another*. Modes do not give new essential features to things; rather, they give an essence a certain manner or way of existing. Thus Suarez posited a mode of dependence of the effect on its cause, a mode of the union of the body and the soul, a mode of the inherence of an accident in its substance, etc. Cf. *MD* VII 1,17.

[12]On this see St. Thomas, *De ente et essentia*, chap. III.

[13]The reason is that the "form" here includes the entire essence of the thing. Thus, if the thing is a material substance, the form of the whole includes both matter and form.

[14]See note 10. For Suarez, as for the whole school of St. Thomas, logic is the science of second intentions, and it bears on relations of reason rather than on real relations. The reason is that Logic is concerned with universals *qua* universals and universals are relations of reason which *distribute* a mentally abstract essence to a class of things thought to exemplify that essence.

[15]That is, Christ's human nature is essentially or specifically whole, but it does not exist or subsist in itself by a proper mode of subsistence of its own. Rather, it shares in the subsistence of the second person of the Trinity.

[16]That is, each of the persons of the Trinity, Father, Son, and Holy Spirit.

[17]According to Aquinas, whom Suarez follows here, God's perfection excludes *any* composition since composition imports some sort of dependency of the whole upon its parts or properties. See *ST* I, Q. 3.

[18]This is simply the substantial form Suarez has been discussing until this section.

[19]*MD* XXXVI, sect. 2.

[20]The reason is that "person" designates an essence or nature existing in itself, i.e., it expresses such a nature along with the subsistence appropriate to it. The Lutheran Chemnitz gave a clear definition of this: "A Person or individual is something peculiar, possessing indeed the entire and perfect substance [i.e., essence] of the same species, but determined and limited by a characteristic and personal peculiarity, and thus subsists of itself.... For a person is an indivisible, intelligent, and incommunicable substance, which neither is a part of another, nor is sustained in another, nor has dependence upon another such as the separated soul has upon the body that is to be raised up." (Schmid, *The Doctrinal Theology of the Evangelical*

Lutheran Church, trans. by C. Hay and H. Jacobs [Minneapolis: Augsburg Press, 1961], p. 297.) In saying that it is the *supposite*, not the nature which generates, Suarez is saying that it is God the Father, and not the Divine Essence, Who begets God the Son.

[21]The imposition of a word comes from what it *first* signified. After that it can, by analogy, be extended to beings of a different nature. Thus "wisdom" first signified an accidental essence since in creatures it is an accident. It can, however, be extended to refer to God's wisdom, which is not an accident but is His very substance.

[22]As attributes or features of substances, accidents are not so much beings, as beings *of* beings; hence, they do not have an essence in the strict sense.

[23]So health is an accident according to nature, disease an accident contrary to nature, and infused charity an accident beyond nature.

[24]That is, though Christ's humanity constitutes Christ as a human being, that humanity does not inform the divine nature as a subject in the way form does matter. If anything, it is rather informed by the divine nature.

[25]Suarez is probably here referring to efficient causality, the causality of which formally resides in action; cf. *MD* XVIII, sect. 10.

[26]That is, form and matter.

[27]Such as the whole human body in relation to its various members.

[28]That is, one comes up with many distinct natures here insofar as one compares an individual thing with many different things of distinct natures. So, by comparing the human being with an animal, I come up with one notion of it; by comparing it with a tree, I come up with another notion of it, etc.

[29]According to Suarez, everything is individuated by its own real entity and so Suarez held that there is only a conceptual and not a real distinction between the essence of a thing and the thing itself. Cf. *MD* V 2,16.

[30]Suarez called such a form the logical form because he conceived of logic as the science which studies certain relations set up by the mind.

[31]*MD* VI 8,7.

[32]The notion is that the genus "animal," for example, represents an essence at a very general and indeterminate level capable of being further specified through various differences, for example, "rational" in the case of humans, to constitute the definition of some particular essence.

[33]That is, both the genus and the species represent a particular essence but at different levels of abstraction.

[34]This clearly shows Suarez's nominalistic leanings. Since only individuals exist and since the difference brings the concept of an essence closer to the individual, the difference represents greater actuality and perfection than the genus. In a Platonic metaphysics, the reverse is true; the genus is more perfect as being closer to the more universal and, hence, more perfect forms.

[35]The human soul can naturally exist without its matter, while the forms of lower corporeal substances can be conserved without matter by God's infinite power.

[36]The genus and the difference are conceptually but not really distinct, i.e., they represent distinct *aspects* of a thing separated by thought but inseparable in reality, so neither can exist without the other.

[37]For example, there can be no animal *simpliciter* which is not a specific *sort* of animal.

[38]According to the scholastics, proper predicates are necessary accidents flowing from the *specific* nature of a thing. The classic example is "risibility" in humans.

[39]See sect. 6,6-7 of this disputation.

[40]One precisively abstracts a certain attribute or feature of a thing (X) from any other attribute of it (O), when one simply attends to (X) but not to (O). In this there is simply a failure to consider (O) but not a positive negation or exclusion of (O).

[41]Suarez is using "mode" here in the loose sense which is roughly equivalent to a manner or way of being which contracts the notion of being to *this* rather than *that* sort of essence. A difference is not a real mode of a genus because neither genera nor species, as universals, actually exist according to Suarez. On the technical sense of "mode" in Suarez, see note 11. The difference is *like* a real mode, e.g., the mode of inherence of a non-modal accident, in that it is united to that of which it is a mode immediately and necessarily.

[42]A thing is really constituted, not by the parts of its definition, but by the real constitutes of it, namely, form and matter, atom and molecule, etc.

[43]The idea is that the term, "corporeal form," can sometimes refer to those forms which only give corporeal being to a thing. In this sense "corporeal form" represents only a part of the human essence. But in another sense "corporeal form" can refer to any form giving corporeal being. In this sense it refers to the whole human essence. Compare "animal," taken in the generic sense, to "animal," taken in the specific sense, where it is equivalent to "brute." In the first, or generic sense, it can be predicated of human beings, while in the specific sense it cannot. Cf. St. Thomas, *De ente et essentia*, II, 6-7.

[44]The argument here is that, depending on what other essences one compares a certain individual essence to, one can come up with more than one legitimate definition of a thing. Thus a human being can be defined as a "rational animal," but she can also be defined as an "incarnate spirit." It all depends upon whether one compares humans to animals or angels. None of this in the least, however, changes the human essence which is really constituted by a immaterial soul and a material body. This may serve as a warning to some contemporary philosophers, such as Quine and Rorty, who seem to think that the fact that we can give more than one legitimate definition of a thing shows that substances have no real essences. If Suarez is right, it shows no such thing.

[45]For example, "being a material thing" entails "being a thing," but the latter property does not increase the perfection of a material thing.

[46]For Suarez's arguments against supposing being is a genus, see *MD* II, sect. 5.

[47]The transcendental predicates are those which apply to all beings and thus *transcend* the Aristotelian categories. Such are "unity," goodness," and "truth," according to Suarez.

[48]In other words, it might not be that just *one* feature marks off cats from other mammals, but a concatenation of them. This concatenation could be taken to be the specific difference in the definition of a cat.

[49]That is, differences which are subordinate to each other.

[50]See above, sect. 10, 65.

[51]This would depend, presumably, on what one compares a given thing's essence to in order to make its genus. Thus, as was said above, one might take either "spirit," or "animal" as the genus of humans, and which one one chooses will determine what one gives as the difference contracting the genus to the human species.

[52]Because the angels are rational but not mortal, while cats are mortal but not rational.

[53]Again, because angels are living but incorporeal while metals are corporeal but inanimate, and cats are living and corporeal.

[54]In this way one and the same predicate, namely, "living" will be higher, so to speak, in the series of essential predicates according to one way of dividing things, and lower according to another way of dividing them.

[55]In other words, "mortal" will be a property pertaining to humans from their genus, and thus will not be constitutive, along with "reason," of the proper difference of "human being."

[56]The argument here is that, as the differences each add a perfection to the finite essence, if they were infinite, the essence would be infinitely perfect. But this is not possible; therefore, the differences are not infinite.

[57]Corporeal living beings are constituted out of form and matter and only their *forms* make them alive. Incorporeal things, however, are constituted *only* by their forms and so are alive by their *entire essences*.

[58]By the time of Suarez the scholastics had developed a very sophisticated theory of predication. According to them, some predicates, while true of certain subjects, do not stand for real properties existing *in* those subjects, but simply for negations, privations, or mental relations. Thus, "blindness," though truly predicated of some things, is not a real property in those things, but rather the *lack* of a property. Again, it is true that Tom Hanks is liked by many people, but the property "being liked by many people" does not name any real property *in* Hanks, but a certain relation set up by the mind based, in fact, upon a real property in the people who like him. On the difference between predicates which refer to real properties in things and those which do not, see St. Thomas *De ente et essentia*, chap. I.

Among predicates that stand for real properties in things, most scholastics distinguished between real properties of things which are nevertheless identical with the very essences of those things, and real properties which are not identical with their essences, but which are, in some way, really distinct from their essences. An example of a property identical with the essence of a human being is "rational," since the very essence of the human is rational as naturally *rooting* the powers of reason and rational volition. On the other hand the property of "reason" is, according to Suarez and the entire school of St. Thomas, really distinct from the human being since reason is a power of the human being which flows from her essence. For Suarez, that one finite thing X is really distinct from another finite thing Y means that X and Y each have their own *esse* and that each can be preserved in separation from the other by God (cf. *MD* VII, sec. 2). The Thomists did not agree with Suarez on this point, while the Scotists posited between real and conceptual distinctions their famous "formal distinction." Suarez defends his theory of distinctions in *MD* VII.

Besides the existence of real properties of things that are identical with them and real properties of things which are not identical with them in the fullest sense, Suarez recognized an in between class of properties he called modes which, though they are not identical with the substances they modify, have no essence of their own and so cannot exist in separation from those substances. An example of such a mode would be the real dependency that the power of reason has on the rational soul. On modes see *MD* VII, sec. 1.

The relevance of this complex doctrine to the question of the nature of definitions is just this: As the definition of a thing is a formula capturing its essence, a perfect definition would not include in it any properties of a thing which are really or modally distinct from it, nor would it include negations or privations. Since Suarez held that reason and all other operational powers of finite substances are really distinct from those substances (*MD* XVIII 3,21-22), he likewise held that no operational power should be included in the perfect definition of a substance. Nevertheless, since we know essences from the outside in, so to speak, we must often settle for definitions of things which take their *differentia* from the operational powers of things. It should be noted here that most scholastics did *not* think that "rational" refers directly to a power of the soul, but to the soul itself as the remote *cause* or *root* of the power of rationality. On this see *ST* I, q. 77, a. 1, ad. 7: "Rational and sensitive, as differences, are not taken from the powers of sense and reason, but from the sensitive and rational soul itself. But because substantial forms, which in themselves are unknown to us, are known by their accidents; nothing prevents us from sometimes substituting accidents for substantial differences." Fathers of the English Dominican Province translation, (Westminster: Christian Classics, 1948) Vol. I, p. 384. In light of passages like this it is hard to make sense of the insistence of some Neo-Thomists, such as E. Gilson and F. Copleston, that Locke's doctrine of substance differed essentially from that of Aquinas or his medieval followers.

Select Bibliography

I: Parts of the *Metaphysical Disputations* available in English.

Disputation 5: *Suarez on Individuation: Metaphysical Disputation V, Individual Unity and Its Principle.* Translated with introduction, notes, glossary, and bibliography by Jorge J. E. Gracia. Milwaukee: Marquette University Press, 1982

Disputation 6: *On Formal and Universal Unity.* Translated, with introduction and notes, by James F. Ross. Milwaukee: Marquette university Press, 1964.

Disputation 7: *On the Various Kinds of Distinctions* (Disputationes Metaphysicae, Disputatio VII). Translated by Cyril O. Vollert. Milwaukee: Marquette University Press, 1947.

Disputations 10 and 11 and part of 23: *The Metaphysics of Good and Evil According To Suarez: Metaphysical Disputations X and XI and Selected Passages from Disputation XXIII and Other Works.* Translated, with introduction, notes, and glossary by Jorge J. E. Gracia and Douglas Davis. Munich: Philosophia Verlag, 1989.

Disputations 17, 18, and 19: *On Efficient Causality.* Translated, with introduction and notes by Alfred J. Freddoso. New Haven: Yale University Press, 1994.

Disputation 31: *On the Essence of Finite Being as Such, On the Existence of That Essence and Their Distinction.* Translated, with an introduction and notes, by NormanJ. Wells. Milwaukee: Marquette University Press, 1983.

Disputation 54: *On Beings of Reason.* Translated, with and introduction and notes, by John Doyle. Milwaukee: Marquette University Press, 1995.

II: Books and Dissertations:

There are no complete book length treatments of Suarez's metaphysics in English. However, Thomas Harper's presentation of scholastic metaphysics was greatly influenced by Suarez (as he himself admits), and with respect to virtually every topic he treats in his book he relates the teachings of Suarez on the matter. Furthermore, the arguments he gives for commonly accepted scholastics doctrines are largely shaped by Suarez (for example, the arguments he gives for the existence of substantial forms in Vol. II, pp. 405-423 are virtually identical to the arguments Suarez gives for their existence in sect. I of *MD* XV). With the obvious exception of the biography, the other books listed here also give rather lengthy expositions of Suarez's views on various controverted points in scholastic philosophy.

Cronin, Timothy J. *Objective Being in Descartes and Suarez.* New York: Garland Publishing, 1987.

Fichter, Joseph H., S.J. *Man of Spain: Francis Suarez.* New York: Macmillan, 1940.

Harper, Thomas. *The Metaphysics of the School, Three Volumes.* First Published, 1879, Reprinted, New York: Peter Smith, 1940.

Kronen, John. *The Substantial Unity of Material Substances.* Doctoral dissertation, State University of New York at Buffalo, 1991.

Murray, Michael V. *The Theory of Distinctions in the Metaphysics of Francis Suarez.* Doctoral dissertation, Fordham University, 1944.

O'Neil, John. *Cosmology, An Introduction to the Philosophy of Matter, Vol. I, The Greeks and Aristotelian Schoolmen.* London: Longmans, Green and Co., 1923.

Phillips, *Modern Thomistic Philosophy, Two Volumes.* London: Burns Oates and Washbourne, 1935

Stengren, George L. *The Doctrine of Being in the Metaphysics of Suarez.* Master's dissertation, St. John's Unviersity, 1956.

————. *Human Intellectual Knowledge of the Material Singular according to Francis Suarez.* Doctoral dissertation, Fordham Unvierstiy, 1965.

Ssekasozi, Engelbert. *A Comparative and Critical Analysis of the Metaphysical Theories of William of Ockham and Francis Suarez as regards the Principle of Individuation.* Doctoral dissertation, Kansas, 1976.

Treloar, John Lawrence. *Francis Suarez: A Metaphysics for Body and Soul.* Doctoral dissertation, Michigan State University, 1976.

III: Articles

Allers, Rudold. "The Intellectual Cognition of Pariculars," *Thomist* 3 (1941): 95-163

Burns, J. Patout. "Action in Suarez," *New Scholasticism* 37 (1964): 453-472.

Copleston, Frederick. *A History of Philosophy*, Vol. III. New York: Doubleday, 1963.

Cronin, Timothy J. "Eternal Truths in the Thought of Suarez and Descartes," *Modern Schoolman* 38 (1960-1): 269-288.

————. "Eternal Truths in the Thought of Descartes and of His Adversary." *Journal of the History of Ideas* 21 (1960): 553-559.

Davis, Douglas P. "Suarez and the Problem of Postive Evil." *American Catholic Philosophical Quarterly* 65 (1991): 361-372.

Doyle, John P. "'Extrinsic Cognoscibility': A Seventeenth-Centruy Supertranscendental Notion." *Modern Schoolman* 68 (1990): 57-80.

————. "Heidegger and Scholastic Metaphysics." *Modern Schoolman* 49 (1972): 201-220.

————. "*Prolegomena* to a Study of Extrinsic Denomination in the Work of Francis Suarez, S.J." *Vivarium* 22 (1984): 121-160.

————. "Suarez on Beings of Reason and Truth." *Vivarium* 25 (1987): 47-75 and 26 (1988): 51-72.

————. "Suarez on the Analogy of Being." *Modern Schoolman* 46 (1969):219-249 and 323-341.

————. "Suarez on the Reality of the Possibles." *Modern Schoolman* 45 (1967):29-48.

————. "Suarez on the Unity of a Scientific Habit." *American Catholic Philosophical Quarterly* 65 (1991):311-334.

Ewbank, Michael. "The Route to Substance in Suarez's *Disputationes Metaphysicae.*" *Proceedings of the American Catholic Philosophical Association* 61 (1987):98-111.

Ferrater Mora, Jose. "Suarez and Modern Philosophy." *Journal of the History of Ideas* 14 (1953):528-547.

Gracia, Jorge J.E. "Evil and the Transcendentality of Goddness: Suarez's Solution to the Problem of Positive Evils." In *Being and Goodness: The Concept of the Good in Metaphysics and Philosophical Theology,* edited by Scott MacDonald, pp. 151-179. Ithaca, N.Y.: Cornell University Press, 1991.

————. "Francis Suarez." *Individuation in Scholasticism: The Later Middle Ages and the Counter-Reformation, 1150-1650.* Albany: State University of New York Press, 1994, pp. 475-510.

————. "Francisco Suarez: The Man in History." *American Catholic Philosophical Quarterly* 65 (1991):259-266

————. "Suarez and the Doctrine of Transcendentals." *Topoi* 11 no. 2 (1992): 121-134.

————. "Suarez's Conception of Metaphysics: A Step in the Direction of Mentalism?" Ibid.: 287-309.

————. "Suarez's Criticism of the Thomistic Principle of Individuation," *Atti. Congresso Internazionale de Filosofia, 1974.* Roma, 1978.

————. "What the Individual Adds to the common Nature according to Suarez." *New Scholasticism* 53(1979): 221-233.

Kainz, H.P. "The Suarezian Position on Being and the Real Distinction: An Analytic and Comparative Study." *Thomist* 34 (1970):289-305.

Knight, David M. "Suarez's Approach to Substantial Form." *Modern Schoolman* 39 (1961-1962): 219-239.

Kronen, John. "Can Leclerc's Composite Actualities Be Substances?" *Process Studies.* 21 1992): 25-43.

———— "Essentialism Old and New: Suarez and Brody." *Modern Schoolman* 69 (1991):123-151.

————. "The Importance of the Concept of Substantial Unity in Suarez's Argument for Hylomorphism." *Amercian Catholic Philosophical Quarterly* 65 (1991):335-360.

————. "Substances are not Windowless: A Suarezian Critique of Monadism." *Americal Catholic Philosophical Quarterly* 71 (1997):59-81.

Maurer, Armand. "St. Thomas and Eternal Truths." *Mediaeval Studies* 32 (1970): 91-107.

Norena, Carlos, "Ockham and Suarez on the Ontological Status of Universal Concepts." *New Scholasticism* 53 (1981):159-174.

Owens, Joseph. The number of Terms in the Suarezian Discussion on Essence and Being." *Modern Schoolman* 34 (1957): 147-191.

Peccorini, Franscisco L. "Suarez's Struggle with the Problem of the One and the Many." *Thomist* 36 (1972):433-471.

Peccorini, Franscisco L. "Knowledge of the Singular: Aquinas, Suarez and Recent Interpreters." *Thomist* 38 (1974): 606-655.

————. "Suarez's Struggle with the Problem of the One and the Many." *Thomist* 36 (1972):433-471.

Ross, James F. "Suarez on Universals." *Journal of Philosophy* 59 (1962):736-748.

Wells, Norman J. "Objective Being: Descartes and His Sources." *Modern Schoolman* 45 (1967):49-61.

————. "Objective Reality of Ideas in Descartes, Caterus, and Suarez." *Journal of the History of Philosophy* 28 (1990):33-61.

————. "Suarez, Historian and Critic of the Modal Distinction between Essential Being and Existential Being." *New Scholasticism* 36 (1962):419-444.

———— "Suarez on the Eternal Truths." *Modern Schoolman* 58 (1981):73-106 and 159-174.

Index of Names

Index of Terms

A

A posteriori
Dependency of matter on form, 107-108, 118
Scotus's argument for the form of corporeity, 130-131
Demonstration of the view that the rational soul is not distinct from the sensitive, 137

A priori
Demonstration of the existence of form, 28
Defined, 41, note 68
Demonstration that temporal priority or posteriority does not change the nature of an action, 67
Dependency of matter on form, 108
Demonstration that God can conserve matter apart from form, 118
Argument of Scotus for the form of corporeity, 130

Abstraction
Predicates multiplied through, 128

Accidents
Form necessary to root, 21
Loss or acquisition of does not constitute substantial generation or corruption, 21
Return of demonstrates existence of form, 22-24
Dispose matter for the reception of a certain form, 21, 46, 51, 82-83
Certain of inseparable from their subjects, 25
Matter of indifferent to, 23
Some inseparable from others, 26
Are perfections of other things, 29
Not the basis of substantial being, 30-31, 46

Definition of, 43, note 92
Truly come to be, 44
Have a proper entity of their own, 45, 57, note 6
Not created, 50-51
Modal not properly educed, 68-69
Compose with their subjects accidental unities, 91, 181
Have less entity than substantial forms, 115
Convertible with accidental forms, 122
Difference from substantial forms, 152
Of the elemental forms remain virtually in the compound, 154-155
Have no essence in the absolute sense, 180

Act
Of existence, 11
Substantial, 21, 28-31
Accidental, 30
Form the act of matter, 21, 30, 77-78
Of existence, 119
Entitative distinct from formal, 119
Soul an act of matter, 140
Of subsistence, 181

Action
Of eduction distinct from creation, 63-64
Nature of not altered by temporal priority or posteriority, 63, 67
Productive of the heaven different in nature from that which produced the matter of the elements, 66
Conserving a composite thing is twofold, 66
Conserving a human threefold, 66
Which educes the form and generates the composite is one, 74
Four kinds of distinguished, 75
Has a reality in the natures of things, 83
The causality of an agent *qua* agent, 84
Of union, 86-87
Productive of matter the same as that which conserves it, 102

Ad hominem argument
Explained, 118, 124, note 24, 132

Mediæval Philosophical Texts in Translation
Complete List

Pseudo-Dionysius Areopagite: *The Divine Names and Mystical Theology.* John D. Jones, Tr. ISBN 0-87462-221-2. (Translation No. 21). 320 pp. $25

Matthew of Vendome: *Ars Versificatoria.* Roger P. Parr, Tr. ISBN 0-87462-222-0. (Translation No. 22). 150 pp. $15

Francis Suárez. *On Individuation.* Jorge J.E. Gracia, Tr. ISBN 0-87462-223-9. (Translation No. 23). 304 pp. $35

Francis Suárez: *On the Essence of Finite Being as Such, on the Existence of That Essence and Their Distinction.* Norman J. Wells, Tr. ISBN 0-87462-224-7. (Translation No. 24). 248 pp. $20

The Book of Causes (Liber De Causis). Dennis J. Brand, Tr. ISBN 0-87462-225-5. (Translation No. 25). 56 pp. $5

Giles of Rome: *Errores Philosophorum.* John O. Riedl, Tr. Intro. by Josef Koch. ISBN 0-87462-429-0. (Translation No. 26). 136 pp. $10

St. Thomas Aquinas: *Questions on the Soul.* James H. Robb, Tr. ISBN 0-87462-226-3. (Translation No. 27). 285 pp. $25

William of Auvergne. *The Trinity.* Roland J. Teske, S.J. and Francis C. Wade, S.J. ISBN 0-87462-231-X 286 pp. (Translation No. 28) 1989 $20

Hugh of St. Victor. *Practical Geometry.* Frederick A. Homann, S.J., Tr. ISBN 0-87462-232-8 92 pp. (Translation No. 29) 1991 $10

William of Auvergne. *The Immortality of the Soul.* Roland J. Teske, S.J., Tr. ISBN 0-87462-233-6 72 pp. (Translation No. 30) 1991 $10

Dietrich of Freiberg. *Treatise of the Intellect and the Intelligible.* M. L. Führer, Tr. ISBN 0-87462-234-4 135 pp. (Translation No. 31) 1992 $15

Henry of Ghent. *Quodlibetal Questions on Free Will.* Roland J. Teske, S.J., Tr. ISBN 0-87462-234-4 135 pp. (Translation No. 32) $15

Francisco Suárez, S.J. *On Beings of Reason. Metaphysical Disputation LIV.* John P. Doyle, Tr. ISBN 0-87462-236-0 170 pp. (Translation No. 33) $20

Francisco De Vitoria, O.P. *On Homicide,* and *Commentary on Thomas Aquinas: Summa theologiae IIaIIae, 64.* Edited and Translated by John Doyle. ISBN 0-87462-237-9. 280 pp. (Translation No. 34) $30. Available as e-book.

William of Auvergne. *The Universe of Creatures.* Edited, Translated, and with an Introduction by Roland J. Teske, S.J. ISBN 0-87462-238-7. 235 pp. (Translation No. 35) $25. Available as e-book.

Francis Suarez, S.J. *On the Formal Cause of Substance. Metaphysical Disputation XV.* Translated by John Kronen & Jeremiah Reedy. Introduction & Explanatory Notes by John Kronen. ISBN 0-87462-239-5. 218 pp. (Translation No. 36) $25. Available as e-book.

Mediæval Philosophical Texts in Translation
Roland J. Teske, S.J., Editor

This series originated at Marquette University in 1942, and with revived interest in Mediæval studies is read internationally with steadily increasing popularity. Available in attractive, durable, colored soft covers. Volumes priced from $5 to $35 each. Complete Set (35 softbound titles) [0-87462-200-X] receives a 40% discount. John Riedl's *A Catalogue of Renaissance Philosophers*, hardbound with red cloth, is an ideal reference companion title (sent free with purchase of complete set). New standing orders receive a 30% discount and a free copy of the Riedl volume. Regular reprinting keeps all volumes available. Recent volumes are also available as ebooks.

See our web page: http://www.marquette.edu/mupress/

Order through:
> BookMasters, Inc.
> 30 Amberwood Parkway
> Ashland OH 44805

Tel. 800-247-6553   Fax: 419-281-6883

Editorial Address for Mediæval Philosophical Texts in Translation:
Roland J. Teske, S.J., Editor MPTT
Department of Philosophy
Marquette Univesity
Box 1881
Milwaukee WI 53201-1881

Marquette University Press office:
Marquette University Press
Dr. Andrew Tallon, Director
Box 1881
Milwaukee WI 53201-1881

Tel: (414) 288-7298 FAX: (414) 288-3300
Internet: andrew.tallon@marquette.edu.
Web Page: http://www.marquette.edu/mupress/

Subscribe to the free *MU Press Enewsletter* for immediate notice of new books. With the word **subscribe** as the subject, email a message to universitypress@marquette.edu